THE CIVIL WAR IN WALES

THE CIVIL WAR IN WALES

THE SCOURING OF THE NATION

TERRY JOHN

PEN & SWORD
HISTORY

AN IMPRINT OF PEN & SWORD BOOKS LTD.
YORKSHIRE - PHILADELPHIA

First published in Great Britain in 2021 by
PEN AND SWORD HISTORY
An imprint of
Pen & Sword Books Ltd
Yorkshire – Philadelphia

ISBN 978 1 39900 476 3

A CIP catalogue record for this book is available from the British Library.

Typeset in Times New Roman 11.5/14 by
SJmagic DESIGN SERVICES, India.
Printed and bound by CPI Group (UK) Ltd, Croydon, CR0 4YY

Pen & Sword Books Limited incorporates the imprints of Atlas, Archaeology,
Aviation, Discovery, Family History, Fiction, History, Maritime, Military, Military
Classics, Politics, Select, Transport, True Crime, Air World, Frontline Publishing,
Leo Cooper, Remember When, Seaforth Publishing, The Praetorian Press,
Wharncliffe Local History, Wharncliffe Transport, Wharncliffe True Crime and
White Owl.

For a complete list of Pen & Sword titles please contact
PEN & SWORD BOOKS LIMITED
47 Church Street, Barnsley, South Yorkshire, S70 2AS, England
E-mail: enquiries@pen-and-sword.co.uk
Website: www.pen-and-sword.co.uk

Or
PEN AND SWORD BOOKS
1950 Lawrence Rd, Havertown, PA 19083, USA
E-mail: Uspen-and-sword@casematepublishers.com
Website: www.penandswordbooks.com

MIX
Paper from
responsible sources
FSC® C013604

Contents

Acknowledgements

The greater part of this book has been written during the Covid-19 pandemic, during which all libraries, county archives and museums have been closed. It has not been possible to access original archives and accounts from the period of the Civil Wars. I therefore owe a great debt of gratitude to the authors of the books mentioned in the bibliography. Particularly useful have been the following: *The Great Siege of Chester* by John Barratt; *Civil War and Restoration in Monmouthshire* by Jeremy Knight; *Radnorshire; from Civil War to Restoration* by Keith Parker; and the writings of the late Norman Tucker. I would recommend all of them to anyone eager to discover more about the Civil Wars in Wales. *Memoirs of the Civil War in Wales and the Marches* by J.R. Phillips, remains the great standard reference work on the subject.

I owe grateful thanks the staff of Pembrokeshire Record Office and the National Library of Wales for their efficiency and patience. A special mention to the staff of Pen and Sword Books, especially Claire Hopkins, who commissioned the book, Chris Evan Brown for careful editing and Paul Wilkinson for the excellent cover design.

For years of encouragement and support, thanks are also due in no small measure to: Eric and Julieanne Audigé; Karen Bentall; Janet Bray; Des and Pam Brown; Margaret Buckingham; Father Gildas of Caldey Abbey; Thelma Golden; Trevor and Mary Goodman; my godsons Glenn and Liam Hewer and their families; Eileen and Richard Horton; Adrian James for many discussions on the Civil Wars; Angela Jones; Rob and Vicky Jones, with whom I walked the battlefield at Montgomery and visited Brampton Bryan; Hans, Christine and Christian Klamm in Landstuhl; Stephen Laugharne; Steve Liddle who supplied photographs; Gareth Preece; Ivy and David Smith; Roger and Rose Withington; and the members of Lord Saye and Sele's Blew Regiment of Foote. Grateful thanks to the Harley estate for permission to use photographs of Brampton Bryan Castle, which is not open to the public.

Abbreviations

AC	*Archaeologia Cambrensis*
BLHC	British Library Historical Collection
CQM	*Cambrian Quarterly Magazine*
CSPD	*Calendar of State Papers Domestic*
DOP	*Diurnal Occurrences in Parliament*
HC	Haverfordwest Corporation
NLW	National Library of Wales
NLWJ	*National Library of Wales Journal*
PCH	*Pembrokeshire County History*
PRO	Pembrokeshire Record Office
WHR	*Welsh Historical Review*

Chapter 1

Wales, Land and People

On 13 July 1652, John Taylor, an eccentric and much-travelled character known as 'The Water Poet', set off on a journey from London to Wales and back. He recorded his experiences in a book entitled *A Short Relation of a Long Journey,* which was written partly in verse and partly in prose. During his wanderings, he visited Flint Castle, which he described as almost buried in its own rubble, remarking that, 'surely war hath made it miserable'. He found Aberystwyth to be in an even worse state, its castle blown up and its houses 'transformed into confused heaps of unnecessary rubbidge.'[1]

Taylor was witnessing the devastation that resulted from almost ten years of civil war. In common with many areas of Britain, Wales had been torn apart, its towns ruined, its fields despoiled and the blood of its people spilt. It would take decades for many communities to recover.

The damage to the infrastructure of Wales seems to have been matched by a slump in population growth. In 1642, at the beginning of the Civil Wars, the people of Wales have been estimated to number about 356,000, a steady increase from the supposed total of 329,000 in 1621.[2] By 1670, over a similar period of thirty years, it had barely reached 376,000, though some of this may admittedly be due to a series of poor harvests in the 1620s and an outbreak of plague in the 1630s. In 1623 Sir John Gwynn of Gwydir in Caernarfonshire found himself £3,000 in debt due to a shortfall in his income from rents and he was worried that his tenants were unable to pay as the cost of bread corn had risen so much 'that a number do die in the country from hunger...the rest have the impression of hunger in their faces exceeding the memory of any man living'.[3] It is worth noting however, that some years earlier, he had been fined for oppressing his tenants in Dolwyddelan and Llysfaen, so it is to be hoped that he now did something to help the hungry.

Most people lived in scattered rural communities. There were no very populous towns. The two largest centres of population were Wrexham,

1

with about 2,500 inhabitants, whilst in South Wales, Carmarthen could boast between 1,500 and 2,000 people.[4] In the years before the Civil Wars, only about ten per cent of the population lived in urban settings and even the rural settlements tended to cluster in the more fertile lands. In the north, the Vale of Clwyd and Flintshire contained the best farmland, and in the south the most fertile land lay in the Vale of Glamorgan, areas of the Gower and most of Pembrokeshire.[5]

Much of Wales consisted of unproductive moorlands and mountain ranges, with shallower soils where the wetter climate made the growing of crops problematic. Farms and villages were sparsely scattered and were huddled against the more sheltered slopes and hollows. Sheep had been grazed in these areas for generations and during the medieval period, several of the larger Welsh abbeys had grazed their flocks on the upland plateaus during the summer months.

Industries

The woollen industry was important to many Welsh counties. At the end of the sixteenth century, George Owen, a Pembrokeshire landowner, recorded a 'great quantity yearly sold' from his area of northern Pembrokeshire through 'Cardigan market to North Wales men' who also sold their own wool to Oswestry and Shrewsbury.[6] The southern part of Pembrokeshire traded to Bristol, Barnstaple and Somerset. In mid-Wales, the flocks provided material for the wool industry at Presteigne and the markets at Knighton and Ludlow.

It was not unusual in the spring and summer months to see the drovers' roads crowded with cattle, sheep and even geese being driven eastwards towards the Midland towns, Bristol and even London. From South Wales, cattle were shipped out from coastal ports along the coast to harbours in the West Country and to Bristol. This movement of livestock was not all one way. Every year herds of cattle were sent into Wales to summer in the countryside, and there was a steady reciprocal trade in fruit, corn and other kinds of merchandise.[7]

A high percentage of the Welsh population was employed in industries that were linked to agriculture. Spinning, weaving, cloth making and tanning were carried on as cottage industries as well as in many towns and villages, though George Owen lamented the fact that in

Pembrokeshire the wool there was 'unwrought', but was sold in a raw state to other countries. Dairy produce was much in demand, so much so that Glamorgan became one of Wales' biggest butter and cheese making regions. Oats, wheat, barley and rye were grown in the fertile lands of the north and south.

The majority of Welsh landowners were eager to exploit the resources that lay beneath their fields. Lead and copper were mined and smelted, with stone and lime being quarried in a number of locations. Sir Thomas Myddleton of Chirk Castle developed an ironworks on his estate, whilst allowing a speculator named Thomas Bushell to mine lead on the family's lands in Cardiganshire.[8] Coal had been extracted for centuries from the coalfields of the south and north east. Opencast mining is recorded as taking place in Pembrokeshire from the fourteenth century, if not before. Coal and culm – a mixture of clay and coal pressed into balls of fuel that burned slowly – were being exported from Tenby to Ireland in regular shipments during the latter half of the sixteenth century.

Woodlands and forests provided timber for pit props and house- and shipbuilding. Neath was regarded as the best place for shipbuilding in Wales[9], though it was possible to find it taking place in harbours and creeks almost anywhere along the coastline. In some cases, the vessels were built on the beaches and a construction site might lie dormant for months until a new ship was needed to replace one that had been wrecked or was no longer seaworthy.

A surprising number of the gentry were involved in some way in sea trade, either by buying shares in a ship, or by financing a voyage. Wealthy merchants also invested in ships as partners or combined their roles as traders with that of captaining a trading vessel. The ports along the South Wales coast had developed close links with Bristol and a number of merchants from Glamorganshire, Carmarthenshire and Pembrokeshire had warehouses in Bristol, mostly in an area of the docks known as the Welsh Quay. Some were willing to send their wives off on voyages to Bristol in order to settle debts or conduct business there, whilst others sent their sons and even their daughters to be apprenticed to a craft or trade.[10]

Chester, because it was linked to the sea by the River Dee, became a major trading centre for Wales and the Marches. Prosperous, of strategic importance, encircled by its medieval walls, much of its wealth was derived from the wool trade, with fleeces being brought in from

North Wales. Welsh cattle also supplied the raw materials for the city's leather workers, tanners, glovers, saddlers and shoemakers. The city had been sending out ships and cargoes to destinations in France, Iberia and Ireland for many centuries. There were, however, concerns that the wealth of the city was threatened by the silting up of the Dee estuary, which during the mid-sixteenth century, had necessitated the building of a new quay nearer to the outlet with the Irish Sea.[11]

Three other cities close to the borders with Wales also relied upon Welsh produce to fuel their industries. Shrewsbury became a major centre of the woollen industry, with its merchants buying Welsh cloth that had been woven and treated in fulling mills but was otherwise in an unfinished state. The resulting friezes and plain cloth were sent regularly by road to markets further east, including London.

Wool from the Marches also found its way to Hereford, where it was woven and fulled. This involved cleaning and thickening it by pounding it in a mixture of water and clay and then stretching it on frames known as tenters, to which it was attached by tenterhooks, to dry before making it into clothing. Gloucester also had a flourishing woollen industry and, as at Hereford, the leatherworkers fashioned animal hides into hats, gloves, leather bottles and saddles.

All four of these cities, to a greater or lesser extent, would shape the course of the Civil War in Wales and the Marches.

Society

Across Wales the most eminent positions in society were held by members of the aristocratic and gentry classes. Some great peers, members of the Stuart court, held lands in Wales, but few of them dwelt permanently in their Welsh houses. In North Wales and the borders, the dominant figures, amongst others, were the Myddleton family of Chirk Castle, and the Salusbury family of Lleweni.

The most influential figures in South Wales were Henry Somerset, fifth Earl and later first Marquis of Worcester, whose magnificent castle at Raglan dominated the landscape, and Richard Vaughan, second Earl of Carbery at Golden Grove in Carmarthenshire. Both were to play leading parts in the Royalist war effort in South Wales, with Lord Worcester's vast wealth and unshakable loyalty to Charles I fuelling the Crown's campaign across Glamorganshire, Monmouthshire and the southern Marches.

Another leading nobleman was Robert Devereux, third Earl of Essex. The son of Robert, the second earl who had been the favourite of Queen Elizabeth I in her elder years, Essex held a number of manors in Wales, including the former episcopal palace of Lamphey, near Pembroke. Many gentry families such as the Powells, Meyricks and Cunys in Pembrokeshire and the Gwynnes and Lewises in Radnorshire, had been drawn into the orbit of the second earl. After his execution in 1601, they had transferred their loyalties to his son. Another group which was to follow Essex's lead when he declared for Parliament at the outbreak of the war were the Gunters, who may originally have hailed from the Brecon area and who in 1642 were renting Lamphey Palace from the earl.

Gentry families such as those mentioned here provided Wales with its Members of Parliament, Justices of the Peace and County Sheriffs, whilst younger sons entered the church or the legal profession. As the ruling class within Wales, they were conscious that within their ranks there existed careful gradations of precedence. First in eminence were the knights and, after the creation of the position in 1611, the baronets. Then came the squires and after them the gentlemen.

All derived their position and influence from services carried out for, and privileges granted by, various sovereigns. Some gentry families could trace their lineage back through countless generations to the time of the early Welsh princes, whilst others rooted their ancestry in the conquering Norman lords. Others combined a descent from both sides.

The Welsh gentry were not as wealthy as their English counterparts. Their riches came from land ownership and whilst some lived handsomely on an annual income of £1,000 or more, others existed quite well on at least £300 per annum. There were those who managed more frugally on amounts of less than £100, but this did not necessarily affect their status as gentry, as it was their pedigree and their ownership of land that buoyed them up.

Certain standards were expected of the gentry, whatever their financial situation. In 1626, William Vaughan, the uncle of Richard Vaughan, second Earl of Carbery, produced a work entitled *The Golden Grove,* in which he set out 'the means to discern a gentleman'. Foremost amongst the necessary qualities were that 'he must be affable and courteous in speech, and behaviour'. A true gentleman must also be 'endowed with mercy to forgive the trespasses of his friends and servants.' Charity to the poor and hospitality to their fellows should be combined with kindness to servants and an adventurous heart to fight for just causes. 'These be the properties of a gentleman, which whosoever lacketh deserveth but the title of a clown or of a country boor.'[12]

A gentleman should also be a patron of the arts, supporting scholars, musicians and poets, perhaps even writing himself, as Sir James Perrot of Carew did in 1630. His book, *Meditations on the Lord's Prayer*, proved to be an influential and respected religious text. This was only one of a number of publications he produced during his lifetime.

Some Welsh gentlemen created private libraries of books. The collections of Sir John Price of Brecon and Sir Edward Stradling of St Donat's were to be envied, whilst one landowner, William Maurice of Cefnybraich in Denbighshire built a three-story addition to his house to hold all his books.[13] In the Vale of Clwyd, Glamorgan and Pembrokeshire there existed scholarly groups which met regularly to exchange ideas and manuscripts.[14]

However cultured they might be, members of the gentry were also proud of their status, touchy over their dignity and rights, and were prepared to take out legal actions against anyone who threatened their titles to land and property. There were long-held grudges against other families and barely concealed resentments over religion. Indeed, it was said that in Monmouthshire few quarrels arose that did not develop out of a difference between Catholicism and Protestantism.[15]

Another prosperous group, almost indistinguishable from the minor gentry, consisted of yeoman farmers. They occupied freehold lands which they worked for themselves, selling corn and other produce in the markets and could count on an income of up to forty shillings a year. Some diversified into trades, owning smithies and running alehouses and bakeries, even investing in maritime trading ventures. The wealthiest amongst them were ready to loan money, livestock, and crops to their less fortunate neighbours. Their dwellings were often stone-built and surprisingly comfortable, furnished with items of furniture such as chairs, tables, beds with mattresses, wooden chests for storage, candlesticks and other household utensils.

Yeoman farmers could often trace their lineage back through many generations, especially where their families had occupied the same lands for a century or more. It was not unknown for a member of a well-respected and prosperous yeoman family to marry into the lower ranks of the gentry.

There were grades within the yeoman class and some freehold families worked much smaller acreages and were much more likely to slip into poverty following a series of bad harvests or the death or illness of the principal breadwinner. This was also true of the husbandman class, a group of tenant farmers who, if fortune favoured them, might work their way upwards to a reasonable level of prosperity, but who were much more likely to feel the harsh effects of misfortune.

The majority of the rural population worked on the land. They paid cash rents to the gentry for the tenancies of a few acres of land each and, in addition, carried out a range of services for their landlords. These services often dated back to the medieval period and might include the gathering in of the lord's crops, the repair and maintenance of the manorial mill or fishpond. The homes of the poorest among them were bare of the furnishings of the yeoman class and there were few household goods except wooden bowls and platters and a few sticks of furniture. They lived in houses that were little better than hovels with no windows and earthen floors, upon which the inhabitants slept on heaps of straw. These dwellings, once left empty, quickly collapsed back into the earth from which they had been made.

Welsh was the everyday language of most people, though English dominated in south Pembrokeshire and in some areas of Glamorgan and Monmouthshire. The Reverend John Edwards of Tredunnock, writing in the aftermath of the Civil War, noted that Welsh was not widespread in his home village of Caldicott, whilst another contemporary claimed that no one in the parish of Caerwent spoke it at all.[16] As a contrast to this, in October 1641 the parishioners of Llanbister approached Sir Robert Harley, their local magnate, to ask if he would request their priest to allow a Welsh-speaking preacher to deliver sermons, since many of them did not understand English.[17]

It would be wrong, as is sometimes claimed, that the aristocracy and gentry regarded the Welsh language with indifference. William Herbert, created first Earl of Pembroke in 1551 by Edward VI, was the son of a Monmouthshire squire, and was said to speak Welsh more easily than English.[18] Some gentry families were fluent Welsh speakers and even amongst those where English was the predominant tongue, the sons were often boarded with Welsh families to become familiar with it, as was Lord Herbert of Chirbury in his youth.[19]

7

The Accession of Charles I

King Charles I succeeded to the throne on 27 March 1625. His accession was greeted with addresses of loyalty from prominent landowners and with expressions of allegiance from a number of Welsh counties – but if he expected that allegiance to be indicative of unquestioning submission, he was soon disillusioned.

As a part of the ongoing Thirty Years' War, a military campaign was being planned against Spain, with a naval attack on Spanish shipping at Cadiz. When the first Parliament of Charles' reign assembled in London on 18 June, he hoped to be granted sufficient subsidies to prosecute the war satisfactorily, but the grants he received were far short of his needs. Many members of the House, such as the determined and hard-headed Puritan lawyer and MP John Pym, were more concerned with possible popish plots against the state and its religion, whilst others were intent on limiting what was regarded as the malign influence of the king's trusted friend and courtier, the elegant and ambitious George Villiers, Duke of Buckingham.

Charles reminded the House of his benign feeling towards all members, but made it clear that, if the Spanish campaign was to be a success, more money was needed. If it was not forthcoming, Parliament would be dissolved. He would order the expedition to Cadiz to go ahead using whatever money came to hand. A range of measures were brought into force to ensure compliance with the king's aims. The Lords Lieutenant of the various counties of England and Wales were instructed to pressurise their wealthier inhabitants to cough up cash in the form of loans which would be used to finance the venture. All loans would be repaid in due course. The names of those who refused were to be reported to the royal council.

Ordinary townspeople who refused to contribute to the loans were told their houses would be demolished, and even those who did pay were likely to have soldiers billeted upon them, with the extra burden of having to feed them.[20] Martial law was declared in the name of national security, but none of this dampened the swell of indignation and resentment that swept the country. More than seventy people were imprisoned for non-contribution and five gentlemen were ordered to appear in court.

The case caused a sensation. As it was not entirely clear what the charges against them might be, the Attorney General attempted to get a ruling, but the judges fudged the issue by denying bail, contending that it could not be granted as there were no charges. They also ruled that the five could not be freed and that the whole issue was 'too dangerous for public discussion'. The king decided not to pursue the matter any further, as the loans might now be regarded as illegal.

The numbers of people refusing to pay grew steadily and some local authorities found themselves in a sticky situation. In Breconshire, only seven out of nineteen possible contributors agreed to send in any money. Flintshire had no cash to spare and Glamorganshire reminded the king that its seaborne trade had been so damaged by pirate attacks that farmers could not pay their rents.[21] Various amounts reluctantly dribbled in from other Welsh counties.

The raising of cash was far from being the only strain placed on the people of Wales. Troops had to be found to serve on the Spanish expedition, so a levy of men was placed on every Welsh county and suitably fit young men were sent down to the seaports along the southern English coast to board the ships waiting to sail for Cadiz.

The campaign was a disaster. A small fort was captured, but the men were poorly led and undisciplined. Many fell ill and by October the fleet was wallowing back towards England with half its complement dead.[22] Less than two years later there was yet another levy of Welsh soldiers, this time for an expedition to southern France. The Huguenot stronghold of La Rochelle was under siege by a French Catholic army and was desperate for aid. The Welsh counties were again expected to supply a body of men, one hundred each from Glamorgan and Monmouth and fifty from each of the others. As 800 Welshmen had been packed off the previous year for military service in Ireland, raising the new levy proved to be a challenge. The Deputy-Lieutenant of Pembrokeshire wrote to the Council of State that they had managed to find fifty men but were 'obliged to impress such men as they are both sorry and ashamed to present'.[23] Other counties found it hard even to achieve the necessary number. Cardiganshire managed forty-seven, with Carmarthenshire sending forty-nine men.[24]

The Duke of Buckingham sailed with the fleet as overall commander of the expedition. His plan was to land on the Île de Ré, close to La Rochelle and attack the French garrison besieging the city. It was another disaster. Heavy rain lasting for weeks caused sickness throughout the camp. The cannon ordered by Buckingham were too few in number and of insufficient power to breach the walls of the French fortress. A fleet carrying reinforcements was delayed and on 27 October it was decided to abandon the project. Of the 7,000 men who had set out for La Rochelle, only about 3,000 returned.[25]

In mounting these campaigns, it was not only men, munitions and supplies that were needed, but the ships to carry them. The City of London was expected to supply twenty ships, more than had ever been requested before, but their protest was quickly dismissed. The Welsh counties also found themselves at odds with the royal demand. Carmarthenshire was unable to provide the expected vessel of thirty tons, being 'an inland county with only a few creeks, in which there was no such ship', but eventually donated the cash equivalent.[26] Pembrokeshire attempted to share the cost of a pinnace with Cardiganshire, were turned down, and had to inform the Council that they could not provide it. Moreover, the county was short of cash because of poor harvests and because of the burdens already laid upon its people. Caernarfonshire, Merioneth and Denbighshire were also in financial straits, whilst Monmouthshire would do nothing without the agreement of Parliament.

The authorities of the maritime counties of Wales may well have been struggling to raise funds, but they also faced another more immediate problem. In August 1628, the Justices of the Peace in Pembrokeshire reported to the Council of State that large numbers of poor Irish people had been landing in the county, some of them secretly under cover of darkness. More refugees came ashore in the following months, all driven to flee from Ireland by a shortage of cattle and corn.[27]

This influx of strangers only deepened the long-standing fears of invasion by the Irish, possibly backed by Spanish or French soldiers. The Milford Haven waterway, with its long, winding channel snaking far into the centre of the county, was recognised by the government as a perfect landing place for an attacking force which once ashore, would prove difficult to dislodge. Anglesey might also prove to be an ideal base for a popish army, so the decision was taken to prepare defences along the Welsh coastline.

Forts were to be repaired or built anew at several places along the Milford Haven waterway, whilst Tenby, with its long, sandy beaches, well-suited as landing places, was to have its fortifications put in good order.

In addition, the trained bands of the Welsh counties were to be augmented by the recruitment of more men. To make them fit for purpose, a group of eighty-four experienced drill sergeants was formed, their pay increased from six shillings to twelve. They were to remain for up to three months at a location, training men in musketry and the use of swords and pikes. The one drawback was the cost of up to date weapons for each county authority and at least one area, Glamorganshire, considered equipping its men with bows and arrows.

The Petition of Rights

In March 1628, a new Parliament convened. In his opening speech, the king made it clear that if the Commons did not do its duty, he would 'in discharge of his conscience, use those other means which God had put into his hands to save that which the follies of some particular men may otherwise hazard to lose'.[28] Despite the veiled threat, it seemed that all might go well. Parliament voted a large subsidy to supply the king's needs, but no act was passed to ensure its payment. Members were muttering amongst themselves that before the passage of any act there would have to be a settlement of any grievances arising between Parliament and the Crown, but they were also aware that to alienate the king might result in a premature dissolution. The Commons therefore took a placatory course. It was willing to offer the king five subsidies, providing that he would agree to give his assent to a Bill of Rights that would make it illegal to apply any loan or tax without Parliament's agreement and to ensure that no subject could be imprisoned without trial. It was also remembered that several statutes issued during the reigns of Edward I and Edward III had made it illegal for the Crown to exact any taxes without the explicit approval of Parliament. The Bill was also aimed squarely at one measure imposed by royal decree, the so-called 'Coat and Conduct money', by which householders were required to house, feed and clothe any soldiers billeted upon them in times of trouble.

The king was concerned that the clauses of the Bill might infringe on the royal prerogative. He was further worried by the news that the House of Commons was to demand the removal of the Duke of Buckingham from the royal orbit. Charles cannot have been made any happier when Sir Edward Coke, one of the most respected lawyers to serve in the courts, stated that the law was the supreme authority in the kingdom and that it conferred upon the Crown all the rights that the monarch legitimately used. If those rights were abused, then Parliament could re-define them through legal means. Amongst those who helped to draw up the Petition was Charles Jones, a lawyer and member of Parliament for Beaumaris.[29]

On 13 May, Charles announced that Parliament was to be prorogued, so Coke suggested that, as the king had refused to countenance a public bill, the whole matter should be presented as a Petition of Rights. This was a long-established procedure by which any subject who felt ill-used by actions of the sovereign or his officials could petition to be allowed to enjoy the rights conferred by the laws of the land.

An argument now ensued, but at a distance, with messages being sent back and forth. Charles, unhappy at the Petition's terms, indicated that he would not receive it. In the event, he did, and returned a long-winded reply which sounded like agreement. The House of Commons demanded a formal assent, to which the king replied that the members should not interfere in affairs of state. There was an eruption of anger from the assembled MPs and the royal assent to the Petition was somewhat grudgingly given – but to the chagrin of the Commons, their bid to oust Buckingham failed.

When it became apparent that Parliament intended to take further measures to redress grievances, the king swiftly prorogued it. Copies of the Petition of Rights that had been printed on the instructions of Parliament, but not distributed, were destroyed by royal command and then reprinted with Charles' first agreement added to it. All of this confusion must have been a salutary lesson for the printer who, having published the Petition and the king's reply to it, found himself accused of misrepresenting both sides of the argument. One of those active in inquiring into the case was a member of the Vaughan family of Trawscoed.[30]

On 23 August 1628, The Duke of Buckingham was stabbed to death whilst staying at the Greyhound Inn in Portsmouth, shortly after hearing that La Rochelle had been relieved by an English army – news which was untrue. His assassin was a former soldier who had been wounded at Île de Ré. The news of the murder devastated the king, but others heard of it with relief.

Parliament reassembled in January 1629 and once again members concerned themselves with a list of grievances. Charles had hoped that his right to collect tonnage and poundage might not become an issue, but it was very much at the forefront of the minds of his subjects.

Tonnage and poundage were customs duties granted since medieval times to the English Crown by successive Parliaments. Tonnage was a fixed subsidy levied on every cask, or tun, of imported wine, whilst poundage was a tax on all imported goods. The two taxes had originally been levied separately but eventually were granted together, with the money collected being used for the protection of maritime trade. King James I had placed surcharges on customs and the Parliament of 1625 had delayed voting through tonnage and poundage until complaints that the surcharges were illegal had been examined. Before the matter was settled, a plague in London caused the prorogation of both Houses, but King Charles continued to apply the taxes as if they were an established prerogative of the Crown.

As soon as the question arose, Parliament denied the Crown's right to tonnage and poundage. When it seemed that the Petition of Rights might again be referred to, the king ordered the Speaker not to place it before the Commons. The House angrily adjourned, but when it met again, the Speaker still refused to let a vote to be taken and announced that Parliament would adjourn again at the king's command and would not meet until 10 March.

A farcical scene now ensued. When the Speaker tried to rise from his chair and leave the House, he found himself held down by several members, whilst a formal protest was drawn up and presented for consideration. The Commons was determined to vote on the problem of tonnage and poundage and also to rule against any new changes to forms of worship in the established Church.

When the king learned of this, he sent an order that the Sergeant-at-Arms should remove the mace, but the messenger was turned away from the doors of the chamber and the Sergeant was held under detention. When a second messenger arrived, the doors were firmly locked against him. Charles lost his temper and ordered the doors of the chamber to be broken down. Before this could be done, the resolution had been passed and the members had left the chamber.

It was inevitable that Parliament should now be closed, which took place in March 1629. Within days, Charles had published a proclamation justifying his actions and blaming everyone else. Several unfortunate members of the Commons were thrown into the Tower of London and heavily fined. Some preferred to remain in prison rather than pay and at least one of them died there.

The Personal Rule of Charles I

Parliament was not to be recalled for eleven years. The king, with the backing of a coterie of advisors who included Sir Thomas Wentworth, later Earl of Strafford, and William Laud, from 1633 Archbishop of Canterbury, began a long period of personal rule. Some of his subjects saw this as a time of tyranny, for others it was no more than the exercise of divine right.

One of the most difficult problems the king faced was a lack of money. The ongoing wars with Spain and France had proved a drain on the Crown's resources. Fortunately, peace was achieved by the close of 1629. Even so, the finances of the royal household were in a mess and Charles was deeply in debt. To find a way out of the financial swamp involved some hard decisions. Lands which had belonged to his predecessors for generations would have to be sold off and the collection of custom dues was rented out at a set rate to anyone who would take over the task.[31] He was also ready to fine gentlemen who enjoyed an income of £40 per annum; men of this rank had in the past been expected to present themselves at a coronation to be knighted. Well over 9,000 men were fined for having failed to do so. Monopolies to trade in a variety of goods were also awarded to those prepared to part with cash to receive the charter. Yet another sore point was that the prerogative rights of the Crown were exploited in order to fine anyone who encroached on the boundaries of royal forests. In one instance, the boundaries of a particular forest were extended in order to bring in more revenue.

Through these and various other means, by about 1634, Charles had managed to restore the fortunes of the Crown. However, a new problem now arose. There was every possibility that the French and Dutch would try to gain control of the waters around the eastern coasts of England.

To prevent this, the Navy needed to be improved and better armed – but how to raise the finances for this?

The answer was provided by William Noy, the Attorney General, who suggested the revival of the Ship Money tax. This was originally a medieval tax, levied on coastal communities in times of war to provide ships for national defence, or if that was impossible, a cash equivalent. It had been attempted in 1628, during the war with France, when £173,000 was demanded, but the opposition was so great that the writs were withdrawn. The difference now was that the country was at peace, but Charles justified the levy by citing the danger to trade and coastal settlements posed by pirates and the possibility of another outbreak of war in Europe. Nevertheless, as news of the imposition became public, there was a ripple of alarm across England and Wales.

London claimed immunity, as set out in the city's charter, but there was, despite concerns, no great surge of protest. In a relatively short time, £104,000 was collected. The howl of outrage came a year later, when the tax was applied again, but this time across the country to include inland communities.

The total amount to be brought in from all over England and Wales was just over £200,000, with £9,000 coming from Wales. Of this sum, £5,000 was expected from the southern areas and £4,000 from the north. Welsh counties with no coastline such as Breconshire and Radnorshire found themselves having to find sums of £933 and £490 10s respectively. Cardiganshire was assessed at £645, Carmarthenshire at £760, whilst Glamorganshire had to pay £1,449. Pembrokeshire was rated at £723 10s, with Haverfordwest chipping in with its own rate of £65 10s. Things were no easier in North Wales; Merionethshire was to find £416, Montgomeryshire £416, Flintshire £738 14s, Denbighshire £1,117, Caernarfonshire £447 and Anglesey £448.

Remarkably, protest was muted in Wales, perhaps because people bore in mind the damage to trade inflicted over the years by pirates. If the money was indeed to be spent on improving the navy, then all well and good. What caused irritation were the amounts to be paid over. In Cardiganshire a letter from disgruntled citizens was received by the High Sheriff, who was to collect the tax, reminding him that in past exactions the county had paid only half of what was expected from their neighbouring counties of Pembrokeshire and Carmarthenshire. Now there was no significant difference. Similarly, Flintshire in the past had only had to deliver half the amount extorted from other nearby counties.

Glamorganshire seems to have been one of the quickest to send its money up to London, as the Sheriff there was informed that the king had taken 'special notice of his forwardness'. Denbighshire's money did not arrive in the royal coffers until November, but this may have been because the Sheriff had entrusted the cash to drovers taking their cattle up to London. It was not unusual for drovers to be employed in this way. They had to hold a licence in order to drive cattle and this was awarded at quarter sessions only to those who were over thirty years of age and were householders. They had to be trustworthy, as they sometimes acted as bankers between the farmers and the merchants who bought the livestock. They were also empowered to buy or sell animals en route. On this occasion, a plague in London had sent the drovers entrusted with the Ship Money hurrying back home.

A sadder story prevailed in Pembrokeshire. The Sheriff, John Scourfield of New Moat, had set off for London on 1 February with the money in his saddlebags, but whilst crossing the river at Eynsham Ferry, the boat sank and he and others were drowned. At least £43 was lost with him.

In Merionethshire, the collection of money erupted into a court case when a poor man, Humphrey Tudor was unable, or refused, to part with any cash. The two collectors appointed by the Sheriff seized some of his goods. Tudor complained to a magistrate, Griffith Lloyd, who immediately granted a warrant for the arrest of the collectors. The case then went before the Council of the Marches, where the Sheriff accused Lloyd of encouraging the non-payment of the tax. The Council listened to Lloyd's explanation of events and found the charge against him to be a malicious falsehood.[33]

Writs for further payments of Ship Money were sent out in October 1635 and again in 1636. These were the years of the highest cash yields, but by now people were beginning to wonder if the tax was becoming an annual affair. Another cause for considerable unease was that the tax, supposedly only to be levied in times of war, was being regularly applied in times of peace.

There was no serious increase in the amounts demanded, but by 1637 it proved harder to collect the money. In Cardiganshire hardly a penny was offered. Rather shamefacedly, the Sheriff complained to the Council that in 'endeavouring to levy the ship-money, he tried by all fair and gentle means, but could not receive one penny, so that he was compelled to distrain oxen, kine, horses, sheep, household stuff and implements of husbandry, the which petitioner can get no money for, nor anyman to offer them one penny, though often set at sale'.[34] In Radnorshire, the Sheriff was also unable to raise funds but this time it was because of an outbreak of illness and the efforts to support the poor. Ship Money continued to be demanded until, as we shall see, in 1641 it was declared illegal by Parliament.

Religious Divides

Taxation was only one of the many problems that faced the king as the decade wore on. There had been concerns about the activities of Queen Henrietta Maria ever since her marriage to Charles in 1625. A devout Catholic, she had made no bones about her efforts to lure members of the aristocracy away from Anglicanism. She was also known to house a number of Capuchin priests in her palaces and to have constructed a sumptuous chapel at Somerset House, designed by Inigo Jones.

To some, it seemed that she was working hand in glove with William Laud, Archbishop of Canterbury. A former Bishop of St Davids, Laud had been raised in 1622 to the highest position in the Church of England. Highly suspicious of Puritans, whom he regarded as disloyal to church and state, he had begun a re-introduction of ceremonial into the Church of England. The celebration of the sacraments was to be observed, altar rails, which had vanished from many churches, were re-introduced and strict adherence to the *Book of Common Prayer* was to be observed. Any clergyman who seemed to be of a Puritan turn of mind, might find himself ousted from his living and Laud was prepared to crack down hard upon those who refused to obey the rules. Two priests in Wales, William Cradock, vicar of Cardiff and John Erbury, his curate, were accused of preaching dangerous ideas to their parishioners and another, William Wroth, developed what amounted to an independent church at his parish of Llanfaches.[35] All three were expelled from their livings.

There was widespread unease about all of these measures, which seemed to foretell a return to popery and the destruction of the established Church of England.

The Bishop's Wars

By far the biggest threat to the king's authority before the outbreak of the Civil Wars came from Scotland, which had its own distinct forms of worship. The Church of Scotland was far more Calvinist than its English equivalent, and hoped to see the bishops appointed by the king replaced by elected Elders. King Charles, like his father, looked to the unification of the Church of Scotland with that of England and in 1637 attempted to impose standard practices on both. The *English Prayer Book* was at his command to be introduced in Scotland and anyone who denied the king's supremacy in church matters was to be excommunicated.

There was immediate uproar. In February 1638 a committee formed of lords, burgesses and others in Scotland formed the National Covenant to resist these measures. There was widespread support, but the king remained adamant. When the Scottish Assembly met in Glasgow Cathedral in December it rejected all changes, expelled bishops from the kirk and affirmed its right to meet annually, not at the king's whim.

The only answer to Scottish intransigence as far as Charles was concerned was military action. An immediate levy of troops was called, with Wales to provide 1,160 men. The largest number came from Denbigh with 150 foot soldiers and Radnorshire, Cardiganshire and Merionethshire sending 50 each.

These and other levies assembled at York. There were some 28,000 men in all, but very few were trained soldiers. Despite the fact that 8,000 muskets had been ordered from Holland to equip them, the men proved difficult to train in the handling of the guns, for few had any knowledge of warfare and the majority were armed only with bows and arrows. Sir Edmund Verney, the king's standard bearer, reviewed them and was horrified at how untrained and unwilling they clearly were. They were stiffened by a number of professional soldiers and mercenaries, but the presence of these men only encouraged the rumour that the king was prepared to use foreign troops against his own people

This ragtag army, with the Earl of Essex in command, marched north to the border, where they came to a halt at Berwick. Here the king joined them, ready to face the 30,000 Scots massing just a short distance away. Charles announced he would not invade Scotland, providing the Scots approached no closer than ten miles from the border. A series of negotiations took place and on 19 June a treaty known as the Pacification of Berwick was signed. Its terms included a clause that all problems would be referred to the Scottish Assembly for resolution. Both armies then marched away without a serious clash of arms, but preparations for war continued.

When the Assembly reconvened in August 1639, it confirmed all the decisions taken previously at Glasgow and passed them into law. A new tax was to be raised to support the Scottish cause and all males were to sign the National Covenant. The Earl of Traquair, the king's representative, attempted to prorogue the Scottish Parliament to no effect and had no option but to return to London.

King Charles had decided to mount a new expedition against the Scots, but the expected cost of about £900,000 could not be met by the Treasury. It would be necessary to recall Parliament in the hope that subsidies would be granted. Members assembled on 13 April 1640 but any hopes that the king might have entertained for a quick granting of his wishes soon evaporated. John Pym, member for Calne, sprang to his feet and reminded the House of all the grievances to be discussed before any subsidies were considered. A debate was triggered that lasted for over a week and an exasperated Charles put an end to it by sending everyone home. The Short Parliament had lasted just three weeks.

Loans were requested, or enforced, in order to raise the necessary cash. The Earl of Strafford, now the king's principal advisor, is said to have handed over £20,000 of his own money. In all some £300,000 was found, by one means or another. The militias from areas to the south of the River Trent formed the bulk of the new army, but proved to be mutinous, ill-disciplined and argumentative. It was in no state to mount an effective opposition to the Scots army, which had crossed the border in August. Within weeks, Northumberland and County Durham had fallen and the English had to retreat.

The news of the invasion of the north caused widespread terror across the nation. William Maurice of Cefnybraich noted that 'there was great preparations for resisting of the Scots, both in England and in Wales. The trained bands were weekly mustered, beacons watched, all the able men in every county viewed and counted, and a general press for Scotland. The trained bands commanded to be ready under 24 hours warning to great trouble of the Commonwealth.'[36]

No doubt to Maurice's relief, and everyone else's, a Treaty was signed at Ripon in October 1640 by which Northumberland was left in Scottish hands, with the English exchequer meeting the costs.

Just before the signing of the agreement, at York, Charles had received a deputation of MPs and peers, who reminded him of their grievances and begged for peace with the Scots. It was clear that the Treaty would have to be ratified by both Houses so, scarcely knowing which way to turn, he capitulated and summoned another Parliament.

The Long Parliament

King Charles returned to London from York in October 1640. His entry into London was witnessed by John Evelyn who noted in his diary that he rode in some pomp, attended by a great cavalcade and with cheers of acclaim. In reality, the situation was much more threatening. Whitehall Palace had been fortified and there were guns placed on the roads leading to the building.[37]

The king was well aware that his opponents in Parliament meant to curb his prerogatives by any means possible. Members of the newly elected House of Commons knew that their wily sovereign would not give up his authority so easily. Both sides therefore began a not particularly subtle campaign of propaganda.

Rumours of a Catholic threat were deliberately circulated. On the night of 2 November, a day before Parliament was due to open, Catholic homes across the capital were raided in a search for arms. So virulent was public anger against so-called Papists that worshippers leaving the queen's private chapel at Somerset House were pelted with stones by an angry mob.

Supporters of the king were active, too. Some were encouraged to come to the opening of Parliament armed with swords, ready to deal with the king's opponents by violence if necessary. So volatile was the situation that, on the day of the state opening of Parliament, the king decided against the usual procession through the streets and travelled by barge along the river.[38]

In his opening speech, Charles made it clear that there would have to be a third campaign against the Scots but, in an effort to allay any fears, he asked members to put aside their suspicions and promised to do the same. It did little good, for most members had their eyes firmly fixed on reform. One eagerly anticipated measure was the drawing up of a Bill of Attainder against the Earl of Strafford, widely seen as the worst of the king's advisors. On 11 November Strafford was formally impeached on charges of high treason, with fifty-nine votes cast against the charge, including the Welsh members for Beaumaris, Caernarfon, Cardiff and Brecon. In December, Archbishop Laud was impeached and he too was hauled off to the Tower to join Strafford.

The king had never wished to sign the order for Strafford's execution, but realised that he had no choice. Huge crowds had gathered in the streets of London, howling for the earl's death. A possible plot to spring Strafford from the Tower was exposed, adding to the public fury. Those MPs who had voted against the Attainder Bill or had abstained from it were threatened, as was Charles and all his family. Eventually, upon receipt of a letter from Strafford urging him to sign the death warrant in order to preserve the public peace, he buckled and appended his name to the document. It was a decision he bitterly regretted for the rest of his life and one which may have strengthened his determination to resist any further machinations by Parliament. Strafford was executed for treason on 9 May 1641, though it was January 1645 before Laud suffered beneath the headsman's axe.

In the summer of 1641, the king travelled to northwards to attend the Scottish Parliament. His entry into the newly completed Parliament House was as regal as could be desired, with his crown carried before him, but what followed was as humiliating as he might have feared. He agreed that the laws passed the previous year by the Scottish Parliament should be published, accepted the National Covenant and even attended Presbyterian church services. He gave up any thoughts of imposing either the *English Prayer Book* or episcopacy on Scotland by signing the Treaty of London, which proclaimed that no military action could be taken against the Scots without the agreement of the English parliament.[39] He had, however, collected evidence implicating members of the Commons in treasonable dealings during the Bishops' Wars.

He was still in Edinburgh in October, when the nation was rocked by shocking news from Ireland. A rebellion had broken out and thousands of Protestant settlers were reported to have been murdered with appalling savagery. Boatloads of refugees were coming ashore in Pembrokeshire and Anglesey, bringing with them news of a possible French involvement in the rising. Indeed, the rebels were said to have the king's warrant for the rebellion and it was also reported that Queen Henrietta Maria regarded it as a defence of the Catholic church.

On 13 January 1642, Parliament sent out warning of a popish plot against the kingdom. Orders were given for all local magazines to be fully stocked with weapons and ammunition, guards were to be set and no castle or fort was to be passed into the hands of strangers without the express agreement of Parliament. There were reports of strange vessels sighted off the coast of Wales at Aberdyfi and Milford Haven and the mayors of Bristol and Pembroke were instructed to seize the ships, goods and persons of anyone coming from Ross, Wexford and Kilkenny.[40] At the end of January, Parliament went further; anyone attempting to enter England and Wales from Ireland was to be sent back and all shipments of arms, ammunition and supplies destined for Irish ports were banned.

Such was the panic that in Bradford, when news of the rebellion was received, it put the congregation of one chapel into such fear that some ran away, others wept and wailed and the preacher prayed for the protection of the Almighty God.[41] In Staffordshire, people went to church armed to the teeth and in Portsmouth it was believed that the fortress there was to be placed at the disposal of French invaders.[42]

The Grand Remonstrance

Covert plans to limit the king's prerogatives had been developing in the shadowy corners of Parliament for some time. Originating with John Pym, and couched in loyal, almost sycophantic, terms, the document that became known as the Grand Remonstrance listed in minute detail the grievances that had mounted up during King Charles' reign and beseeched him to carry out a series of reforms and the reversal of previous policies. Keynote clauses included the right of veto over all royal appointments and the curtailing of episcopal power. Members of the Commons were also invited to add their own pet grievances to the list.

When it was presented on 8 November 1641, there was considerable discussion in the House. Not everyone was accepting of it and it went through several readings. It was finally passed in the early hours of 18 November having been voted on by those weary MPs who still remained awake; there were 159 'ayes' and 148 'noes', a majority of just eleven. When it was presented to the king for his approval, he expressed some fury that it had already been published. Recognising the limits that it would place on his authority, he turned it down flat. In what may have been meant as a conciliatory gesture, he then offered to raise 10,000 troops to deal with the Irish rebels, but the question that most concerned members of the House was whether the king would use the troops against the rebels or against his opponents in England. The offer was rejected. Anxieties were heightened when the king ordered the guard around Parliament to be removed.[43]

Events now developed an unstoppable momentum fuelled by several serious blunders committed by the king. The first of these was to remove from the Lieutenancy of the Tower of London Sir William Balfour, a man known to sympathise with the aims of Parliamentary reformers. Balfour was replaced by Colonel Thomas Lunsford, a swaggering lout whose enemies accused him of eating children. Such was the outcry that within four days Lunsford had been replaced by Sir John Byron.

The king had decided on the arrest of five members of Parliament who were known opponents and who he had reason to believe had encouraged the Scots to invade Northumberland at the outbreak of the second Bishops' War. Accordingly, charges were drawn up against John Pym, Denzil Holles, John Hampden, William Strode and Arthur Haselrig. On Monday, 3 January, the Attorney General presented the impeachment articles to the House of Lords but it was decided that a committee should be appointed to look into the legality of the charges. The Sergeant-at-Arms was dispatched to the Commons to arrest the five, but was sent packing.

On the following day Charles set off for Parliament, apparently having been ordered by his wife 'Go, you coward, and pull those rogues out by the ears, or never see my face more.' The Commons however had received at least two warnings of what was intended and the five men were hustled away. When the king strode into the chamber, backed by an armed guard, he was greeted by a horrified silence. As *The Diurnall Occurrences in Parliament*, a newsbook published in London, noted, 'At which the House being much amazed to see his Majesty, who had never before been at their House, and having no notice of his coming'.[44] It was an unprecedented action. Though the members hastily rose to their feet, uncovered their heads and bowed, Charles had only humiliated himself and as he left the Commons empty-handed it was to angry cries of 'Privilege! Privilege!'

An ancient and long-standing tradition of Parliament had been breached and because of it, the House unanimously decided to adjourn for six days. The situation went from bad to worse on the next day, when the king went to the Guildhall to demand that the five members, who were in hiding nearby, should be handed over to him. As he made his way through the crowded, jeering streets, he was met with such hostility that he was forced yet again to withdraw. On 10 January, beset by fears for his own safety and that of his family, he abandoned the capital in favour of Hampton Court Palace.

In the succeeding weeks, the queen left England for Holland, laden with the crown jewels which she intended to sell in order to raise armaments. Charles accompanied her to Dover and after a sad farewell, made his way in stages to York. During his journey he received a number of messages from Parliament, urging him to return to London. He refused, perhaps reasoning that any laws enacted during his absence would have no legal force.

At some point he was presented with the Militia Ordinance, drawn up by Parliament in his absence. It proposed that the country's militia bands should be placed under command of men nominated by the Commons, a move that would guarantee that armed force would not be used against MPs. He refused to sign it. Irritated by this lack of cooperation, the House of Lords passed the Ordinance as a legally enforceable law without the Royal Assent

Negotiations between sovereign and Parliament were long, drawn out and bitter. Both sides made their arguments public by publishing them in pamphlets and tracts. The Commons had decided to carry on its business with or without the king and began enacting laws as it saw fit. The king made accusations of illegal conduct and was charged with the same by his opponents.

During the spring months, Parliament began appointing deputy lieutenants and commissioners to every county in the land who, under the terms of the Militia Ordinance, were to be responsible for the militia. By July and August, the nominees had received orders to set about training men for war. The king regarded this as illegal and created his own Commissions of Array, by which nominated men were to call out and prepare the trained bands and other military units in their vicinity. Parliament responded by declaring the Commissions of Array to be illegal and a danger to the peace and liberty of the subject. Neither side seemed to find it ridiculous that they had sometimes nominated the same people and had no idea which side, if any, the nominees would support.

On 12 July, Parliament passed a vote to raise an army, with the Earl of Essex as General-in-Chief. In a tit for tat move, the king appointed the Marquis of Hertford as Lieutenant-General for the western counties of England and the counties of South Wales. He was to have the authority to order the Commissioners of Array to levy forces, train them and lead them out to war.

Not surprisingly, some communities preferred to stand back and take a more measured approach to what they saw as an unnecessary catastrophe. The city of Chester declared that 'it is a sacred truth that a Kingdom divided cannot stand, so it is a legal principle that His Royal Majesty is the head, and the Parliament the representative body of this Kingdom, and that in the cordial union of his Majesty and Parliament consists the safety, glory and hope thereof.' They went on to say that the people of Chester did not wish to foment any difference between king and Parliament and were ready to 'obey his Majesty as their most dear and dread Sovereign, according to their due allegiance and their resolution to defend the privileges of Parliament, according to their free and just protestation; and that as God and the fundamental laws of this Kingdom have joined his Majesty and the Parliament together, so they cannot agree to a disjointed obedience, but do declare themselves enemies to all such as shall go about to put his Majesty and the Parliament asunder... .'[45]

Chester cannot have been alone in its desire to avoid war. No doubt in many parish churches prayers for peace were offered up and in the privacy of their own homes, men and women were fearful for the safety of themselves and their families. Samuel Wood, the steward of Sir John Trevor of Trefalun in Flintshire wrote that 'our fears do daily increase here, whether upon just grounds or not God knows'.[46]

There was to be no miracle, no avoidance of what was about to overtake the nation. The people of the British Isles would have to cleave to one side or the other. From the humble peasant in his rickety house to the nobleman in his fine mansion, all were expected to declare a loyalty. Brothers and fathers and sons, mothers and daughters, all were about to see the very foundations of their lives smashed around them.

Chapter 2

1642

Loyalties

In the summer of 1642, as the peoples of the British Isles prepared themselves for war, an uncomfortable choice faced them. For which side should they declare? On the one hand there was King Charles, whom many believed to be ordained by God to govern the nation. To oppose him was surely to oppose God; attempts to alter or subvert an ordained hierarchy in which everyone's place had been set by divine command could only result in chaos. A victory of the Parliamentary party would inevitably lead to the destruction of that orderly world. It was not surprising therefore that Charles claimed to be the defender of the church and an upholder of the traditional laws and customs of the realm.

On the other hand, there was Parliament, which also sought to preserve and enhance the laws and liberties of the nation and to place a limit on the powers of the Crown. There were few opponents of King Charles who envisaged the destruction of the monarchy or his death. Parliamentarians went into battle with the cry 'For God and Parliament', envisaging a time when, the fighting over, the role of the sovereign could be redefined within a new framework, its constitutional place guaranteed by the rights and privileges granted by the law, tradition and Parliament. The Church could be reformed, all traces of Papist influence removed and the clean, pure forms of Anglican worship preserved.

There were many who agonised over what to do. Sir Thomas Salusbury of Lleweni, MP for Denbighshire, sat down with his Bible and carefully studied all the references within it to monarchy and the role of kings. He was particularly inspired by Jesus' commandment to render to Caesar those things that were Caesar's and to God those things that were God's. Sir Thomas became a devoted follower of the royal cause. Others were guided by the First Book of Samuel, 26 verse 9: 'And David said to

Abishai, Destroy him not: for who can stretch forth his hand against the Lord's anointed and be guiltless?'[1] There were no doubts as far as the Royalist William Price of Rhiwlas in Merioneth was concerned; he spent large amounts of his own fortune in providing uniforms for the king's men but handed them over to his tenants until he could find someone to wear them. A slight hint perhaps as to what he expected his people to do, but a wasted one. The uniforms were discovered by a Parliamentary patrol, along with a good deal of cash.[2]

For others, it was the Parliamentary cause that engaged their loyalty. The Earl of Pembroke, the owner of extensive lands in Monmouthshire and Glamorganshire, adhered to the Parliamentary cause from the beginning, as did Sir Hugh Owen of Pembroke. Only two or three miles away from Owen's home the Lort brothers, Roger and Sampson of Stackpole Court, dithered over which side to choose. Indeed, they and others in the locality changed sides so often during the conflict that they were to become known as 'the West Wales Weathercocks.'

The majority of the upper classes moved, however sluggishly, into the Royalist camp. Their wealth and influence had been dependent for many generations on the Crown, and they had transferred their traditional loyalties to the Stuart dynasty upon the death of Elizabeth I. It has also been suggested that a subsidiary reason was gratitude for the measures taken by the Crown against pirates, who had for over a century caused such havoc to Welsh ships and coastal communities. There's no doubt too, that fears of invasion had been sharpened in Wales by the influx of so many refugees from Ireland and the refusal of Parliament to hand control of the military to the king only deepened those concerns.[3]

The attitudes of the ordinary people of Wales are harder to discover. Few of them left a record of their thoughts and it would be facile to say that they made their opinions clear by the side they chose. Many could not read and, as the newssheets and pamphlets of the day were all in English, the texts could not be understood. It's probable that the agricultural workers, miners, tradesmen and craftsmen who took up arms for one side or the other did so because they followed the lead of their local squire, who was in all likelihood, their employer and landlord.

King Charles, however, had no doubt about the loyalty of his Welsh subjects, declaring that he had utter confidence in them because no other part of his realm had done so much to support him. In fact, so many Welshmen flocked to his banner that North Wales became known as 'the nursery of the king's infantry'. This rush of enthusiasm for the royal cause dismayed many opponents, who believed that it confirmed the king in his decision to fight. At least one Roundhead supporter believed that the Welsh had 'done their best...to destroy three kingdoms'.[4]

Preparing for War

In July 1642, Parliament discussed the possibility of war. There were few Royalist members still sitting and on 12 July a vote was passed to raise an army of 10,000 men, but it was also stated that there was no evil intended against the king's person. This was to be a war of ideals, not a persecution of one man. The Earl of Essex was chosen as General-in-Chief of the Parliamentary army, with the Earl of Bedford as General-of-Horse. Warrants and commissions were handed out to supporters and instructions were given to raise and train men for the militias.

The Militia Ordinance to call out the militia in the county of Pembroke is one of the few to have survived. It was addressed to sixteen of the most prominent gentlemen in the area and began with the words: 'Whereas it doth appear to the lords and Commons in Parliament now assembled, that the King, seduced by wicked council, doth make war against the Parliament, and for that it is not improbable that under the colour of raising a guard for his Majesty's person, or some other pretence, the knights, gentlemen, freeholders and inhabitants of the county of Pembroke and town of Haverford the West may be drawn together. Therefore, you and every of you shall take special care that the ordinance concerning the militia be forthwith put in execution through the county; and the Sheriff, and all other officers, are hereby enjoined to assist you and every of you therein... .'[5]

Similar orders were issued by the king. He appointed the Marquis of Hertford as Lieutenant-General for the western counties of England, the six counties of South Wales and for Monmouthshire and Herefordshire. Hertford was to order Commissions of Array, to levy, train, and arm men and conduct them against the enemy. In the three counties of South-West Wales, the king's supporters formed the Royalist Association. At its head was Lord Carbery, despite the fact that he had been nominated by Parliament to implement the Militia Ordinance in the area.

In North Wales, a number of prominent figures were busy on the king's behalf. Chief amongst them were the Bulkeley family in Anglesey, Hugh Wynne of Bodysgallen and Roger Mostyn, who was said to have raised a regiment of 1,500 men for the king in just twelve hours, many of them lead and coal miners from his Flintshire estates.[6] Sir John Owen of Clenennau, however, found it much harder to recruit men in North Wales, despite the fact that he was trying to form a bodyguard to serve the twelve-year-old Prince of Wales.

The county of Flintshire had already assured the king of its loyalty with an address in which it promised that its people were prepared to hazard their lives and fortunes to maintain the honour and person of their monarch. The gentlemen of Flintshire and Denbighshire had met at Wrexham, where they resolved to raise a regiment of volunteers for the king's service and also to subscribe to a sum of £1,500 for the same purpose. They elected Sir Thomas Salusbury as the regiment's commander and, as we know, his deliberation over his Bible had already convinced him that he could not serve the Lord unless he served the Lord's anointed.

Commissions were granted by both sides to gentlemen across England and Wales, who exhorted their estate workers and tenants to fight for the side they favoured, or organised recruiting drives in their localities to swell the numbers. The regiments were frequently named after the gentlemen who created them, who would also appoint a number of officers, often men they were acquainted with, who might provide their own companies for the regiment. The average number of men in a regiment was about a thousand, and in the weeks and months following its creation, a regiment might not be well equipped or uniformed. The soldiers would practice with whatever weapons came to hand – axes, ditch digging tools, long knives or bows and arrows. Money to buy more up to date weapons would come out of the colonel's pocket, but once the regiment had joined the main army, its payment, equipment and training became the responsibility of the overall command. As the fighting began, the majority of men, whether they were officers, foot soldiers or mounted troops, had very little experience of warfare.

In addition to raising troops, supporters on both sides were frantically repairing, fortifying and provisioning their ancient castles and mansions. Town councils looked anxiously at the defences surrounding their settlements and hastily set about improving them. At Tenby, David Hammond the Mayor obtained guns from the guardship *Lyon,* at anchor in Milford Haven, and employed workmen to make cartridges and a new bolt for the carriages of one of the ship's cannon. He ordered culm, sand, gravel and limestone for repairs to the walls, timbers for bars and door lintels, and iron for chains, locks and bolts. The town's gates were put into repair and the ruined sections of the town walls were rebuilt, a tree was sawn down to make a pair of wheels, possibly for the cannon, and candles and coal were supplied to the town watch.[7]

There were similar moves in North Wales; the ruinous state of Conwy Castle was swiftly repaired by John Williams, Archbishop of York, who used it as a base for much of the war. A few miles away, Thomas Bulkeley of Baron Hill strengthened the defences of Beaumaris Castle.[8]

Whilst all these frantic preparations were taking place, King Charles was moving steadily northwards towards York. He arrived there with a small retinue on 19 March 1642, and set about raising troops, calling upon individual noblemen on their allegiance to attend the king in person. Soon there was a steady influx into the city of peers and men from all walks of life. A setback occurred in April when Sir John Hotham, governor of Hull, where a great store of munitions was kept, refused his sovereign entry into the town, as he had strict instruction from Parliament to hand over the armaments only on the orders of the Commons.

Nevertheless, the king continued to recruit and in August summoned all true supporters to attend him at Nottingham. There, on 22 August, in heavy rain, he raised his standard to a fanfare of trumpets and shouts of 'God save the king!' It was a declaration of war, but not one that enthralled some of his advisers, who a day or two later suggested that he should attempt negotiations with Parliament. Charles refused point blank.

Within a short time, it was decided to move to Derby, and once there, to move on to the Welsh Marches. Shrewsbury was said to be entirely favourable to his cause and there was every prospect that men would flock to his standard from the counties of Wales. The king was probably also aware that on 7 September, the Earl of Essex had left London with an army of between 15,000 and 20,000 men and was shadowing his line of march.

Before he set off for Shrewsbury, the king sent ahead Francis Ottley with orders to raise a force of 200 men and to march them as quickly as possible to the town. Possibly, Charles wanted to forestall any likely demonstrations of disloyalty and he must have been delighted when the town council promised him 'the best entertainment the troublesome times could afford'.[9]

Charles entered Shrewsbury on 20 September to a warm reception and was housed at the Council House, where he remained for several days. During his stay, he gave the town two pieces of ordinance and toured the fortifications. On Friday, 23 September the king moved on to Chester with a small escort, leaving the bulk of his army behind at Shrewsbury.

He may have felt some concern about his reception at Chester. On 8 August, the day on which the city had proclaimed its unwillingness to take sides, it had been visited by Sir William Brereton. This convinced Parliamentarian, with a fiery dislike of the Established Church, had sent drummers through the town to encourage support for Parliament. Unfortunately for him, a number of prominent Royalists lived in the town and their objections to the drummers led to a riot. Brereton and two of the city's officials were dragged off to face the authorities at the Guildhall, but luckily were discharged.

No such tumult welcomed the king. He was cordially received by the mayor and aldermen, who escorted him at the head of a large procession to the Bishop's Palace, where he was to stay. In the succeeding days he received a gift of £200 from the city, with another £100 for the Prince of Wales, who had accompanied him. There were inspections of the city walls and gates, and the king welcomed several regiments of trained bands, including the men raised by Roger Mostyn and another under the command of William Salesbury. Equally eager to attend his king was Lord Grandison, who on his way to Chester had diverted to attack Nantwich, a town suspected of Parliamentary sympathies.

Two of the most welcome arrivals were the king's nephews, Prince Rupert and Prince Maurice. The sons of Charles' sister, Elizabeth, Queen of Bohemia, these young men had already experienced warfare. Given command of cavalry units, Rupert had proved his worth by a military action near Worcester. Learning that Essex's army was approaching Worcester, Rupert had been ordered to take a force of about 1,000 cavalrymen to protect a Royalist convoy but on 23 September they encountered the vanguard of Essex's army at the village of Powick, just outside Worcester. A sharp skirmish ensued in which over 150 of the Parliamentary force were killed. It was touted as a glorious victory, though the losing side saw it somewhat differently.

On 26 September, Nehemiah Wharton, a foot soldier with Essex's army, sent a detailed account of the action to his family and friends in London. 'This day our horse forces…kept all the passages over the Severne, and by that means kept in the Cavaliers, who often assayed to fly but were repelled…. Towards evening, Prince Robert (sic) entered the city at a bye passage with eighteen troops of horse, most of the city crying "Welcome, welcome", but principally the mayor who desired to entertain him; but he answered "God damn him, he would not stay, but would go and wash his hands in the blood of Roundheads" and immediately sent some to lye in ambush, and with the rest sallied out upon our forces…the battle was very hot and many fell on both sides…our wounded men they brought into the city and stripped, stabbed and slashed their bodies in a most barbarous manner and imbued their hands in their blood.'[10]

Already tales of atrocities and barbarism were circulating on both sides, deepening the divisions between them.

On 25 September, King Charles issued instruction to the Commissioners of Array in Caernarfonshire to pay all the money collected for the war effort to Sir John Owen of Clenennau. Two days later he left Chester and travelled to Wrexham to address a large crowd of people from Denbighshire and Flintshire, explaining his motives for declaring war on Parliament. He then returned to Shrewsbury, where he refused a request from the Earl of Essex for another round of negotiations.

All was not well at Shrewsbury. Daily complaints were made about the conduct of the king's soldiers. Their pay came in irregular amounts, with long gaps between payments. They had to forage for their own food and some were prepared to resort to theft and violence if they did not get what they wanted. In an attempt to calm tempers, meetings of the soldiery were held and addressed by the king, who also convened meetings of the people of Shrewsbury and did his best to calm their fears. Their anger unassuaged, the more prominent citizens held their own meeting at the George Hotel and bluntly told their sovereign that they did not approve of his behaviour or that of his soldiers.

Determined to ensure a steady flow of cash, Charles ordered the establishment of a Mint at Shrewsbury. He placed it under the direction of Thomas Bushell, who had been mining lead on the lands of the Myddelton family in Cardiganshire and who had been allowed to create another Mint at Aberystwyth. Bushell was a trusted figure in Royalist circles, having supplied troops, clothing and lead for shot to the army.

Supplies of silver and other metals for the Mint were in short supply, so the king held a large public meeting in fields outside the town. He assured his listeners that he was fighting for their rights and liberties and promised to melt down his own plate and convert it into money if only they would do the same. Many people are said to have agreed, but whether the meeting was as successful as hoped is unknown.

There were other sources of income at Charles' disposal. Sir Richard Newport of High Ercall in Shropshire is said to have paid £6,000 for a peerage, whilst others handed over varying sums of money for knighthoods.

Events in South Wales

Across South Wales, supporters of both sides were hurriedly trying to prepare for what might come. The Earl of Worcester in his mighty stronghold of Raglan Castle was concerned to ensure that the defences would hold against a possible siege. He ordered the building of earthworks in the park around the castle and set up a powder mill. The surrounding area was scoured for likely recruits and he appointed his fourth son Charles to command the garrison.

The Somerset family, of which Lord Worcester was the head, had been influential in Monmouthshire for several generations. Wealthy and devotedly Catholic, they also enjoyed the confidence and trust of successive English monarchs since Henry VIII. Their Catholicism also made them a focus of Protestant and Parliamentary suspicion. During the fractious years leading up to the Civil Wars, it was claimed that the earl was plotting rebellion and in 1636 he was deprived of the Lord Lieutenancy of the county, which included command of the local militia, despite the fact that he had lent the king the staggering amount of £40,000. Rumour also suggested that he had planned to place fellow Catholics as officers of the militia.[11]

Gossip intensified in 1640, when King Charles wrote to the Deputy Lieutenants of South Wales mentioning that Worcester had been entrusted with 'some secret service' but did not specify what that service might be. It was possibly the raising of troops for the Bishops' Wars, but the earl was now seen as a highly dubious character by many Parliamentary supporters.

On 29 August 1642, the House of Lords ordered the Commons to disarm all Papists, including the Earl of Worcester. A few local Protestants thought that they were the men for the job and marched to Raglan Castle, where they demanded entry. They had come, they told the bemused earl, to search for arms. According to legend, the earl allowed them into his home, insisting that they must carry out their search. He led them into the great keep, where an ingenious piece of machinery had been set up by his eldest son, Lord Herbert, to pump water from the moat to a tank at the top of the keep. At a secret sign from the earl, the machinery was put into motion, its rumblings and grindings terrifying the visitors. A second later, one of the castle workmen came flying into the keep screaming 'Look to yourselves my masters, the lions are got loose.' The men wasted no time in putting a considerable distance between themselves and the castle.[12]

Lord Herbert, who would be described in 1655 as one of the foremost scientific geniuses of the day, was an enthusiastic inventor who set up a laboratory within the castle to study mechanics and mathematics. He was a favourite of the king and hoped to be given a command in the South Wales area, but Charles was unwilling to promote him as he knew it would invite accusations of pro-Catholic leanings. Instead, he chose the Marquis of Hertford who, as we have seen, was appointed Lieutenant-General for the western counties of England and for the six counties of South Wales. It was an appointment that reportedly caused tensions between Herbert and Hertford.

Despite his disappointment, Lord Herbert continued to work hard rallying men and funds for the royal cause. Then, towards the end of September, a small fleet of coal ships arrived in Cardiff, but they were not carrying coal. Instead, their cargoes consisted of the Marquis of Hertford and a detachment of his troops. Initially active in the south-west of England, they had lost an encounter with Parliamentarian forces near Sherborne in Dorset and had been pushed westwards towards Minehead in Somerset.[13] The marquis hoped to be able to transport his men across the Bristol Channel to Wales, but there was an insufficient number of available ships, so he split his force, sending half his men to Cornwall under the command of Colonel Hopton. The rest scrambled aboard the coal ships and sailed into Cardiff.

Now that they were face to face, Hertford and Herbert seemed to understand the need to cooperate and worked together to solve a confused situation that had arisen at Cardiff. The castle was the property of the Parliamentarian Earl of Pembroke. The king had ordered it to be seized and had appointed a man named William Herbert, apparently no close relation to Lord Herbert, to oversee the task. William Herbert was also instructed to confiscate all the rents of Pembroke's properties in the area.

When the Marquis of Hertford and Lord Herbert joined up, they were supposedly admitted into Cardiff Castle without problem, though a contemporary pamphlet claimed that the Royalist force had been attacked by people fearing that they had come to plunder. Whatever the truth, the marquis and his men remained at Cardiff for some weeks, where he levied more men for the Royalist army. Rumour stated that he soon had a force of some 10,000 men. In his endeavours, he was aided by the Earl of Worcester, who lent him up to £2,000 to further the war effort.

The drive to recruit more troops must have been greatly encouraged by the arrival in Raglan of the Prince of Wales. Sent by his father to stay with Lord Worcester, the Prince was welcomed enthusiastically and honoured with a banquet. Gifts were lavished upon the twelve-year-old by local worthies, who were probably impressed by the aplomb with which he carried out his duties. The same excitement seems to have attended him as he passed through Radnorshire on his way back to re-join his father.[14]

It's tempting to wonder if the prince's departure from Raglan was hastened by rumours of a possible Parliamentarian advance on Abergavenny. The city of Hereford had recently been occupied by the Earl of Stamford in the name of Parliament and he was expected to march westwards. To counter this, Hertford sent 900 of his foot soldiers and a troop of horse to garrison Monmouth.[15] There was every reason for Hertford to be concerned. On 27 October, Stamford had launched a surprise raid on Presteigne, where a gathering of Royalists was planning an attack on Hereford. In the confusion, three Royalist soldiers were killed and Charles Price of Pilleth and Francis Rickards, two of the originators of the plan, were captured.[16]

On 4 November, Hertford set off towards Hereford, accompanied by Lord Herbert. Just over a week later, at Pontrilas, Hertford's advance guard of 350 men came face to face with a detachment of Stamford's troops led by Colonel Robert Kyrle. In the initial skirmish, six of Hertford's men were killed and another fifteen of them fell in the ensuing firefight.

Reaching the banks of the River Severn, Hertford's force pushed on into Herefordshire. It seemed likely that Hereford itself was threatened, so Lord Stamford hurriedly summoned together the local trained bands, but before he could challenge the enemy approach, he learned that Hertford had re-crossed the Severn and was now marching in the direction of Tewkesbury. Stamford, with a force of some 4,000 men set off in pursuit and on 16 November caught up with the Royalists just outside Tewkesbury. In the fight that followed hundreds of recent Welsh recruits, poorly trained in the use of their muskets, were mown down by Parliamentary guns. The rest tossed aside their weapons and fled, despite the pleas of Lord Herbert to stand their ground. Over 2,500 men from both sides died that day and the surviving Royalists took refuge back in Wales.[17]

Despite the losses his men had suffered, Hertford was determined to press home an attack on Hereford. On 27 November he launched an assault on the city, which was said to be defended by only 1,500 troops. It was again a defeat for the Royalists, with the Welsh driven back with losses of up to 2,000 men, that being the number claimed by the newssheets. It was an unnecessary loss, because just a short while later, Lord Stamford left for Gloucester to help in its defence and the whole of Herefordshire fell to the Royalists.[18]

The Road to Edgehill

King Charles had remained at Shrewsbury for much of September but was giving careful consideration as to his next move. He knew that the Earl of Essex was occupying Worcester with an army of some 16,000 men. It might be possible to challenge Essex somewhere near Worcester and bring him to ruin. Alternatively, the king could slip away from Shrewsbury with his forces and head for London before Essex was even aware that he was gone. A quick decision was needed as winter was not far off and neither army would wish to move along muddy roads in cold, wet conditions.

On 12 October, the king's forces set out for London in a bid to capture the capital. Travelling as swiftly as conditions allowed, the route took them through Bridgnorth, Kenilworth and on towards Banbury.[19] Essex was caught napping, for it was several days before he realised that the king had left the Marches. Scrambling out of Worcester, he and his men set off to intercept the Royalist force. It was not certain exactly where the royal army was and neither did Charles have an exact knowledge of Essex's whereabouts. The king must have been encouraged, however, by the daily sight of more and more recruits hurrying to join him.

By 22 October, the royal army was just a few miles short of Banbury. Encamped over a wide area, it now numbered some 15,000 men, with twenty or so cannon. Amongst the foot soldiers were more than 700 men from South Wales, arranged into eight blue-coated companies, under the command of Sir Edward Stradling of St Donat's Castle. Another body of Welsh troops was commanded by Sir Thomas Salusbury and had been formed as a result of the meeting at Wrexham, where Salusbury had been elected as their colonel. These were the men who were famously described by one of their countrymen, Robert Evans, as '1,200 poor Welsh vermin, the offscourings of the nation'. It is worth noting that a contemporary account describes some of the troops as still wearing the same garments they had worn in the fields at home. Very few of them had adequate weapons, and instead clutched old knives, wooden cudgels, scythes, pitchforks, sickles or any kind of sharp-edged tool.[20]

As night drew on, the countryside to the west and north of Banbury was lit by pinpricks of light as the Royalist army huddled around campfires to await the dawn. Incredibly, just a few miles away near Kineton, Essex's army had also settled down for the night. As already noted, his force numbered some 16,000 men, of which about 12,000 were infantry, with maybe 1,000 dragoons. The artillery train contained over thirty guns of various sizes. There was still uncertainty in each camp as to exactly where the other was and it was not until nightfall that Prince Rupert and his cavalry, riding back to the house he occupied in the village of Wormleighton, came across a party of Essex's men and captured them, that the positions were finally known.[21]

The following morning, at Prince Rupert's suggestion, the king's army took up position just below the crest of a steep, north-westwards facing escarpment known as Edgehill, which lay across the route to London. There was already disagreement amongst the army's commanders as to how the troops should be disposed. The Earl of Lindsey wanted the regiments in the five brigades drawn up in lines two or three abreast, whilst the Earl of Forth argued that it was better to place the musketeers on the wings of the army, with the pikemen forming a solid central block. Urged by Prince Rupert, the king eventually ordered Forth's plan to be adopted.

It took much of the morning to deploy the troops, but by noon the king's army was in place. In the centre stood three brigades of infantry, with two more in reserve behind them. The brigades were flanked by cavalry units. In the centre of the line was a block consisting of Richard Feilding's Brigade of Foot, which included Sir Edward Stradling's regiment. To the left of Feilding's Brigade was Henry Wentworth's Brigade, in which was positioned Sir Thomas Salusbury's regiment.

The Parliamentary army had drawn up in formation on the plain below the Royalist position. Amongst the troop waiting anxiously there was a unit commanded by John Gunter, Lord Essex's tenant at Lamphey Palace. It is possible that some of Gunter's soldiers included men from the Lamphey estate. Both sides would have seen the flags of the opposition fluttering in the breeze and the flash of sunlight on breastplate and helmet and both would have heard the distant sound of the enemy drums rolling wave-like through the autumn air.

Each side seem to have waited for the other to make the first move, though the Parliamentary inactivity may have been because they were awaiting the arrival of some of their regiments. At about 2.00pm, Essex's artillery opened fire, supposedly aiming at the king and his retinue, who were observed to be riding from regiment to regiment to encourage the men. This cannonade was answered by the six-gun Royalist battery situated on Bullet Hill.[22] The bombardment lasted for up to an hour, during which time it is possible that some men deserted the field. The Royalist infantry had moved slowly down the slope from the crest of the ridge, flags waving jauntily above them, until they came to the foot of the hill.

There was fighting between the dragoons of both sides and between opposing groups of musketeers as they struggled for possession of a hedge that ran across the battlefield.[23] At about 3.00pm, Prince Rupert ordered a cavalry charge against the Parliamentary mounted troops, who let loose a crackling fire from their pistols before some turned to flee. Cutting down the remainder and killing some of the gunners of the Parliamentary artillery, the Royalist cavalry set off in an enthusiastic pursuit of the retreating enemy. The chase is said to have reached as far as Kineton, many fugitives being hacked down on the way, before the horsemen began plundering the Parliamentary baggage train.

The absence of their cavalry left some units of Royalist infantry exposed to attack. Feilding's Brigade found itself receiving a charge from a Parliamentarian cavalry unit and in the bloody struggle that followed, Stradling's regiment suffered serious casualties. Amongst the dead was Lieutenant-Colonel William Herbert, the man entrusted by the king a few months earlier to seize Cardiff Castle. A number of prisoners was taken, including Richard Feilding himself and Sir Edward Stradling, who was dragged away to be imprisoned in Warwick Castle.

Wentworth's Brigade had moved forward to clash with large groups of Parliamentary infantry, which did not give way easily. Half blinded by smoke from volleys of musketry, men clubbed at one another with cudgels and musket butts, or slashed wildly with swords, both sides unwilling to give ground.

By now, it was late afternoon and, as the light began to fail, fighting petered out across the battlefield. The fields were littered with corpses and wounded men lay calling for help. The two armies had fought to a standstill, their troops shocked, bloodstained and bewildered. As night wore on it became bitterly cold, but few fires were lit and survivors huddled together for warmth. Many men had eaten no more than a crust or two of bread for over forty-eight hours and hunger must have added to their exhaustion.

As dawn began to break, there was a suggestion by some Royalist officers that a cavalry charge might settle the battle for good, but in view of the state of the army, the idea was abandoned. Neither side was willing to abandon the battlefield and at some time during the morning the king sent a proclamation to the Earl of Essex, promising a pardon to all soldiers who were willing to lay down their arms. It was rejected and eventually the two armies began a withdrawal from the area. Essex's troops made their way to Warwick, whilst the king's army headed for Banbury. Two days after the battle, Prince Rupert raided the rear of Essex's column and took about twenty-five wagons loaded with ammunition. His men also slaughtered a large number of wounded men who were being nursed in Kineton.

Both sides claimed Edgehill as a victory, but it was actually something of a stalemate. Over 1,000 men from both sides had perished, their bodies tumbled into huge burial pits across the battlefield. There was probably an equal number of wounded, some of whom were too badly injured ever to fight again. There must have been many who, for the rest of their lives, were haunted by what they had seen that day.

It was also noted by some contemporaries that many men fled the battlefield during the fighting, terrified for their lives. Amongst them, it was said, were large numbers of Welshmen. Lord Clarendon, writing years after the battle, hinted that their conduct had been disappointing, but he may have drawn his view from pamphlets published in the immediate aftermath of the battle. One such, entitled *The Welshman's Public Recantation, or her hearty sorrow for taking up arms against her Parliament*, was a set of verses, one of which ran:

> 'Their Grievous fight,
> Did make day night,
> O Taffy, Taffy;
> Her would be flying,
> Liked not dying,
> 'Twas bad Epitaphe;
> Her sword and spear
> Did smell for fear,
> And her heart were
> In a cold plight;
> Made Taffy outright,
> His poore britches beshite,
> O Taffy, O Taffy.'[24]

This sort of view of the Welsh, highly derogatory and contemptuous, was as we shall see, not unknown at the time. There can be no doubt that Welshmen and Englishmen on both sides deserted before and during the battle. The fact that many of them, Welsh and English alike, were inexperienced, poorly armed and clothed and badly fed, must not be forgotten.

The Storming of Brentford

A few days after Edgehill, the king had established himself in Oxford, which from this time became the Royalist headquarters in England. It was decided that the advance upon London should continue, and in the following days Reading was taken without opposition. Prince Rupert, in a series of raids across the surrounding countryside, approached almost to the limits of London. This alarmed Parliament to such an extent that it was decided to send a message to the king suggesting negotiations. After initial reluctance, Charles agreed, but did not halt his army's march towards the city. Frantic preparations were made at Brentford to halt his approach, a series of barricades and fortifications being thrown up across the line of approach. These hasty defences proved strong enough on 12 November to resist Rupert's cavalry when he attempted to breach them.

Unwilling to accept failure, the Prince regrouped and sent forward the infantry. These included Sir Thomas Salusbury's regiment which, in the initial clash that opened the fighting, found itself in front of the strongly fortified house of Sir Richard Wynne. The house was occupied by an advance guard of the Parliamentary army, commanded by Denzil Holles, one of the five MPs whom the king had failed to arrest the previous January. Holles' soldiers now opened up a devastating fire upon the approaching enemy. Salusbury's infantry soldiers were ordered to clear the building and were inspired to fight like lions by Sir Thomas' words to them: 'Gentlemen, you lost your honour at Edgehill. I hope you will regain it here.'[25]

The Royalist attack was successful in driving the Parliament forces out of Wynne's house and back into the town itself, out onto the road to London. Casualties were said to number between 150 and 500 men, with a great many more Parliamentarians drowning in the River Thames as they tried to escape along its banks. Meanwhile the victorious Royalist army set about looting the town, carrying away almost everything they could, from money and clothing to household items and livestock. Some of the inhabitants of Brentford were left in such a state that they had to beg the Royalists for bread.

The news of the fall of Brentford was received in London with horror. Parliament was quick to issue a call for volunteers to protect the city and within two days, the Earl of Essex, who had reached London by a roundabout route, was able to inspect an army of 24,000 men at Turnham Green. News of this impressive force must have filtered through to King Charles who, fearing an attack, withdrew to Oxford. It was a decision which many of his commanders regretted, for had he been able to take the capital, the war might have been over within weeks. As it was, with winter now upon them, both sides preferred to await events.

Chester Defenceless

In the Welsh Marches Lord Hertford, perhaps spurred on by news of the indecisive result at Edgehill, was busy raising troops for the king. Lord Worcester, soon to be raised to the rank of Marquis by the king, was pouring money into this effort. At Shrewsbury, the departure of the king had left the city undefended. Shortly afterwards, Sir Francis Ottley, one of the king's Commissioners of Array, was appointed as governor and he set about preparing a defence. Repairs were carried out to the castle and town walls and the council voted the sum of £200 for the purchase of two pieces of ordnance.

Further north, Chester was also defenceless. It was known that Sir William Brereton, one of the MPs for Cheshire, was in London recruiting a regiment intended to seize the county for Parliament. A campaign in the neighbourhood of the city could only be a threat to the prosperity and wellbeing of the inhabitants, a likelihood which many of its people were eager to prevent.

On 21 October 1642, it was agreed by an assembly of citizens that a band of 300 men should be raised for defence. These should be inhabitants of Chester and they were to be armed with muskets and other weapons. The guns were to be supplied by a group of sixty-one citizens, each of them providing between one and three muskets. The mayor and others would decide exactly how the other armaments were to be supplied.[26]

Three weeks later it was agreed that a city watch was needed. On each of Chester's six gates a guard of eight men were to be stationed, two of the soldiers with muskets, the others armed with halberds. Another guard of twelve men was to be placed permanently at the High Cross.[27] All the guards were to be intensively trained and eight members of the trained bands were to instruct them in the use of their weapons.

In December, much of central and eastern Cheshire fell to Parliament. This seems to have panicked the assembly in Chester into drawing up an Agreement of Neutrality, its terms intended to underline the city's unwillingness to be involved in the war. The Agreement stated that there should be a cessation of arms; that there should be a disbandment of armed troops; that prisoners should be exchanged; that the fortifications of Chester, Nantwich, Slopford and Knutsford should be demolished; that all plundered goods should be restored to their owners; and that ratification of the terms should be procured from the king and from Parliament.[28]

The king apparently disapproved of the Agreement, saying that he 'did not like this kind of measuring out of treason by the month.' Parliament refused to countenance it, believing it set a bad example to other towns.

In contrast, on 20 December, the gentlemen of Shropshire put their names to a resolution to raise and maintain forces 'at their own charge for the defence of his Majesty, their country, and more particularly the Fortunes, Persons, and Estates of the Subscribers undernamed.'[29] By the end of the month, they are said to have raised a troop of 2,000 dragoons.

At the close of 1642, the Royalists were supreme in much of Wales and the Marches. Chester might seem to waver in its allegiance and in some parts of Glamorgan and in South-West Wales there were pockets of Parliamentarian resistance. In Pembrokeshire, John Poyer, ex-mayor and merchant of Pembroke, had set about improving the defences of Pembroke, the only town in Wales to have actually declared for Parliament. With the support of the influential Laugharne and Owen families, it was possible that he could hold back for a time the advancing tide of Royalism. On the whole, however, King Charles had good reason to feel confident as he celebrated Christmas with his court at Oxford.

Chapter 3

1643

January to March, South Wales; Battles and Skirmishes

There was little festive goodwill to be had at Raglan as the new year of 1643 was ushered in. Lord Herbert and the Marquis of Hertford were at odds and relationships between the two men grew so bitter that the king was forced to dispatch Colonel Arthur Trevor to South Wales to try and mend fences. The quarrel may have had its roots in Herbert's resentment over Hertford's appointment as Commander-in-Chief of South Wales and Hertford's distrust of Herbert's Catholicism. Whatever the cause, Trevor's tact seems to have healed the breach as he was able to assure one of his correspondents that he thought the two men could at last cooperate.

Early in January 1643, Hertford marched out of Wales towards Worcester with an army of 2,000 horse and foot, continuing on to Burford, where he hoped to join up with Gloucestershire Royalists. He became convinced that, with a strong Parliamentarian garrison based at Cirencester, nothing could be done in the area, so headed for Oxford where he presented the king with a plan to capture the town. Charles must have been impressed because he ordered the Princes Rupert and Maurice to help. By 7 January, a Royalist force of 6,000 horse and foot, many of them Welsh, had appeared before Cirencester.

A summons to surrender was sent into the town, but when it was refused, the decision was taken to postpone an attack.[1] Hertford's force marched back to Burford, whilst the two princes retired to Oxford with their men to drum up more support.

On 1 February, the Royalists were back before Cirencester, numbering now some 4,000 troops, with reinforcements drawn from the Oxford garrison.[2] There was no hesitation in storming the town, which was taken after heavy fighting and thoroughly plundered in the same manner as Brentford. Over 1,100 prisoners were taken. The Welsh troops in

44

Hertford's army had been at the forefront of the attack and suffered many casualties. There were claims that the Welsh had been deliberately placed at the forefront of the fighting, driven on by the Royalist cavalry, 'to suffer the greatest slaughter, who in that army were a continual sacrifice to the sword.'[3]

From Cirencester Prince Rupert moved on to Gloucester, which he ordered to surrender early in February. Lieutenant-Colonel Massey, in command of the garrison, was unimpressed and replied that he held the city for Parliament and would only give it up on the instructions of that authority. A second summons met with no better response, so Rupert abandoned any idea of an attack and marched back to Cirencester.

In South Wales, Lord Herbert had been energetically raising more troops and by mid-February had gathered together 1,500 foot and 500 horse. They were provided with a good selection of arms, supposedly at a cost to Herbert of about £60,000, though money had also been raised through a 'Benevolence' tax levied on the local gentry.[4] The fact that Herbert had been able to raise so many men so quickly suggests that there was still a groundswell of loyalty to the king, though not everyone proved so enthusiastic. Thomas Morgan of Machen near Caerphilly refused to serve under Herbert, offended by his Catholicism.

Although the majority of the soldiery were from the areas under Herbert's influence, there was a group of professional soldiers, with officers from as far afield as Herefordshire, Yorkshire and Devon.[5] Herbert placed the infantry under the command of Sir Richard Lawley, or Lawdly, an experienced soldier from Exeter. The cavalry was commanded by Lord John Somerset, Herbert's brother.

By the middle of February, they were on the road to Gloucester, hoping to succeed where Prince Rupert had failed. Gloucester, as we have seen, was an important trading centre, with links to the iron-producing industries of the West Midlands and its capture would seriously affect supplies of arms to the Parliamentarians.

At Coleford in the Forest of Dean, Herbert's army encountered a small enemy garrison led by Colonel Burrowes, a local gentleman loyal to Parliament. The skirmish that followed was hard fought, Burrowes' men being driven back through the village, with forty of them taken prisoner.[6] Several of Herbert's officers were killed though, strangely, there appear to have been no casualties amongst the common soldiers. Sir Richard Lawley was apparently shot dead by a silver bullet fired from a window of the King's Head Inn.[7] He was replaced as commanding officer of the infantry by Sir Jerome Brett.

By early March, Herbert and his army had arrived before Gloucester, where they encamped at Highnam Court, the home of Sir Robert Cook, a Parliamentary MP. Across the intervening River Severn, the walls and spires of Gloucester were clearly visible and to ward off a surprise attack from the garrison there, entrenchments and barricades were quickly thrown up. A message was sent to Lieutenant-Colonel Massey demanding surrender, and was turned down. Perhaps the citizens were terrified of falling into the clutches of a group of 140 ferocious women who were said to be accompanying Herbert's force. These 'Amazons' were believed to be armed with knives two or three feet long with which they intended to carry out mayhem and massacre.[8]

For a month or more, there was little action. Massey occasionally sent out raiding parties, and there was the odd exchange of musketry, but it was not the glorious campaign that Herbert might have hoped for. Indeed, he was not even at Highnam at this time. He had made his way to Oxford, having turned over the conduct of the siege to Brett, who in turn seems to have been unaware that a Parliamentary relief force was closing in on Gloucester.

Sir William Waller, one of Parliament's best soldiers, had captured Malmesbury just a few days earlier and, passing north of Gloucester, had reached Framilode on the River Severn. Ferrying his men across the river by means of a fleet of thirty flat-bottomed boats sent down from London on carts, he attacked the Welsh encampment from the rear. Already under fire from Massey's garrison, who had been warned of Waller's approach, Jerome Brett had apparently urged his infantry to escape under cover of darkness, but they refused, leaving him little option but to accept terms of surrender on 25 March.

It was a humiliating disaster for the Royalists. Several hundred men had been killed and over 1,500 officers and men taken prisoner. The cavalry managed to escape and headed back towards Wales.

The prisoners were taken into Gloucester, roped in pairs, and were incarcerated in two of the city's churches. Amongst them was a lad known as Welsh Thomas, a seventeen-year-old who came from Carmarthen. Locked up with hundreds of others in the church of St Mary Lode, he soon became sickened by the daily diet of cabbage leaves, turnip tops and bread upon which he and his companions were fed and achieved his freedom by switching his loyalty to Parliament. He fought with Massey in the defence of the city later in the war and in 1717, at the age of 90, was still living there.[9]

In the aftermath of the defeat at Highnam, Herbert was heavily criticised, as much for his absence from the battle as for anything else. His brother Lord John, with three or four troops of his horse had during the closing stages of the battle, gone 'fairly off and saved themselves for better times'.[10]

With Gloucester safe, Waller marched into Wales, hoping to deal a final blow to the remnants of Lord Herbert's army. He may have expected support from some of the Monmouthshire gentry, who were rumoured to be changing sides. His arrival at Monmouth caused a hasty evacuation by the garrison, who took refuge at Caerleon. Usk fell next, but lacking sufficient men and artillery to mount a siege of Raglan Castle, Waller fell back towards Chepstow. He allowed his men a day or two of rest, but sensing the possibility of becoming trapped between approaching enemy forces, he left Chepstow on 10 April, sending his baggage and ordnance across the Severn at Aust Passage. He then moved through the Forest of Dean, fighting a sharp skirmish at Little Dean, before achieving his target of Gloucester, where he remained for a few weeks.

The day after Waller's departure from Monmouth, the town was re-occupied by a Royalist force of 180 mounted troops and not long afterwards Abergavenny was taken over by two companies of infantry loyal to the king, a Royalist triumph which can only have delighted Lord Worcester at Raglan.

January to March; Hard Fighting in North Wales and the Marches

At the beginning of January 1643, news was received in Chester that Sir William Brereton had raised a regiment in London and was marching north-west to seize his home county of Cheshire for Parliament. Brereton had served as MP for Cheshire and would be in almost continuous action from this point until July 1646, proving himself to be a strategist of note.[11] It seemed likely to his opponents that he would set up a base at Nantwich, known for its Parliamentary sympathies, so towards the end of the month a large force of Royalist troops set out from Chester under the command of Sir Thomas Aston to seize the town.

Unfortunately for Aston, the enemy was closer than expected and had been forewarned of his intention. The two sides came together at Congleton, near Nantwich, on 28 January and in a short, sharp engagement, Aston was forced into a chaotic retreat in which a large haul of weapons and horses fell into Parliamentary hands. Aston escaped capture by good luck and one of his officers, named as Sir Vincent Corbet, had to crawl to safety on his hands and knees.[12] When the result of the engagement became known in Chester, the houses of Parliamentary supporters in the city were damaged. On 2 February, Brereton's own home, known as the Nunnery or Noons, was sacked, its windows smashed, the contents carried off and sold, and what could not be removed was burnt.

The city authorities, fearful of more disturbances, did what they could to recover the stolen property. At the same time, searches were made of the houses of those whose loyalties were suspect and a few known Parliamentarian sympathisers were imprisoned. Others fled to Nantwich.

Because of the destruction of his property, Brereton was said ever afterwards to have held a grudge against Chester, but he busied himself at Nantwich by setting apart a day of thanksgiving to the Almighty for his victory. Nor did he neglect the defences of Nantwich. Trenches were dug around the town and the earth piled up to form a series of mud walls. All males between the ages of sixteen and sixty were called out for the militia. The new defences were put to the test when a raid was launched on the town by an impressive force of infantry and horse from Chester, which actually achieved very little.

Chester was active in preparing its own warlike stance. Colonel Mostyn had arrived in the city with a large force of Welsh infantry, some of whom were involved in the sacking of Brereton's house. A further two regiments of foot, consisting of about 1,000 men, had been brought in from North Wales by Orlando Bridgeman, the son of the Bishop of Chester. Aston's own cavalry were also back from Nantwich and the presence of so many armed men within the city walls caused problems of discipline and difficulties over the supply of food. Bridgeman, with the king's permission, appropriated all the supplies in the Chester area for the maintenance of the garrison.[13] Aston's cavalry was reduced to plundering for food wherever they could find it.

One of the officers commanding the regiments in Chester, Robert Ellice of Gwasnewydd near Wrexham, was an experienced soldier who was described as 'a vigilant, sober, active and valiant commander'.[14] He had served with the Swedish army in the Thirty Years' War and was chosen to improve the defences of Chester. Many stretches of the wall surrounding the city had fallen into disrepair, and these were now put back into a serviceable state. Earth ramparts were erected immediately behind them to absorb the effects of cannon fire and new drawbridges were fitted to the gates. Outworks of earth and timber were created around the suburbs, with projecting salients to provide flanking fire and pits lined with stakes were dug before the walls.[15]

The people of Shropshire were also concerned for their safety. In the spring, they sent a letter to the Commissioners of Array for Denbighshire, reminding them that Shropshire stood sentinel on the borders of Wales and was a 'guard from any force of the Parliament'. It was suggested that a contribution of some kind might be made to the county's defence by North Wales.[16] Within a short time, Colonel William Wynne of Melai, near Llangernyw, had arrived with his regiment to support Lord Capell, who had been appointed Lieutenant-General of Shropshire, Cheshire and North Wales by the king.[17]

All these preparations were soon followed by military action. Sir William Brereton, eager to recruit more men, sent out warrants summoning all persons liable to serve in the militias to gather on 11 March at Tarporley, between Nantwich and Chester. The King's Commissioners of Array learned of this and called their own meeting of recruits on the same day, at the same place and sent a large body of troops commanded by Sir Nicholas Byron, recently appointed as governor of Chester by the king. Brereton seems to have been ready for them, as he turned up with a force of 1,500 men. The fighting that followed was indecisive and both sides retreated without having recruited the numbers they hoped for.

After his recent defeats, Sir Thomas Aston was eager to prove his mettle. On 11 March, he left Chester at the head of a considerable band of mounted troops and foot soldiers, most of them Welsh, under the command of Colonel Robert Ellice, who had done so much to improve the defences of Chester. Their intention was to seize Middlewich, a quiet town to the east of Chester. The following day being a Sunday, it was spent in prayer and preparation. A few miles away, at Northwich, where he was supervising the building of fortifications, Sir William Brereton was alerted to the possibility of an attack and sent frantic messages to Nantwich summoning reinforcements.

By the time these arrived at Middlewich on the morning of Monday, 11 March, the battle had already begun. Aston's troops, surprised by the appearance of an unexpected enemy force, were driven back through the streets of the town, where they took refuge in the church, all 'wedged up like billets of wood, no man at his arms'.[18] Aston always blamed the defeat on his Welsh foot soldiers, who he claimed threw away their weapons and bolted. He could not even deploy his cavalry in the narrow streets and most of them fled into the side roads, making off into the countryside. He was forced to gallop away himself, heading for nearby Whitchurch. Colonel Ellice was taken prisoner, along with other officers and more than 600 infantrymen and he was eventually released on exchange in September.

April to December, South Wales in Arms

On 8 April, Lord Herbert received from the king the command for which he had been hoping. He was appointed as Lieutenant-General in South Wales. If he believed that this would be a help to him in recruiting more men for the royal army, he was to be disappointed. There were some potential recruits, particularly in Monmouthshire, who refused because they did not wish to serve under a Papist.

In South-West Wales, Lord Carbery continued to be active in the king's name. His wholehearted devotion to his sovereign marked him down as a dangerous enemy to Parliament which, on 19 April, impeached him for high treason. Named with him were Roger Lort and Archdeacon Rudd, both resident in Pembrokeshire, who were ordered to be arrested as delinquents. All three had been encouraging attempts to erect a fort on the shores of Milford Haven in the hope that it would provide cover for the landing of troops from Ireland.

The news of Carbery's impeachment did nothing to dampen his enthusiasm. To be certain of repelling any local opposition to the new fort, Carbery and Lord Herbert were proposing to raise an army of 3,000 men to invade Pembrokeshire. He was prepared to use underhand methods to raise funds for his king, though in this he was no different to many officials on both sides. Three months earlier, in January 1643, he and his supporters ensured that a Grand Jury serving in the Carmarthenshire Quarter Session was full of sympathisers, which 'prepared a presentment

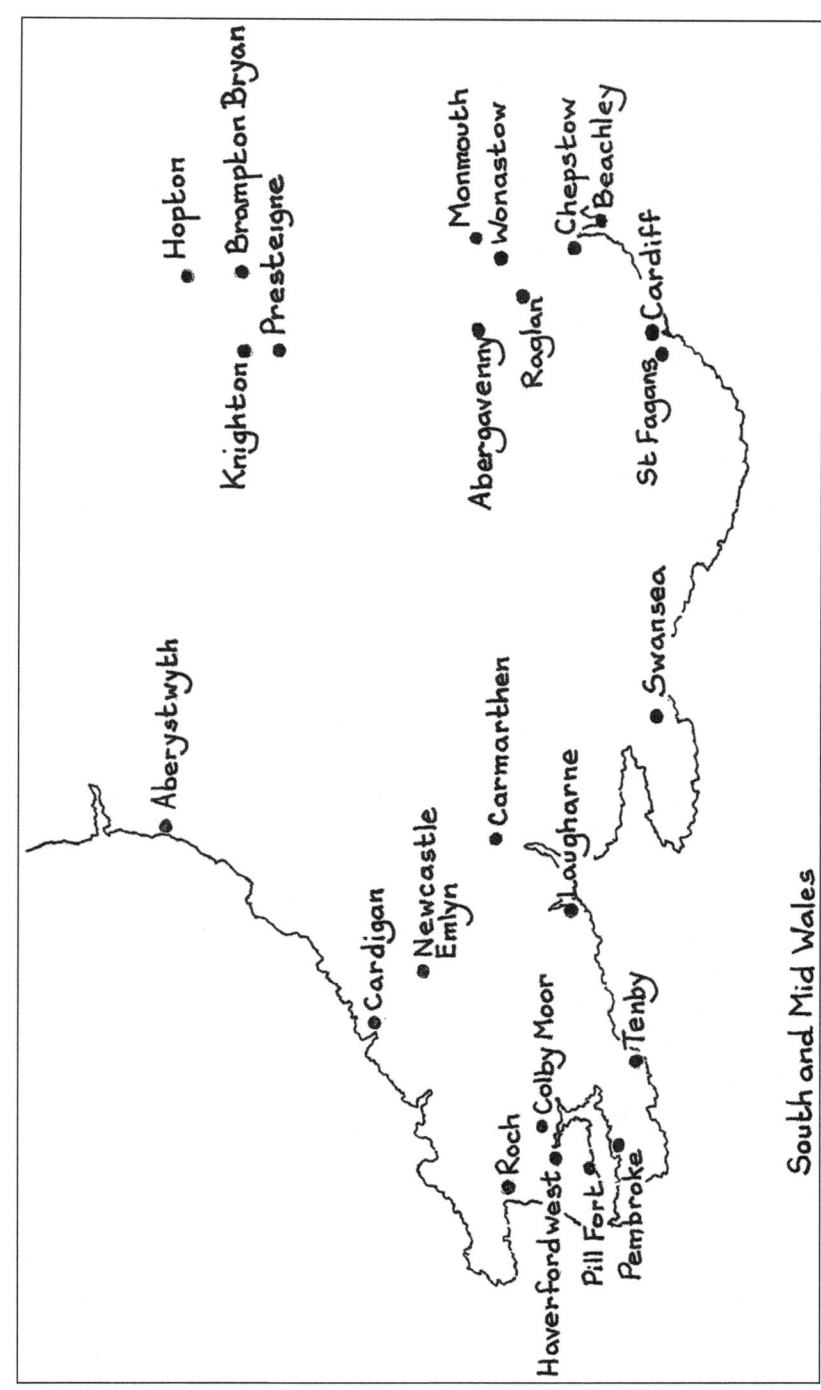

South and Mid Wales

A map of South Wales

for raising money and suppressing Parliament's friends.' In this way over £2,600 was poured into Carbery's war funds.

Further east, Lord Herbert was having to deal with a number of problems. Although William Waller's retreat to Gloucester in April had cleared Monmouthshire of any direct Parliamentarian threat, a spirit of neutrality or even indifference seemed to be affecting recruitment. A group of about 150 men based near Hereford had mutinied and disbanded, leaving their commanding officer to load their abandoned weapons onto a cart. Work on Hereford's defences had all but come to a halt because the citizens proved unwilling to provide the labour. In order to create some sort of defensive association in the area, a meeting was called at Abergavenny and another at Hereford but all efforts collapsed when it was learned that William Waller was again advancing across the border. On 23 April, Monmouth was occupied in the name of Parliament and two days later Waller entered Hereford, capturing most of the local gentry and the military commanders.[19]

Lord Herbert, in Oxford, managed to persuade King Charles to send more help to Herefordshire and Monmouthshire, where it was sorely needed. As if to emphasise the point, on 28 April, a naval attack was made on Royalist-held Chepstow by warships from Bristol, then in Parliamentary hands, but the town and castle were quickly re-taken.

It had become obvious that some sort of re-organisation of the Royalist forces in Monmouthshire and the nearby Marches was necessary. Towards the end of June, Sir William Vavasour of the Royal Lifeguards was appointed as Colonel-General under Lord Herbert. As Herbert was vain and conscious of his status and Vavasour, in the words of King Charles, 'a man that could agree with no one in the kingdom', it was hardly a match made in heaven.[20]

The king's Commissioners of Array for the area were re-organised as the Commissioners of Safeguard to defend the locality and raise taxes for war. The king was closing in on Gloucester, intending to besiege it, so fresh levies were called for. Vavasour, with a large force of Welshmen, blocked all the approaches to Gloucester from the west and Richard Bassett, High Sheriff of Glamorgan marched into the royal camp with 2,000 soldiers. They were determined to storm and hold the city against all odds, driven to do so by the 'inveterate hatred, derived by fabulous tradition' that had long existed between the citizens and the Welsh.[21]

The siege continued until September, when the arrival of the Earl of Essex with an army of 15,000 men forced the king to withdraw. William Vavasour was expected to remain, blockading the city from the west, but did so without the cooperation of Lord Herbert, who was instrumental in his eventual dismissal from the royal service.

In the immediate aftermath of the relief of Gloucester another cat and mouse game developed between the two armies, much as it had done before Edgehill. With Essex occupying Gloucester, the king was determined to prevent any possible move back to London and bring the enemy to battle. Essex was equally determined to avoid that likelihood and made a northerly move towards Tewkesbury, as if he intended to invade Wales. The king realised that this was probably a trick and placed his army to block any march that Essex might make to London via Worcester. In days of heavy rain, both armies slogged along muddy roads until, on 20 September 1643, they came face to face outside the Berkshire town of Newbury. It was the first of two celebrated battles that would take place there and lasted for much of the day. Many Welsh soldiers were involved in the fight, with Lord Herbert's regiment suffering particularly heavy casualties.

During the night hours following the battle, the king ordered a retreat to Oxford, perhaps influenced by the fact that only ten barrels of gunpowder remained to his army. At daybreak, the Parliamentary army was still in position, its road to London still open, so Newbury was claimed as a victory for Essex and his men.

Herbert's regiment was ordered back to Hereford, but no sooner had they arrived there than it seemed that they were to be sent north to Cheshire. The news brought about a near mutiny, with officers complaining bitterly that 'the soldiers would hardly keepe together further than Worster' and probably less than 200 of them would reach Shrewsbury. There were, too, agonised demands from communities in South Wales that 'noe more contributions could be expected from those parts...unless their men returned to secure them from the irruptions of Gloucestermen'.[22]

The Commissioners for Glamorgan soon found themselves in receipt of an exasperated letter from the king, who told them in no uncertain terms, 'that some of your county and others have lefte their collers (colours) and basely run away.' They had betrayed their king and those who led them; such conduct deserved death, but Charles magnanimously promised to forgive them if they re-enlisted in Vavasour's regiment at Cardiff. Few appear to have done so.

Naval Action in Pembrokeshire

In the summer of 1643, Pembrokeshire saw its first military action. On 7 August, Captain William Smith, a Vice-Admiral of the Parliamentary navy, brought his warship *Swallow* into Milford Haven. Smith had been regularly patrolling the Irish Sea, on the lookout for Royalist troop movements and had learned that a Hamburg ship carrying an unknown number of Jesuits had been wrecked near St Davids. The survivors were thought to be in hiding somewhere in the county and Smith was determined to apprehend them.

His plans abruptly changed when he discovered that two Bristol ships, the *Hart* and the *Fellowship,* were already at anchor in the Haven, and were unloading supplies for the fort proposed by Lord Carbery, which was nearing completion. Smith also learned from a local fisherman that all the local gentlemen had been summoned on board the *Fellowship,* to be told that Bristol had fallen to the king and that the war was over. The gentlemen had agreed to send a petition to the king in which they promised to supply a sum of money to him.

Smith was visited by Captain Brooks of the *Fellowship* under a flag of truce, but when Smith demanded the surrender of the two vessels, Brooks returned to his own ship and attempted to sail off. Unfortunately, the *Fellowship* ran aground and surrendered when the *Swallow* opened fire. Two men on board the *Hart* were killed by a cannon shot, the first known casualties of the Civil War in Pembrokeshire. The *Hart* also ran aground whilst making a run upriver, perhaps hoping to reach the protective walls of Haverfordwest, and was captured the next day.[23]

Within a short while, however, there was a serious reverse. Roger Lort of Stackpole, still touting his Royalist sympathies, contacted the town council of Tenby on behalf of Lord Carbery. He offered a choice; a security of £50,000 to the mayor and his brother-in-law, Thomas Bowen of Trefloyne, for an acknowledgement of the king's authority, or a complete blockade of Tenby, thereby ruining its seaborne prosperity. The town council, despite their previous declaration of loyalty to Parliament, agreed to accept any forces sent by Carbery on the king's behalf.

An immediate attack on Tenby was launched by local adherents of Parliament. Rowland Laugharne, a local gentleman who, during the first Civil War, was to prove a main bulwark of opposition to the king in South Wales, brought a force out of Pembroke, but it proved unequal to the challenge of seizing the town. Meanwhile, Captain Richard Swanley, appointed Parliament's Vice-Admiral for the seas around the Welsh coast, arrived off Tenby with a fleet of six ships. A furious bombardment now took place, with an estimated one hundred cannonballs tearing into the medieval walls and houses of the town. The gun batteries on Castle Hill fired back, inflicting such damage on one of Swanley's ships that the fleet sailed off.

Royalist hopes in West Wales were now at their highest. The townspeople of Haverfordwest pledged to provide £2,000 as a promise of their loyalty to the king and when Carbery visited in person he was welcomed by the ringing of church bells. On 18 September, at a meeting in Haverfordwest, a group of forty-seven members of the local gentry signed what became known as 'The Protestation of Pembrokeshire'. This document promised to bring the disloyal town of Pembroke to an obedience to the king by denying help or victuals to the garrison or to any Parliamentary ships attempting to bring relief to the encircled stronghold. As a result, on 26 September 1643 the Royalist broadsheet *Mercurius Aulicus* boasted that Pembroke had swiftly fallen, news that was soon proved untrue.

It may have been Pembroke's intransigence that caused the king to award £20 towards the expenses of raising men for the Royalist Association in West Wales. The defiance of the town and its people seem to have enraged Carbery to such a pitch that he swore to 'plunder the town of Pembroke and the houses of the gentlemen that adhered to that party and that their persons should be put to death by cruel tortures'. John Poyer would be thrust into a barrel and rolled over the cliffs into the sea and Carbery's own men would 'kill the dogs and ravish the bitches and root them out in the third and fourth generation'.[24] Not surprisingly, these words caused consternation amongst the Parliamentary loyalists in South-West Wales.

April to December, North Wales

As events unfolded further south, the people of North Wales found themselves facing unprecedented difficulties. The war was steadily draining men away from the towns and villages of the area, as the demand for fresh levies increased and the local economy, dependent on the sale of

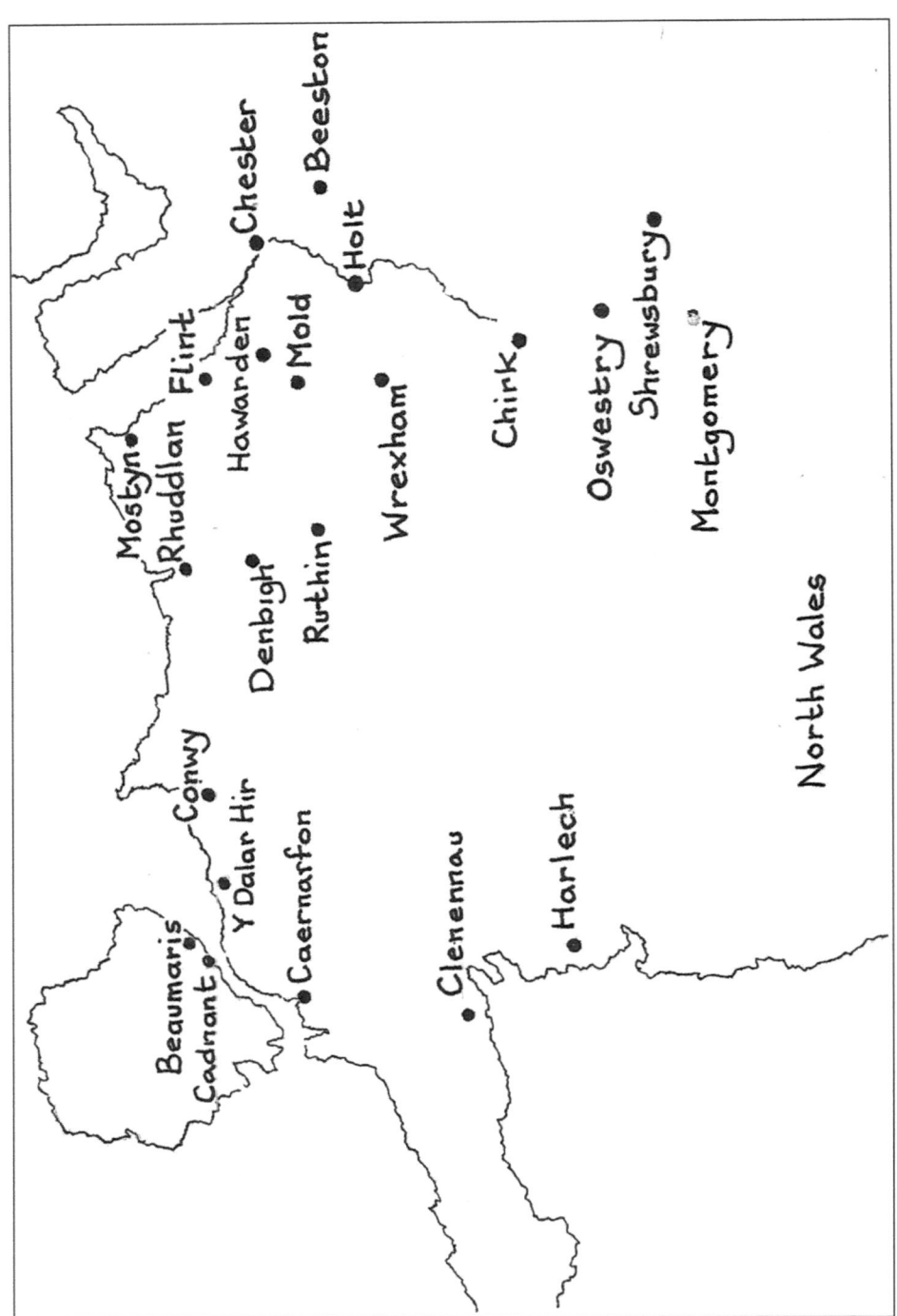

A map of North Wales

cattle and wool, had staggered almost to a halt. A petition was addressed to King Charles requesting safe conducts to allow clothiers and drovers to pass unmolested through the lines of his Majesty's army. It was signed by many of the most notable citizens of the northern counties of Wales.[25]

A demand from Prince Rupert for money was met by a blunt refusal from Archbishop Williams in Conwy Castle, who pointed out that there were no funds to pay them, as there had been no free sales of cattle, many animals having been taken to feed the armies.

As well as a shortage of cash, the soldiers of both sides were desperate to ensure a steady supply of arms and ammunition. The mint established at Shrewsbury was busy melting down plate and other metals for arms. Thomas Bushell, who was overseeing the running of the mint, had donated his own family plate to the cause. Gunsmiths from across the northern Marches and North Wales were taken into the city, which became an armoury producing weapons for the king's army. That other necessity, gunpowder, was also to be provided. Robert Dolben of Denbigh was given his own protective guard whilst he manufactured the powder, but he was to carry out the commission at his own expense and was to offer the finished product as cheaply as possible.[26]

On 10 April Parliament appointed two officers to command counties adjacent to the Welsh Marches. Sir John Corbet was nominated as Colonel-General of Shropshire and Basil Feilding, Earl of Denbigh, who had fought at Edgehill, became commander of forces in Warwickshire. A man of powerful convictions, Feilding had not hesitated to stand against his own father at Edgehill, who had volunteered as a member of the King's Lifeguard-of-Horse. Basil Feilding would prove to be a figure of some note in the struggles that were to engulf the Marches.

All through spring and early summer, raids took place along the borders of England and North Wales. A typical skirmish was that which occurred in Flintshire on 20 June 1643, when a party of Parliamentary troops, led by Colonel Bulkeley, set out from Nantwich to attack the village of Hanmer. They were ambushed by some of Capel's troops and over a hundred were killed, with many more taken prisoner. That the raiders had intended to plunder whatever they could was confirmed when a surplice from Hanmer church was found stuffed into the breeches of one of the prisoners.[27]

Two months later, on 12 June, Sir Thomas Myddelton was appointed as Parliament's Sergeant-Major-General for the six North Wales counties.

His association with Sir William Brereton was to prove a formidable combination in the months to come.

Wem, a small township in Shropshire not far from Oswestry, had been chosen as a base by the Parliamentarian groups in the area. Colonel Mytton had begun to fortify it with the help of Myddelton and Brereton, who arrived from Nantwich, bringing with them some of the men of that garrison. Learning of their presence there, Lord Capell decided that it was an opportune moment to attack Nantwich, an easy target with so many men absent. Capell gathered together an army of some 4–5,000 men and, marching through the night, arrived at Acton, about a mile from Nantwich, during the morning. Here they were challenged by the Nantwich garrison, which had left the town defences intending to fight. So fierce was their advance that the invaders were driven back into the church itself but, lacking the manpower to storm the ancient building, the garrison took refuge behind their defences and awaited a full-scale attack. It never came. Brereton had learned of the battle at Acton and marched to the relief of Nantwich. What followed was a cat and mouse game that might have seemed farcical had it not resulted in so many deaths.

Lord Capell was now heading towards Wem, where Colonel Mytton had at his disposal only about 300 soldiers. An epic fight took place on 18 October, with Mytton's men driving off a force more than ten times their size. Their victory owed much to the efforts of the townswomen, who fought alongside them to such effect that their heroism was afterwards celebrated in rhyme:

'The women of Wem, and a few musketeers,
  Beat the Lord Capel and all his cavaliers.'

The attack on Wem had cost Lord Capell dear. One of his most popular officers, Colonel William Wynne of Melai was killed, his death so disheartening his Welsh soldiers that they gave up the fight. More than sixty Royalists were slain by the discharge of a 'case of drakes' and cartloads of dead bodies were dragged off for burial.

Brereton, on discovering the whereabouts of Capell, had set off hotfoot for Wem from Nantwich, but their arrival was delayed because the exhausted soldiers refused to go any further until they had rested. They finally arrived long after the battle was over. Lord Capell found safety behind the walls of Shrewsbury.

If the defeat at Wem was not enough, the King's Commissioners of Array were finding it hard to raise more men in the Marches and in North Wales. One of the Commissioners, John Edwardes, was forced to write to Sir Richard Lloyd, the King's Attorney General for the area, informing him that 'I have hastened the soldiers you desired, the delay has been caused by the illness of Mr John Trevor (another of the Commissioners) who could not assist me...I have no arms with which to furnish the men.'[28]

A similar problem was being encountered in Radnorshire. Various committees were formed during 1643 to coordinate the raising of men and money for the king's army. Members at one time or another included the sheriff, Hugh Lloyd of Caerfagu, Sir Richard Lloyd the Attorney General, and other prominent Royalists. Eventually, a commission of inquiry was set up to list the lands and assets of all Parliamentary loyalists within the county, in order to sequester their properties to finance the war effort. The confiscations could not, however, be carried out unless the Crown agreed. In the event, the money may not have been used, as the supply of volunteers began to dwindle, and another committee was created to carry out the forced impressment of men for the king's service. Most enthusiastic Royalists had probably already volunteered, and efforts to raise cash to pay or equip troops brought in relatively small amounts. In addition, quarterly amounts were expected from the county in order to finance the billeting of troops In Presteigne and other garrisons.[29]

The Battle of Holt Bridge

On 7 November 1643, a combined force led by Brereton and Myddelton marched out of Nantwich, intent on invading North Wales. On their march, they were joined by a company of Lancashire men commanded by Colonel John Booth and soon afterwards came to Holt, where the enemy were already in wait. The governor of Holt Castle, Lieutenant-Colonel Robinson had been warned of their approach and had placed a party of soldiers to block any advance. The Welsh bank of the River Dee was lined by Major Marcus Trevor's regiment of horse and by musketeers from the regiment of Colonel Ellice, who had been released from imprisonment in September.

Brereton and Myddelton knew that they must gain the far bank of the river if their invasion of North Wales was to continue. The Dee was at that point crossed by a bridge with a central gatehouse defended by a drawbridge and by formidable gates. It was considered unlikely that a passage could be forced over the bridge. An attempt to ferry troops across the river by boat was met with vicious fire from Ellice's musketeers, so that there was no option but to retreat. It was decided to try to hoodwink the enemy. A large group of musketeers marched off along the bank of the river as if searching for another crossing point. With the defenders' attention diverted, Brereton's men made a determined dash across the bridge and threw up ladders against the gatehouse, whilst another group hacked away at the ropes of the drawbridge. When that came crashing down, hand 'granadoes' were hurled at the defenders, who fled. The gates were smashed in and the royalists were driven back from the earthworks along the river banks.

A good haul of prisoners was made – one captain, several lieutenants, one cornet and about forty common soldiers. Others had taken refuge in the castle, which was put under siege. William Maurice of Cefnybraich recorded the event in his notebook: 'The 9th day of November followine, Holy-brige was taken by Sir Th. Midleton and Sir Wm Brerton, who presently entered Wrexham; and shortly after Hawarden Castle was delivered to them. After the taking of Holt-brige, Wm Salusbury (sic) of Rug, fortified the Castel of Denbigh.'[30]

William Salesbury of Bachymbyd and Rug was described by King Charles's secretary as a man who 'under cover of a countryman, he had more experience, courage and loyalty than many who made for greater professions.' He was known to his family, friends and tenants as 'Hen Hosannau Gleision', Old Blue Stockings, and when on 14 November Sir Thomas Myddelton wrote in a kindly manner to Salesbury, with whom he was well acquainted, inviting him to surrender Denbigh Castle, he received a defiant reply: 'But to be plaine – to betray soe great a trust as the keeping of Denbigh Castle, tho' upon ever so fayre pretences, may be acceptable to them that desire it, but in my opinion, it itself is abominable.'[31]

Hawarden Castle was surrendered to Brereton on the day after the battle at Holt Bridge. As he approached with his army, the gates of the castle were opened wide on the orders of its governor, Colonel Thomas Ravenscroft. Brereton's advance through the rest of Flintshire was swift and within a short time Flint, Mold, Holywell and Mostyn were all in Parliamentary hands. There was a certain amount of vandalism on the part of the victors. No private homes are said to have been plundered, but anything that smacked of Popery or High Anglicanism was given short shrift. Stained glass windows were shattered into fragments, monuments were damaged, religious paintings torn to pieces and the ornamented robes of the clergy were stolen. At Wrexham, the lead pipes of the two organs, described as the best in the land, were melted down to make bullets for Sir Thomas Myddelton's musketeers.

At Chester, the news of these successes caused considerable alarm. All roads into Wales were blocked and supplies of coal, lime and food were suddenly halted. It seemed to the nervous citizens that an attack was imminent, especially when a demand for surrender was received from Sir William Brereton. The deputy governor, Sir Abraham Shipman replied that if Brereton wanted the city, he 'must win and wear it'. There must have been considerable consternation amongst the townspeople of Chester when, on 16 November, Sir Abraham gave orders for the outlying suburb of Handbridge to be set ablaze, along with two or three large mansions, so that they might not afford cover to the enemy.[32] The inhabitants of Handbridge flooded into the city, adding to the overcrowding that already existed.

At Conwy Castle, Archbishop Williams was equally concerned by the apparently unstoppable progress of the Parliament forces. On 12 November he sent a letter to the Marquis of Ormonde in Ireland, who was overseeing the dispatch of troops to Wales, asking for urgent reinforcements. He added as a footnote, 'If your Excellency shall send over with Capt Bartlett one company of Yorkshiremen or Welshmen, I will find them meat, drink, and some shoes and stockings, until their rendezvous, provided they come armed with some ammunition, which I will pay for.' Six days later, the Archbishop sent Ormonde another letter, still pleading for help: 'But alas! we grow daily in more uncertainty of the landing of the forces from your parts than we were – some giving out that they are not for these parts but for Bristol, which, if it be true, these parts are quite lost, and will think themselves deserted by his Majesty...I do not care of what country they are, so as they come with arms and competency of ammunition, which shall be paid for or returned.'[33]

The Parliamentary triumph was not to last long. On 18 November, the same day that the Archbishop penned his second letter, a fleet of ships dropped anchor at Mostyn at the mouth of the River Dee. They carried over 2,500 men of the king's army, who had originally been sent into Ireland in 1641 to put down the rebellion there. Their presence in North Wales immediately tipped the balance in favour of the Royalists. Within days of receiving this long-feared news, Brereton had withdrawn his forces across the Dee back into Cheshire. He also lost a part of his command when the troops from Lancashire, fearing an attack on Liverpool, hastened home. Perhaps it was the sudden diminution in his numbers that encouraged Brereton to send a message to the new arrivals, praising their conduct against the Irish rebels, hoping that they meant to fight for Parliament and promising them arrears of pay. His offer was not accepted.[34]

The only Parliamentarian troops still in Flintshire were the 120 men in the garrison of Hawarden Castle, left isolated by Brereton's swift withdrawal. Within days they were under siege by about 500 soldiers, mostly Welsh, from the newly landed forces. The rest had been marched south to reinforce the nervous defenders of Chester. The appearance of these so called 'Irish' troops must have been ragged indeed, because the housewives of Chester immediately began knitting socks for them.

Meanwhile, Hawarden Castle was now surrounded by over 1,000 men, following the arrival of extra forces, though some of these deserted and found their way into the castle. The defenders received a threatening letter from Colonel Thomas Sandford, commanding a detachment of musketeers, which said, 'If you put me to the least trouble or loss of blood to force you, expect no quarter for man, woman or child. I hear you have some of our late Irish army in your company – they very well know me and my forelocks use not to parley.'[35] The reply which was sent back was equally forthright: 'We fear the loss of our religion more than the loss of our dearest blood'.

The determination of the garrison soon weakened and after a further exchange of letters, articles of surrender were signed on 4 December. The men were allowed to march away with half the number of their weapons and £25 worth of goods. Some were ill-treated by the victorious Royalists, perhaps those who had deserted and fled into the castle, though none appear to have been murdered.

The threadbare state of the army from Ireland was causing concern in Chester. The mayor made an appeal for items of clothing and enough was received to comfortably clothe about 300 of the troops. By scouring the towns and villages of North Wales, Orlando Bridgeman obtained enough cloth to be made up into suits for the remainder, as well as shoes and stockings. This apparent goodwill did not last long. Some of the soldiers were found in a drunken state, having sold their newly made clothing to buy alcohol. Others were accused of looting property and stealing cattle. The situation became so bad that on 1 December the Chester assembly decided to donate £100 worth of the city's plate to the officers, as long as the men were removed from the city to a camp elsewhere.[36]

On 6 December, John, first Baron Byron of Rochdale, arrived in Chester, bringing with him 1,000 horse and 300 foot. He had been appointed as Field-Marshal of Cheshire, Shropshire and North Wales, under the authority of Lord Capell. Described by Lord Clarendon as coming from an ancient family and of unblemished reputation, Byron was to play a prominent role in future events. Upon his entry into the city, he was welcomed by the governor, who happened to be his uncle, Sir Nicholas Byron. The family reunion was augmented a week or so later when Byron's brother Robert marched in at the head of his regiment, accompanied by another regiment under the command of Colonel Henry Warren. Both of these units were part of fresh reinforcements from Ireland which had recently landed from Dublin.

With Chester now swollen with troops, it was easy to overawe the surrounding countryside. Raids were carried out deep into the Cheshire countryside. On 13 December, the Parliamentary garrison of Beeston Castle, perched on a rocky outcrop not far from Holt, was forced to surrender to an encircling Royalist army. The capitulation was a civilised affair. Captain Sandford, who had taken Hawarden, managed to enter the upper ward of the castle by a side gate, perhaps through an act of treachery. The governor of the castle, Captain Thomas Steele began a parley and welcomed Sandford into his own lodgings, where the pair dined together. A generous amount of beer was sent out by Steele to Sandford's soldiers and shortly afterwards the sixty men of the garrison marched out with colours flying. They made their way to Nantwich, where Steele, found guilty of betrayal, was shot in the churchyard.

Another raid by Byron's troops ended in a much bloodier fashion. On 23 December, just two days before Christmas, Royalist soldiers entered the village of Barthomley, where about twenty men, led it is said by a schoolmaster, had occupied the church tower. A shot seems to have been fired by one of those in the tower and Byron's soldiers lit a fire at its base.

As the frightened, bewildered villagers stumbled out, they were dragged into the porch and there hacked with swords, at least twelve being killed in cold blood and the others seriously wounded. Although Byron was not present, he seems to have regarded the massacre as justified, remarking 'I put them all to the sword, which I find to be the best way to proceed with these kind of people, for mercy to them is a cruelty.'

News of the atrocity horrified the Parliamentary community and not a few Royalists too. It was unsurprisingly used as propaganda by many opponents of the king, who pointed it out as an example of what might be expected from Lord Byron, who was described as 'Bloody Bragadochio Byron'.[37] It was also to become one of the charges laid against King Charles at his trial.

Almost all of Wales was now in the grip of the Royalists. In the south, there were still individuals and small groups who hoped to see a resurgence of Parliamentary fortunes, but who lacked the means to achieve it. In the south-west, Pembroke was still defiant, but the fort on the north shore of Milford Haven was complete and waited to welcome a landing of troops from Ireland. In the Marches, the border cities of Chester and Shrewsbury were held in the king's name. Gloucester remained loyal to Parliament.

The Parliamentary troops had withdrawn into Nantwich, now encircled by hastily constructed earthen walls. Sir Thomas Myddelton was in London, hoping to recruit another army and Brereton was anxiously trying to raise more men in Lancashire for the defence of Nantwich. It appeared to Lord Byron that an opportune moment had arrived to crush Brereton and Nantwich once and for all. On 28 December, Byron left Chester at the head of an army of 1,000 horse and 300 foot. At Middlewich he encountered Brereton, who suffered a crushing defeat, losing over two hundred men and was forced to retreat towards Manchester. Byron closed in on Nantwich and by the beginning of the New Year, the town was under siege.

Despite the determination of Lord Byron to prosecute the war until Nantwich, and indeed, the whole of the Parliamentary movement had been overthrown, there was a growing resentment over the demands for more cash and men. In particular, the number of enforced loans and taxations levied upon communities and individuals was increasingly resisted. In Parliament itself, members were voicing a desire for peace, or at least a truce until some sort of agreement could be negotiated. Others were determined to prosecute a war until Parliament brought the king to some sort of settlement. John Pym was one who realised that would never be achieved without military help from Scotland. In August 1643, a request for assistance had been tendered to the Scottish Parliament and on 17 August, the Solemn League and Covenant was signed. It consisted of six articles, that guaranteed to uphold the Protestant Religion, eradicate all traces of Popery, to preserve the rights and liberties of the Scottish and English parliaments, to apprehend all false advisors to the king, to observe the terms of previous treaties between the two nations, to lend mutual help whenever needed and not to fall into 'detestable indifference or neutrality'.[38]

The signing of the Covenant was to have a profound impact on the course of events in England and Wales.

Chapter 4

1644

North Wales, January to June

The Fate of Nantwich

During the opening days of the new year, the fate of Nantwich looked decidedly shaky. Protected only by mud walls and ditches and with a garrison of about 300 men, it was unlikely to withstand an assault from its Royalist besiegers, who numbered about 7,000 men. A summons to surrender, couched in frightening terms, was sent into the town by Thomas Sanford, Captain of the Firelocks, who had sent a similarly sinister note to the garrison of Hawarden Castle in December.

'Your drum can inform you Acton Church is no longer a prison, but now free for all honest men to do their devotions in; wherefore, be persuaded from your incredulity and resolve! God will not forsake his anointed. Let not your zeal in a bad cause dazzle your eyes any longer, but wipe away your vain conceits that have too long led you into blind errors. Loath am I to undertake the trouble of persuading you into obedience, because your erroneous opinions do most violently oppose reason amongst you; but, however, if you love your town, accept of quarter; and, if you regard your lives, work your safety by yielding your town to Lord Byron for his Majesty's use. You shall see how my battery is fixed, from when fire shall eternally visit you, to the terror of the old and females, and consumption of your thatched houses. Believe me, gentlemen, I have laid by my former delays, and am now resolved to batter, burn, storm and destroy you. Do not wonder that I write unto you, having officers-in-chief above me. It is only to advise you for your good.'[1]

The defenders were not impressed by this overblown rhetoric and ignored it.

Prospects brightened a little on 12 January, when Colonel Mytton surprised an ammunition convoy travelling through Cheshire, all of whom, as William Maurice noted in his diary, 'were taken at Elsmeare at night in their Quarters, as they marched from Welshpoole to Nantwiych.' Among the prisoners Mytton took was Sir Nicholas Byron, who was returning to Chester.[2]

On the early morning of 18 January, a full-scale assault was launched over snow-covered ground onto the mud walls of Nantwich. There was fierce fighting on the barricades, with no quarter given. Amongst those who defended the outworks was a Nantwich woman named Brett, who exhibited the greatest courage. An estimated three hundred of the attackers perished. One of them was the fire-eating Thomas Sandford. As the enemy fell back, the garrison, battered and exhausted, may have felt a sense of cautious elation, but they knew their ordeal was not over. They were still surrounded by a numerically superior force, there was no sign of relief and their reserves of food and ammunition must have been drained by the two weeks of siege they had already endured.

Nantwich had not been forgotten by Parliament. Brereton had written to the Commons from Manchester, where he had retreated after the battle at Middlewich, appealing for assistance for the beleaguered town. The only troops available were a unit of 1,500 horse and dragoons under the command of Sir Thomas Fairfax. At that time based in Lincolnshire, Fairfax wasted no time in rousing his men and set off for the Midlands, where he was intercepted and attacked by Lord Byron at Ashton-under-Lyne.

Despite that setback, Fairfax continued to move through a frozen and snowy landscape towards Nantwich, picking up more troops on the way. By 24 January 1644, he was within a short distance of the town. Byron had hoped to challenge him some miles to the west of Nantwich, but the first action took place on 26 January in the Delamere Forest, where about thirty of Byron's men were taken prisoner. As Fairfax's advance continued, he came under cannon fire from Acton Church, where a large body of the enemy had gathered. The inclement weather now played into Fairfax's hands, for a sudden thaw in the icy conditions meant that the River Weaver, which flowed between Acton Church and Nantwich, burst its banks and swept away the bridge of boats that spanned it. Unable to ford the river at that spot, Byron was forced to cross at a point further along its course.

Fairfax abandoned plans to attack the church and instead decided to fight his way through a network of lanes and hedges into Nantwich itself. The delay in doing so allowed Byron to seize an advantage, sending units of his troops to block the Parliamentary advance. Fairfax had not gone far before his men came under fire from the front and from troops that had caught up with the rear of the column. Luckily Colonel Booth, in charge of the garrison at Nantwich, ordered a sally from the shelter of the walls and after two hours of bloody fighting, Byron was in retreat towards Chester. Fairfax, who could have claimed the victory, was in no doubt where the credit lay. In a letter written to the Earl of Essex three days after the battle, he described how 'the Lord of Hosts hath done great things for us, to whose name alone be ascribed all the glory... .'

Fairfax also appended a list of about seventy Royalist officers captured in the aftermath of the fighting, plus a regimental chaplain, forty-one sergeants, forty drummers, four cannoneers and 1,500 common soldiers. There were also '120 Women that followed the Camp; of whom many had long knives, with which they were said to have done mischief.'[3]

Byron, however, felt that his God had deserted him. In a letter to the Marquis of Ormonde, he was sure that, 'It hath pleased God of late to turn the tide of our good fortune here... .' He went on to describe how, 'Colonel Warren's men and Sir M. Ernely's at the same time (notwithstanding all the endeavours of their officers) retreated without almost fighting a stroke... .' He provided a list of the guns and carriages that were lost and of most of the regimental colours taken. He put his losses at about 400 men.

Those of Byron's soldiers who had straggled back to Chester included many wounded. They were cared for in the city, but some, when healed, refused to return to duty. Others ignored military discipline and there were brawls in the streets, acts of robbery and one soldier was hung for murder. Others, it was said, had deserted to the Parliamentarians. Many of the townsfolk resented having to give free quarter to the troops and the list of complaints to the city assembly mounted steadily. When two more regiments of foot under the command of colonels Tillier and Broughton arrived from Ireland in February, they were swiftly packed off to Shrewsbury.[4]

There were also arguments over who should succeed the captured Sir Nicholas Byron as governor of Chester. The name of Francis Gamull, one of the city's aldermen, was put forward. He had been appointed as captain of the city's Trained Band in 1642 and, though serving at Oxford as a member of the Royalist Parliament, he was well aware that, back in Chester, his own regiment was in need of pay and had become, in his own words, 'careless'. Gamull did what he could to ensure his own selection for the governorship, even approaching the king. There was considerable opposition to the possibility from Lord Byron, who wanted no interference in military matters from the town corporation. Byron lobbied Prince Rupert, signalling his opposition to Gamull and no more came of the idea.[5]

On 5 February, Prince Rupert was appointed Captain-General of Wales and the Marches. This enabled him to re-organise military matters in the area as he saw fit. He wasted no time in exercising his powers. He had already dispatched a letter to Sir Francis Ottley, governor of Shrewsbury, advising him that he should prepare the castle to receive provisions and ammunition for storage. This should be done with all possible speed, as fifty barrels of gunpowder were on their way to the town and 'all other kind of ammunition will speedily be brought thither, and for the better security of the stores which are the sinews of the King's business... .' Rupert intended to make Shrewsbury his headquarters and was concerned that a plan to betray it to the enemy had recently been uncovered. Various people implicated in the plot had been imprisoned but the prince wrote that, 'I do not hear they are brought to justice by any proceeding against them, so that the punishment may go to some the example and terror to all.'[6]

On 31 January, Ottley penned a reply, assuring the prince that 'Our country is heartily glad that his Majesty has entrusted the care of the country into your hands. I shall be obedient to perform your commands. All things shall be performed with expedition, so far forth as time will permit, against your Highness' coming. Justice has been executed, and one of the corporals under my command hanged for neglect of duty in his place that night as the enemy approached. The huts and the court of guard shall be ready before your Highness's coming. There is one other condemned, but judgement is deferred till your Highness's coming hither. Our hearts do long for your presence to settle the distractions and complaints against us. I rest your servant, ready upon all occasions humbly to serve you.'[7]

Rupert made his entry into Shrewsbury on 18 February. He was gifted the exceptional sum of £1,000 for the war effort by the city corporation.

He remained in Shrewsbury for about a fortnight, making plans to relieve the siege of Lathom House in Lancashire, at that time hard pressed by large Parliamentary force. On 4 March, he marched out, accompanied by some 600 foot soldiers and 300 horse, heading for Chester. On the way, he diverted towards Market Drayton, where he dispersed some of Fairfax's men in a lightning raid.

Rupert entered Chester on 11 March and received a grand civic welcome. The dignitaries of the city gathered at the High Cross wearing their robes and the mayor, Randle Holmes, offered him the best entertainment possible, given the reduced state of the city. He also recited a list of complaints, which the prince apparently accepted in good grace.

The warmth of the welcome seemed to have vanished the next day, when the mayor, suffering from a 'payne in his legg', failed to appear, despite having been asked to do so by Rupert. None of the justices of the peace, also invited to the meeting, turned up either. The prince spent the day inspecting the defences with Lord Byron.

Rupert's stay in Chester was brief. On the day following his arrival, he received instructions from the king to send aid to Newark, the town being exposed to possible attack by Parliamentary units of the Scots army, which had marched 20,000 men over the English border on 19 January. Rupert ordered Major Legge to hasten back to Shrewsbury in order to select as many as possible of Tillier's and Broughton's regiments as were deemed fit for service at Newark. About 1,000 men were chosen, along with 120 members of Colonel Fulke Hunckes's regiment. They were sent to Bridgnorth, where they were joined by Rupert with 800 horse, before setting off for Newark. On 21 March at Newark, this hastily cobbled together band smashed into Sir John Meldrum's regiment and after bitter fighting, forced the Scottish soldiers to surrender on terms. Over 3,000 muskets were taken, along with eleven brass guns and two mortars.

Most of Rupert's army were sent back to Shrewsbury to ensure the safety of the town and Rupert himself made his way to Oxford, before returning to the Marches. The victory at Newark was celebrated, both in Shrewsbury and Chester, by bonfires and the holding of services of thanksgiving. In the succeeding days, Rupert made his way across North Wales, visiting as many garrisons as possible. One of his destinations was Conwy, where he appointed Sir John Owen of Clennenau as governor, to the great annoyance of Archbishop Williams, who had spent a great deal of his own money in improving the defences of the town and castle.

This tactless move was only one example of the prince's policy of replacing Welsh nominees appointed by Lord Byron with Englishmen of whom he approved.[8]

These appointments were resented by the Welsh, who felt they were represented by men who did not understand them or their language. They were prepared to make clear their feelings in their dealings with their new governors. This in turn led to a growing distrust on the part of Rupert's men, who communicated their concerns to the prince. These mutual misunderstandings were to affect attitudes for the rest of the conflict. Prince Rupert also toured areas of South Wales where, as we shall see, he made his presence equally felt.

Fighting had also continued further south in the Marches, where two Parliamentarian enclaves existed at Brampton Bryan and Hopton Castle, near Knighton. In March 1644, efforts were made to destroy them.

Brampton Bryan Castle was the home of Sir Robert Harley, one of the MPs for Herefordshire and a staunch supporter of Parliament. He had remained in London at the outbreak of war, leaving his wife, Lady Brilliana, in charge of the castle. She was well aware of the dangers she faced as the representative of a Puritan family in an overwhelmingly Royalist area. Her worst fears were justified when the castle endured a prolonged siege from 26 July to 9 September 1643. Packed into the castle were some fifty soldiers and as many civilians, and surrounding them were 1,200 men of Sir William Vavasour's command. Despite several summonses to surrender, Lady Harley would not countenance the idea and on each occasion returned a defiant refusal. Eventually, the siege was abandoned in September 1643, though a renewal of it seemed a possibility in the autumn. By then, Lady Harley was seriously ill and died on 29 October. Her body was stored in a lead coffin in a tower of the castle until it could be taken up to London for burial. She was mourned as a Parliamentary heroine, Brampton Bryan being described as 'the saddest garrison in the three kingdoms, having lost their head and governor.'

Command of the castle now fell to the Harleys' friend, Dr Wright, who faced a second siege towards the end of March 1644. This time the garrison was opposed by the troops of Sir Michael Woodhouse, an experienced professional soldier, who had been sent by Prince Rupert specifically to root out the Parliamentarian boltholes of Brampton and Hopton. His troops consisted of men from the Irish campaign lately landed in North Wales, stiffened by units of Lord Herbert's

Monmouthshire levies. The second siege lasted for three weeks, before Dr Wright decided to accept terms of surrender on 17 April. Dr Wright was imprisoned at Ludlow and exchanged for a Royalist prisoner a few months later. It was decided not to install a Royalist garrison at Brampton, and the castle was burned down.

Hopton Castle, the home of the Parliamentarian firebrand Robert Wallop, had been established as an outlying garrison to Brampton on 18 February 1644. Occupied by thirty-one men and two maidservants, it was commanded by Major Phillips. It came under siege on 25 February by the forces of Sir Michael Woodhouse and Lord Herbert and over the next two weeks there were at least four serious assaults on the defences. Four summonses to surrender were sent into the castle, each one refused, despite the fact that the last offer made it clear that further resistance would mean no quarter in the event of a successful attack.

Major Phillips finally agreed to give up the castle on 13 March, on condition that the fate of the garrison was left to Woodhouse's mercy. Phillips was taken to a nearby house, not knowing that almost his entire command had been slaughtered, their bodies, according to one version of events, tossed into a pool below the castle. Major Phillips was then brought back to the castle where he, too, was murdered, despite offering his captors twenty pounds to spare his life.[9] The only survivors were a soldier who had secreted himself in the cellars and the two maids, one of whom was so traumatised by the horrors she witnessed that she never recovered her sanity.

South-West Wales, January to June 1644

In South Wales, Pembroke was still defiantly proclaiming its loyalty to Parliament. John Poyer, having repaired the defences of town and castle, was joined by Rowland Laugharne, a local gentleman who had served as a page boy to Lord Essex and may have attended his lordship in that capacity in 1620, when the earl joined Sir Horace Vere's regiment and fought on the Continent in the opening phases of the Thirty Years' War. He later became one of Essex's most trusted servants and played a part in arranging the earl's second marriage.[10]

Although no definite moves had been made against them by Lord Carbery, Poyer and Laugharne knew that their situation was serious.

There were only sixty foot soldiers and thirty mounted troops holding the castle. Surrounded by a chain of Royalist garrisons, and with the fort on the northern shores of the Haven now complete, ninety men were not enough to hold off an assault, especially if the enemy was reinforced by a landing of troops from Ireland.

On 11 January 1644, the king's supporters in the three counties of South-West Wales issued a second protestation, in which they affirmed their determination not to allow Parliamentary control of the area. They believed that 'great forces designed to land and in readiness to enter and invade the said counties in a hostile manner, in no way commissioned by his Majesty, such forces being thereunto more especially encouraged by the present withstanding of his Majesty's authority, now exercised by sundry persons, who having possessed themselves of the Town and Castle of Pembroke, do in a hostile manner keep the same... .' The king should be assured that the signatories to the protestation would 'withstand, resist, and repulse all such forces, as aforesaid, attempting or acting any such entry and invasion or hostility.'[11]

It is probable that, even before learning of this protestation, Poyer and Laugharne had already decided to appeal for help. Poyer sent out one of his own vessels, armed with eight guns, to warn Richard Swanley, the Admiral of the Parliamentary fleet patrolling the Irish Sea, of the desperate situation of the Pembroke garrison. A short time after leaving the protection of the Haven, it encountered and was taken captive by two Royalist warships, the *Globe* and *Providence,* bound for Milford with a cargo of cannon for the fort there. On board one of the ships was Captain Richard Steele 'who pretended much to be an ingenier' and who would doubtless make the Haven an impregnable stronghold.

There seemed little hope for the survival of Pembroke but then, on 23 January, the weather came to their aid. Storms forced the Parliamentary fleet patrolling the Irish Channel to seek shelter in the calmer waters of the Haven. Laugharne immediately went on board the flagship, the *Leopard* and informed Admiral Swanley of the dangers facing Pembroke. Swanley promised two hundred seamen to augment Pembroke's defenders, as well as three guns and all the powder and shot necessary for use against the strongholds surrounding Pembroke.

Before any military action was undertaken, Swanley sent out a letter to the gentry of Pembrokeshire, calling upon them to offer allegiance to King and Parliament and encouraging them to drive out 'that malignant rout, who seeks to enslave this nation under the yoke of the Anti-Christian beast' but it evoked no answer.

The Royalists had built their fort on a prominent headland on the western side of a narrow tidal inlet known as Prix Pill, or Castle Pill, on what is now the edge of the modern town of Milford Haven. The two warships, *Globe* and *Providence,* withdrew into Prix Pill, sheltering beneath the guns of the fort. During the night of 27 January, the gunners of the fort had managed to drag one of their cannons to the high ground on the opposite, eastern bank of the Pill. This now opened fire on the *Swallow,* one of the Parliamentary fleet, and might have done considerable damage had it not exploded from its own charge. There was also a change in the weather and two of Swanley's ships were forced to take shelter in Angle Bay. The garrison of the fort, seeing the retreat of these vessels, was delighted to claim that they had been forced to do so because of the power and accuracy of the royalist cannon. The news must have spread quickly, because on 2 February, Swanley sent a letter into the fort:

'To the Commander-in-Chief of the forces of Prickspill under the command of the Earl of Carbery.

Gentlemen, I understand you have reported that you have frightened me away with the noise of your guns, assure yourselves had I been acquainted with the Channel, as I make no doubt but I shall be afore I go hence, I had tried which had been strongest, my ships' sides or your mud walls, and having some other business now in hand I refer that to a fitter opportunity. I came not hither to build castles in the aire, nor in any hostile manner, to make a division in this Country, but only for Peace, which at this time I am willing to proffer you, and if you please to send a man or two to treat upon Propositions which shall tend to the glory of God, the honour of the King and the happiness of the subject.... . If you desire a friendly parley I promise you upon the faith of a Christian and the word of a Commander that you shall as safely return as come, of which if you doubt, I will send Hostages of such quality as you send to me.'[12]

No reply was apparently received, and the fort and the warships continued to exchange fire for the next three weeks. Swanley's men managed to ferry one of their cannons to shore on the south side of the Haven and, from there, within the protection of a temporary earthwork, it was able to fire directly into the fort. One lucky retaliatory shot from the fort smashed the empty bunk of the *Leopard*'s captain, but otherwise damage to either side seems to have been minimal.

Meanwhile, Laugharne had decided upon the capture of all the Royalist garrisons surrounding Pembroke. These scattered castles and fortified houses were garrisoned with men from Carbery's command, which effectively meant that he could field no strong force to march to their defence. On 30 January Laugharne attacked Stackpole House, the home of Roger Lort, about three miles south of Pembroke. Stoutly constructed, with thick walls, the mansion was no easy target. The sixty-strong garrison mounted a spirited defence and managed to hold off their enemies for over eight hours. It was only when a gap in the walls was opened with pickaxes and crowbars that a surrender was achieved. Every man of Laugharne's command was allowed to take what he wanted from the contents of the house, an action that John Poyer justified with the words, 'What was taken by the soldiers in the heat of blood cannot be imputed to our dishonour.'[13]

The next target was Trefloyne House, the residence of Thomas Bowen, on the banks of the Ritec stream, just outside Tenby. The stream flowed into the sea through the mouth of a wide creek crossed by a causeway near the village of Penally. Laugharne knew that the house would prove a tougher nut to crack then Stackpole, as Lord Carbery had garrisoned it with 150 foot soldiers and fifty mounted troops, all of whom were well-armed. As Laugharne's men approached Trefloyne along the Ridgeway, a narrow spine of high ground stretching between Pembroke and Tenby, he encountered a mixed force of Carbery's horse and foot near the village of St Florence, and quickly dispersed them with a blast of cannon fire.

Trefloyne fell only after a fierce exchange of musketry and the breaching of the walls of the house by artillery fire. Two of Laugharne's men were killed in the action and six wounded. Forty saddled horses were discovered in the outbuildings, as well as a cannon and all the weapons of the infantrymen.

With two victories to their credit, the Parliamentary forces now considered their next move. At a conference held aboard the *Leopard*, Laugharne and Swanley agreed upon the destruction of the fort at Prix Pill. Before dawn on Friday, 23 February, a force of soldiers and artillery gathered near Pembroke Ferry, on the south side of the Haven and were ferried across to the north shore. The majority of the 250 infantrymen and some sixty horsemen were carried in a great gabbard, a barge-like sailing vessel used for inland navigation, 'that God sent accidentally out of Ireland.'

By 8.00am in the morning the men had been put ashore on the eastern side of Prix Pill and in their efforts to drag two cannon up onto the high ground overlooking the fort they received help from eager groups of local people. By late afternoon, the guns were able to open fire on the fort, adding to the bombardment already taking place from four of the Parliamentary warships at anchor in the Haven.

Laugharne had previously dispatched a group of mounted men round the head of the Pill to prevent the advance of any reinforcements from the Royalist garrison of Haverfordwest. A further detachment of twenty musketeers occupied the tower of Steynton church and in the late afternoon, these men detected movement on the road leading northwards. A mixed unit of horse and foot under Sir Francis Lloyd was approaching from Haverfordwest but, possibly spotting the mounted dragoons drawn up near the church, they retreated.[14]

By now dusk was falling and Laugharne's men were forced to camp out overnight in bitter cold. As dawn broke, the bombardment of the fort was renewed. Laugharne now sent his troops from Steynton towards 'an Ambuscado the enemy had placed in a hedge a little distant on the Stainton (sic) side from Pill, and having divided ourselves into three parts, the Horse furiously and disorderly charged upon them and routed the whole, took officers and most of the soldiers, the rest fled into the fort; hereupon we presently possessed the village of Pill and the ruines of an ancient chapel that stand above the Fort.'[15]

Laugharne now prepared his men to storm the fort but, according to a Parliamentary account, 'the Gentlemen in the Fort hung out a Flagge of Truce, by which they obtained quarter, in rendering us possession of the Fort and themselves prisoners.'[16] Between 240 and 300 soldiers were taken prisoner, along with eighteen great guns and the two royalist vessels, *Providence* and *Globe*, which had remained in Prix Pill throughout the action.

There was panic in Haverfordwest when news of the capture of the fort was received. The day before, when it was learned that Laugharne was disembarking his troops on the north shore of the Haven, a Captain

Steele had been sent to Milford under a flag of truce to discuss peace terms, but when he arrived the fighting had already begun. He made his way back to Haverfordwest and related the news to Sir Henry Vaughan, the uncle of Lord Carbery, and the man in charge of the Royalist troops in Pembrokeshire. Vaughan exploded in rage and vowed vengeance 'on the round-headed Parliament dogs', gathering 450 men and preparing to march towards Milford Haven. Sir John Stepney, governor of the town, went into the churchyard to see if he could spot an enemy advance. On the slopes to the south of Haverfordwest, adjacent to the road to Milford, a farmer named Wheeler was grazing a herd of cattle and these, perhaps alarmed by distant cannon fire, bolted down the hill. Convinced that these were the approaching enemy, Stepney and his men ran through the streets shouting, 'God's wounds! The Roundhead dogs are coming.' There was a confused exodus of the town, with terrified soldiers abandoning a hundred new red coats, stocks of food and ten pieces of ordnance, whilst the boys of the town picked up over sixty muskets from the roadways.

On 25 February, Rowland Laugharne marched his men into Haverfordwest. Two days later, he accepted the surrender of Roch Castle, but he knew that he must now turn his attention to the capture of Tenby. Just over a week later, on 6 March, he set out to wholly 'extirpate and root out the anti-Christian malignant party' from that town and from Pembrokeshire.

The Fall of Tenby

Until the Civil Wars, Tenby was a prosperous seaport, its ships trading around the coasts of Britain, across to Ireland and even along the western shores of France and the Iberian Peninsula. Defended by medieval walls which encircled the town, it could be entered on the landward side by two main gates, the West Gate, called today the Five Arches, and by the massive North Gate, where the road ran out northwards through the suburb known as Norton. A moat, the South Pool, ran along the walls at the West Gate, which was accessed over a wooden footbridge. The town defences continued along the cliff edges overlooking the sands of the North and South Beaches and were dotted at regular intervals by some fourteen towers, with two more gates, the Whitesand and Haven gates leading to the castle and the harbour. The castle occupied a rocky promontory at the south-eastern edge of the town, its steep cliffs acting as a natural defence.

As Laugharne marched towards Tenby at the head of some 600 men, including all the seamen who could be spared from their ship-board duties and Admiral Swanley's master gunner, three ships of Swanley's command, the *Swallow, Prosperous* and *Crescent,* dropped anchor in Caldey Roads, off Tenby, their guns trained on the town.

A polite exchange of letters now took place between Swanley, Governor Gwynne in the castle and Richard Wyatt, the Mayor. The admiral hoped to obtain a surrender without resort to violence, and reminded Wyatt that in a previous appeal, the town council had been asked to 'Joyne with us in the preservation of the Gosspell, the kings Honour, and the Kingdomes Safetie, to expel the Forces brought into the Counties by the Earle of Carbery... .' As no answer to that epistle had been received, immediate obedience was expected to the new demand. The council should therefore waste no time in replying to Swanley, 'that by your timely adhering to us, you may prevent the demolishing of your town by the battering it about your eares with our Ordnance, and hoping you will preserve it as also the effusion of much blood by your sweet compliance.'

The letter to Governor Gwynne was couched in much plainer language. If he did not straight away yield up the castle, he and his men should 'expect to proceeded against as Traytors to your King and Country and enemies to God and the Protestant religion.'

The mayor and the councillors returned a reply in which they reminded Swanley that the town was not theirs to dispose of, but the king's, and they referred him to the answer he would shortly receive from Governor Gwynne. They signed their names underneath, citing themselves as 'Your loving friends if you please'. Gwynne's letter was much less polite:

> 'Gentlemen, This Towne we hold as loyall Subjects to the Kings Majesties use, for defence thereof we have his Majesties gracious Commission, which we will endeavour to maintaine with the hazard of our lives and fortune against all opposers, by what colour or pretence soever. This is the resolution of John Gwynne, David Gwynne, Thomas Botler'.[17]

Laugharne arrived on the landward side of the town in the late afternoon of 6 March, after this exchange of letters had taken place. He set up camp in the fields to the north and west of the town and passed the chill hours of the night in reviewing his plans. At about 8.00am the next morning, the guns of the warships began a bombardment, their shot falling 'very thick upon the town'. At the same time, the land forces closed in upon the ancient walls, driving off the royalist pickets that had been stationed behind the hedges along the roads.

The crackle of shots and the shouts of the men were suddenly stilled by the blast of a trumpet. Laugharne was making a last attempt to obtain the submission of the town, but his messenger was sent away empty-handed by a resolute Colonel Gwynne. By 1.00pm on the afternoon of Thursday, 7 March, Laugharne ordered his cannon to open fire on the town.

The great North Gate came under particularly heavy fire. Governor Gwynne, realising that it would form a focus of any attack, had strengthened it by piling up a mixture of dung and refuse, packed against the inner stonework of the gate, where it had hardened into a rock-like consistency. The exposed outer face of the gate was lined with baskets of woven willow and hazel rods known as gabions, their interiors rammed full of earth and stones to deaden the impact of cannon fire. A narrow passage twisted its way through the gabions, leading to a small doorway in the timbers of the main gate.

After a three-day bombardment from land and sea, during which an unknown number of people were killed and many houses damaged or destroyed, it was decided to launch a final attempt to storm the town. Laugharne was aware that his men were impatient for an end to the siege, especially the seamen, who were believed to respond better to 'a hot and sudden action'.

All artillery fire was now concentrated on the North Gate, where a lucky shot smashed down a strong door in one of the breastworks, whilst the wicket gate in the main gate was demolished by further fire. The foot soldiers stormed their way through the suburb of Norton, taking possession of a turnpike that blocked the way. The mounted troops were now able to gallop forward, their progress marked by cheers and trumpet blasts. The fighting was fierce and there was no certainty of success until Governor Gwynne, leading out a file of musketeers to challenge the attack, was shot and mortally wounded. Within minutes, Tenby's master gunner was also a casualty. As he was training his cannon, loaded with grapeshot, on the advancing enemy, he shouted to his gun crew, 'Now you shall see me make a slaughter of these Roundheads,' and was shot in the head.[18]

Within minutes, the parliamentary troops were inside the town, the garrison surrendering with little further resistance. Over 300 soldiers were taken prisoner, and eight guns were captured. The number of possible casualties amongst the townsfolk caused by the bombardment and storming of Tenby is unknown. A certain amount of looting certainly took place in the days after the surrender and, hiding away in one of the houses was Archdeacon Rudd, described as a 'malignant priest', who had been proscribed for high treason by Parliament. He was taken to Milford Haven and imprisoned on board the guardship *Lyon*.

A few days later, John Poyer arrived at Carew Castle to demand that it should be given up to Parliament. The garrison complied forthwith and were allowed to march away with all their equipment. All the strongholds held in the king's name within Pembrokeshire had fallen to Laugharne's advance, but there was still a threat from outside the county.

A demand was promptly sent to the commissioners of Cardiganshire and Carmarthenshire that they should accept the authority of Parliament. An outright refusal was received from Cardiganshire, whilst the soldiers of Carmarthen, numbering some 150 horse and 300 foot, dithered. Any spirit of defiance amongst them was tempered by the fact that they were poorly armed and that Carmarthen itself was surrounded only by an earthen wall. To drive home his message, Laugharne ordered the muster of 400 infantrymen and 150 mounted soldiers at Colby Moor, four or five miles to the east of Haverfordwest. It was only a day's march to Carmarthen and the council quickly signified their willingness to accept the authority of Parliament. Carmarthen's garrison had already set out for Lord Carbery's castle at Newcastle Emlyn, so any serious threat to Parliament in West Wales had been neutralised. To underline this, Laugharne and Swanley next called a meeting of all the leading gentlemen of the area and persuaded them to accept the Solemn League and Covenant, which had been signed between the Scots and the English on 17 August 1643. Most did so willingly enough, though Thomas Lloyd of Ynysmaengwyn wrote angrily to a friend, 'Pembrokeshire urged the traitorous Covenant also in Carmarthen and Glamorganshire.'

Any triumph felt by Parliament over its successes in South-West Wales was quickly soured by an event which was reported to have occurred on

23 April, St George's Day, 1644. After the fall of Tenby, Captain Swanley had resumed his patrols of the Irish sea, seizing vessels suspected of carrying royalist troops from Ireland to swell the king's garrisons in England. In addition to the numbers landing in North Wales, it was feared that further detachments of infantry were shortly to be landed at Bristol to take the city in the name of the king. The parliamentary press insisted that these men were the very ones who had carried out the slaughter of the Protestant settlers in 1641, a view so widely accepted that the king received a flood of pleas begging him to stop the landings.

In April, a Colonel Anthony Willoughby embarked with 150 soldiers on a ship bound from Dublin to Bristol. They had been called to the king's service as part of a levy imposed on all quarters of Ireland in a scheme that allowed individual officers to create fresh regiments.[19] Not long after clearing the Irish coast they were intercepted by Swanley's fleet and brought into Milford Haven. Efforts were made to persuade the Englishmen amongst the soldiers to enlist in the service of Parliament, but there was no such offer for the Irish. Swanley decided to 'try whether they could tread the seas as lightly as their Irish bogs…and, binding them back-to-back, cast them overboard to swim or drown.' Seventy defenceless men and two women were murdered in this way, though *Mercurius Aulicus,* the Royalist newssheet, suggested that all 150 of the soldiers had been killed. Parliament appeared to be unworried by Swanley's cruelty, summoning him to London, where he was awarded a gold chain for his services since the beginning of hostilities.

Reports of the atrocity were received with particular horror in Ireland, where soldiers were awaiting transportation to England. Few were now willing to chance the journey. The Marquis of Ormonde explained to a correspondent that many men 'were fearful to venture upon the voyage…soe that until these seas be cleared…Anglesey can expect little (indeed noe) succour out of Ireland.'[20] A substantial detachment of about 300 troops landed in Wales in July, with another eighty coming ashore at Conwy in April 1645, but very few others are recorded.[21]

South East Wales, January to June

The activities of the Pembrokeshire Parliamentarians were causing considerable concern in Brecon, which felt itself open to raids from the west. In April, Herbert Price, the royalist MP for Brecon Borough, and a member of Queen Henrietta Maria's household, wrote to Prince Rupert to warn him that 'If the enemy possess Carmarthen and the frontier counties, it is not in the power of man to recover them without ten times the force that may preserve them.'[22]

Since his appointment as Captain-General of Wales, Prince Rupert, as already noted, had been determined to appoint professional soldiers into positions of authority in Wales. One of his first choices was Colonel Charles Gerard, who in May, was sent down to crush Parliamentarian Pembroke. He was to leave a lasting impression in the south-west and he also continued the prince's policy of appointing outsiders to the command of local garrisons. Meanwhile, Rupert ordered a strong force to be placed at Abbey Cwm Hir between Knighton and Aberystwyth under the command of Colonel John Barnard, an experienced and trusted Royalist.

Rupert may have had doubts about the suitability of Lord Herbert in South Wales, because he nominated Sir Nicholas Mynne as Colonel-General of Herefordshire and Gloucestershire whilst allowing Herbert to retain control of the Raglan and Goodrich areas. An increase in the number of soldiers was felt desirable, so plans were developed to raise a force of 2,500 impressed men from South Wales and Herefordshire. These would be added to the already existing four regiments based in the Marches.

The need for more troops was emphasised during the early hours of 20 January, when Colonel Massey, the Parliamentary governor of Gloucester, launched a waterborne attack on Chepstow. Slipping into the town in the darkness, he and his men captured twelve officers and killed another in his room at the George Hotel, before making off with a haul of £300 in cash.

Massey was obviously determined to give his enemies no respite, because in May he seized Ross-on-Wye and moved towards Hereford, sending a further body of troops to challenge Monmouth. Some advance warning seems to have reached the Monmouth garrison, as it was quickly reinforced by the arrival of Major-General Scudamore and a section of Herbert's regiment. Scudamore was clearly a man who liked to lead from the front as, whilst out on patrol with a small escort of a dozen soldiers, he came unexpectedly upon a force of some 500 Parliamentary troops advancing along a lane towards Monmouth. There was a brief exchange of shots which soon sputtered out as heavy rain soaked the gunpowder. Swords were drawn and Scudamore and his troop succeeded in holding the lane until Herbert's men came to his aid. Massey, having lost the element of surprise, retreated and soon abandoned Ross-on-Wye.[23]

Rowland Laugharne had marched eastwards, well beyond the borders of his home county, and by May had placed a strong garrison in Cardiff Castle. There is some evidence that he did so with the help of the Parliamentary navy, which could have landed troops at Cardiff earlier in the month. In seizing Cardiff, Laugharne had bypassed Swansea, which was determined to adhere to its loyalty to the king.

On 15 May, Captain Robert Moulton, on board the *Lion*, then at anchor in Milford Haven, addressed a letter to the mayor and gentlemen of Swansea in the name of Robert, Earl of Warwick, the Lord High Admiral of the navy. He demanded that they yield the town to the forces of Parliament to the 'obedience of the King and Parliament'. Failure to do so would result in a trade embargo on the town 'till your forced obedience bring you to the mercy of him that tendereth your grace and favour.'

The mayor and gentlemen of Swansea returned a blistering reply:

> 'We cannot understand how we may, with any justice or loyalty, return you the name of gentleman to your rude and rebellious paper, in the front of which you have the boldness and presumption, in the name of the right honourable (as you term him) (whom we do and must account a dishonest and most insulting rebel), Robert Earl of Warwick (by you styled) High Admiral of England, Wales and Ireland, and his Majesty's Navy Royal at Sea (the which we do and ought to protest he hath most traitorously betrayed and rebelliously possessed) to will and require us forthwith to yield the town and garrison of Swansea into the obedience of the King and Parliament (a most foul treason, masked under a fair and specious show of a most loyal and just adherency of subjection to his Majesty and his Parliament at Oxford), in defiance of which your traitorous summons we send you this our fixed resolution, that we will neither yield town nor garrison, nor any the least interest we hold of life or fortune (under the protection of his sacred Majesty), but will defend

the same and our country against any your proud and insolent menacings (wherein your proper trade is exhibited) and in the account of a rebel and traitor we leave you to your fearful destruction.'[24]

This tirade seems to have had its desired effect, because no further action was taken against Swansea and towards the end of the month the Parliamentary warships sailed out of Milford Haven. Their departure left the garrison of Pembroke and their followers without the protection they had come to expect and a letter was quickly sent up to Parliament, asking that Swanley be sent back to the Haven. Their concern was fully justified, because Colonel Gerard, at the head of a large force, was heading in their direction.

Mid and North Wales, June to December

On 19 June, the royalist forces suffered a surprise defeat at the hands of Colonel Mytton at Duddlestone, near Oswestry. Mytton had been awoken from sleep the night before to be told that a convoy carrying ammunition to Prince Rupert was in transit. Knowing that Rupert was desperately short of munitions at that time, Mytton set off with a mixed force of twenty-five dragoons and the same number of horsemen and came up behind the convoy without being observed. As the ground was uneven and thickly wooded, it was impossible to use the horses, so the dragoons dismounted and prepared to charge the rear of the ammunition train. The element of complete surprise was lost when one of the troopers accidentally discharged his pistol, but the enemy did not stand their ground, and fled. Twenty-seven were captured, all of them Welshmen, as well as all the ammunition.

The Royalist garrison of Oswestry began to strengthen their fortifications, understanding that an attack was imminent. The town was surrounded by a wall, but its chief defences were the stoutly built church, situated outside the defences, and the nearby castle. Both were well garrisoned. Two days after the debacle at Duddlestone, at about midday, the men peering out over the walls saw the Parliamentary forces advancing towards them.

Accompanying Colonel Mytton was Basil Feilding, Earl of Denbigh, with mounted troops and 200 foot soldiers. Denbigh had already sent out scouts onto the surrounding hills to watch for any possible advance of Irish soldiers from Shrewsbury. Some sort of movement was seen, but never developed into any real threat. As Mytton and Denbigh encouraged their men forward, they received a 'hot salute' from the defenders, but the church was soon taken. The gates of the town were battered down by cannon fire and the Parliamentarian soldiers poured into the town. They found the streets deserted, as most of the garrison had retreated into the castle, though one unfortunate woman was disembowelled by a shot from the cannon.

A fierce firefight followed, with the 'great sacre' of Denbigh's force hammering at the mighty walls of the castle. Some of the men inside attempted to escape over the battlements, one of them falling and breaking his arm, but all were captured and imprisoned. As dusk fell, the gunfire dwindled and it was decided to set the castle gates ablaze. The men detailed for this task were, however, so tired that it was postponed until the morning light. Somehow, news of the planned conflagration spread amongst the townsfolk and, to the surprise of Mytton and Denbigh, the women of Oswestry came to plead on their knees for the lives of their husbands in the castle. Most of the women were Welsh and spoke no English, so an interpreter had to be found. Denbigh agreed to offer quarter to the garrison, but this was turned down. As the cries of the women increased, their menfolk at last agreed to surrender, providing that they could march away unmolested, leaving behind their arms. 'And so', wrote Colonel Mytton in his account of the action, 'they marched out and we found 100 great muskets, besides others stolen away eight halberds...one barrel of powder and suitable match, many swords and some few pistols....'[25] There were numerous prisoners, including some 200 soldiers and the town, to avoid plunder, consented to pay the sum of £500 to the victors. Colonel Mytton took on the role of governor of Oswestry.

Lord Denbigh was anxious to leave the town in order to join Sir Thomas Myddelton at Nantwich. From there, it was proposed that their combined forces should march into Lancashire in pursuit of Prince Rupert, who was on his way to join King Charles in the north. The absence of Denbigh presented the Royalists with an unmissable opportunity to regain Oswestry. It was known that Mytton's troops were few in number, so Sir Fulke Hunckes, governor of Shrewsbury, began to collect reinforcements from surrounding garrisons. Soon he had assembled a force of about 2,600 men, with more expected to join him.

The gathering in of so many men could not be kept secret. Lord Denbigh soon learned of it and directed Sir Thomas Myddelton to take three of his companies and as many men as could be spared from Wem to supplement Mytton's garrison at Oswestry. Over 400 musketeers and a full troop of horse, with 'a good ingenier' marched into the town There was also the hope of further reinforcements as Denbigh, after consultations at Manchester with Sir John Meldrum of the Scottish army, had decided to return with several companies of horse.

By now, the royalist forces were closing in on Oswestry. Colonel Marrow, one of the officers who had arrived in North Wales from Ireland, was preparing to besiege the town. He was assisted by Sir Fulke Hunckes and their combined force numbered some 4,000 men.

On Tuesday, 2 July, Hunckes heard that Myddleton might be moving out of Oswestry towards his camp and instructed Colonel Marrow to take a small party of horse to discover the enemy's strength. Marrow, perhaps eager to mount a real challenge, took out the entire troop. He was completely routed by Myddleton, his men scattered and pursued all over the countryside. So sudden was the defeat that Hunckes only learned of it when a messenger brought the news and Marrow himself staggered in covered with dust.[26] Hunckes, his advantage lost, could do nothing but retire to Shrewsbury.

Prince Rupert Returns to the Marches

On the same day as Marrow's blunder, the king's army had suffered a catastrophic defeat at Marston Moor, near York. Prince Rupert, having been ordered by the king to march to the relief of York, then under siege by Parliamentary forces, had managed to enter the city without opposition on 1 July, but decided to give battle the next day. He hoped to take the enemy by surprise, but in the event suffered a crushing reverse. Rupert abandoned York and began a long, weary retreat back towards the Welsh borders.

He arrived in Shrewsbury on 20 July, having been pursued by Brereton and Meldrum for much of the way. He immediately issued fresh demands for more men and money. By the beginning of August, he had moved to Chester, where he directed a request to Lord Bulkeley for £100 to be paid as a loan to Archbishop Williams 'for my use and his

Majestie's service'. Another demand followed on 8 August, this time for the loan of 'two peeces of brasse cannon' which were to be added to the defences of Chester.[27]

The prince's efforts met with a mixed response. So much had been expected from Wales in terms of money and men that Rupert had become known as the 'Duke of Plunderland'. One Parliamentarian newssheet stated that 'the Welsh have been over and over pricked and pulled that there is not a man left but is a cousin to one Array man or other, and can be got off without bribes.'[28] To add to their troubles the people of North Wales had seen their herds of cattle steadily diminishing in number as the animals were taken to feed the hungry troops.

Rupert had decided to make Chester his winter quarters. Letters were sent to the principal gentlemen of the surrounding counties, requesting their allegiance. Some, whose loyalties were doubtful, were summoned to face to face meetings. Some came, others pleaded a variety of excuses and stayed away.

On 5 August, Rupert's plans received an irritating check. He had sent a body of horse to quarter at Welshpool, but Colonel Mytton, hearing of this, set out to force a confrontation. He was joined by Myddelton, their combined army numbering about 550 horse and foot. In the skirmish that followed some 40 of Rupert's men were taken prisoner along with several officers and Rupert's own cornet officer was killed. Sir Thomas Dallison, the commanding officer, was surprised in his bed and fled without his breeches, in which was found a letter he had intended to send to the prince the next day. In a further reverse, Myddleton raided the park at Powys Castle and drove off 200 head of cattle.

There was a further disappointment on 21 August, when Colonel Marrow, who had been busy with continuous raids across the Marches, decided to quarter his men at Tarvin, just outside Chester. Inevitably, news of fresh troop movements soon reached Brereton at Northwich and he set off with Myddelton to attack the Royalist force. As they approached, they came across some of Marrow's scouts and pursued them back into Tarvin. A sharp but brief engagement followed, in which some of Marrow's men fled into the church, whilst others bolted back to Chester, chased thither by Captain Sankey almost to within pistol shot of the city defences.

Brereton meanwhile concentrated his efforts on the church, his men coming under heavy fire from those trapped within its walls. Several of

The ruins of Brampton Bryan Castle, held for Parliament by Lady Brilliana Harley in 1643. (*Author's Image*)

Above: The impact of musket balls is still clearly visible on the stonework of Brampton Bryan Castle. (*Author's Image*)

Below: Caernarfon Castle was a Royalist stronghold during the first and second Civil Wars. (*Gwyndafh/Pixabay*)

Above: Cardiff Castle, the target of several small local rebellions during the civil wars. (*Daryus Chandra/Pixabay*)

Below: Chepstow Castle was seized and held for the king by Sir Nicholas Kemeys in 1648. He was killed when it was stormed by Parliamentary troops in May of that year. (*silentsal10/Pixabay*)

Above: King Charles I watched the defeat of his troops at Rowton Heath from the cathedral tower. He was almost killed by a stray cannon ball. (*Stephen_UK/Pixabay*)

Below: Colby Moor, where Rowland Laugharne defeated a numerically superior force of Royalists on 1 August 1645. (*Author's Image*)

Rowland Laugharne successfully drove the Royalists out of South Wales in 1645, but changed sides in 1648, a move which brought about the second Civil War. (*Wikimedia Commons*)

A convinced Royalist, Carbery hoped to build a fort at Milford Haven to protect the landing of troops from Ireland. (*Wikimedia Commons*)

Hopton Castle, the scene of an infamous massacre on 13 March 1644. (*Author's Image*)

The memorial in the churchyard at Wiston commemorates the Battle of Colby Moor. Some of those who fell are said to be buried there. (*Author's Image*)

Above: John, 1st Baron Byron, was a leading figure in the wars in North Wales and Chester. Portrait by William Dobson. (*Wikimedia Commons*)

Right: King Charles I. This miniature portrait captures the melancholy air that increasingly seemed to surround him as the war continued. (*lisby1/ Creative Commons*)

Above: Chirk Castle, the home of Sir Thomas Myddelton, which was taken by Royalist forces early in the war and only returned to him years later. (*Etrusia UK/ Creative Commons*)

Left: Prince Rupert was one of the most outstanding Royalist commanders of the first Civil War, until he lost the king's confidence after the fall of Bristol. Portrait by Gerard von Honthorst. (*lisby1 at Creative Commons*)

Right: An opponent of King Charles, Fairfax was nevertheless respected by the monarch, who described him as a man of honour. (*Wikimedia Commons*)

Below: Laugharne Castle capitulated to Rowland Laugharne on 3 November 1644, its garrison shouting out of the windows for terms of surrender. (*Author's Image*)

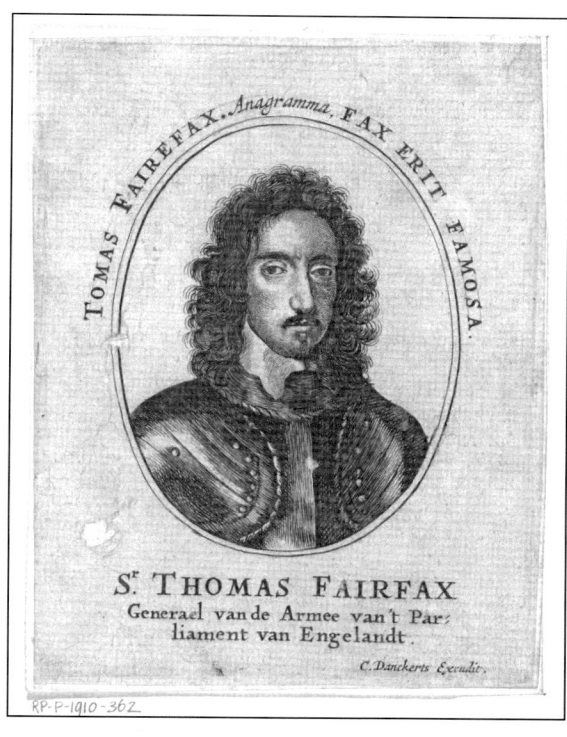

TOMAS FAIREFAX. *Anagramma*, FAX ERIT FAMOSA.

Sᵗ THOMAS FAIRFAX

Generael van de Armee van't Parliament van Engelandt.

C. Danckerts Excudit.

RP-P-1910-362

Known as Red Castle during the Civil Wars, Powis was captured by Sir Thomas Myddelton's forces after its gates were blown down by an explosive petard. (*Meatle/ Pixabay*)

Raglan Castle, the magnificent home of the Marquis of Worcester, played host to King Charles I on two occasions. (*Allie Ford/Pixabay*)

Above: This ruined building is said to have been used as a wound dressing station during the Battle of Rowton Heath. (*chestertourism/Creative Commons Licence*)

Below: The town walls still encircle Pembroke, though on the south side, the ground level has risen considerably, as evidenced by the arrow slit at the bottom of this tower. (*Author's Image*)

None of this was known in North Wales, where towards the end of August there was further fighting in the Marches. Sir Marmaduke Langdale was leading a large Royalist force, the Northern Horse, through Lancashire intending to reach Shrewsbury, but every inch of his progress seems to have been disputed. By the time he entered Cheshire he was said to have lost almost two thirds of his men. That did not prevent him from widespread plundering in the countryside around Chester. Sir William Brereton knew it was vital that Langdale should be stopped from penetrating any further south. Accordingly, he sent Colonel Jones with a small army of 800 men to block the Royalist route. On 26 August the two forces met at Malpas. Despite furious resistance, Jones might have been driven back had not Brereton arrived and turned the tide. In the fight that ensued, Langdale was wounded and two colonels and three majors were killed, plus an unknown number of soldiers. Langdale was driven back into Chester.

Towards the end of August, Sir Thomas Myddelton was ordered to march into Montgomeryshire to disperse any possible Royalist gatherings that might be taking place. There was also the likelihood of capturing a large amount of powder that was being sent up from Bristol to North Wales, where it was urgently needed by Royalist garrisons.

On 3 September, during the night hours, Myddelton marched his men out of Oswestry and by dawn they were close to Newtown. At this point, Myddelton apparently divided his force, sending forward a Lieutenant-Colonel Till with 250 men to surprise the garrison, while he held the rest of his force, including the infantry, in reserve. At some time during the morning, Till succeeded in catching the garrison by surprise, even though its commander, Sir Thomas Gardiner, had apparently been forewarned that 'the enemy had a design upon him'. Forty or fifty men were taken prisoner, along with thirty-six barrels of the powder en route from Bristol, twelve barrels of brimstone and a large quantity of match and bullets.

Later in the day, Myddelton moved towards Montgomery. The castle there was a powerful stronghold, perched at the end of a long ridge overlooking the town and the undulating landscape that stretched northwards to Welshpool and Powys Castle. Montgomery Castle was the home of the literary-minded and eccentric Lord Herbert of Cherbury, who should not be confused with the Lord Herbert of Raglan Castle. Lord Herbert of Cherbury was famous for his book *The Life and Times of Henry VIII* amongst other equally well-received literary works. He had taken little part in the war, and though he had professed a lukewarm Royalism, he had remained neutral. He had been one of those summoned to attend Prince Rupert at Shrewsbury but had excused himself on the grounds of 'the course of physic he had entered upon'. He did suffer from an eye complaint, so perhaps the physic was a treatment for that condition.

Myddelton had already contacted Herbert, demanding the surrender of the castle. Herbert is said to have returned a 'very good and satisfactory answer'. A series of negotiations then followed, conducted on Myddelton's behalf by Captain Samuel More. Lord Herbert proved to be obstructive, whether because he hoped for the sudden arrival of Royalist forces, or because he did not wish to be accused of cooperation with the enemy is uncertain. He was given until 9.00am on 5 September to decide upon a surrender.

Despite this, the Parliamentarians seized the castle outworks on the night before. At about midnight, Lieutenant-Colonel Till, at the head of a storming party, clambered into the ditch in front of the middle ward and loosened a few planks at the foot of the drawbridge, which had been raised to prevent entry. Using this hole, they managed to squeeze through into the entry passage leading to the main gate. There was no resistance from the sentries and Till awoke the sleeping Lord Herbert by blowing fiercely on a trumpet. Presumably still in his nightshirt, Herbert ordered Till to leave, reminding him that he had broken the agreement concluded the day before. Till flourished a petard, an explosive device, promising to blow up the gate. The sight of this small bomb convinced Herbert to surrender the castle.[31]

Herbert made no apparent objection when all the captured gunpowder was stored in his cellars, alongside his own cache of munitions. Nor did he do anything to prevent Myddelton from bringing in some provisions, most of it commandeered from the surrounding countryside, in order to withstand a siege.

The Battle of Montgomery

The occupation of Montgomery Castle urged the Royalists into action. Summoning troops from Chester and Shrewsbury and any adjacent garrisons that could spare men, Sir Michael Ernely, in command of Shrewsbury, determined to attack before Myddelton could consolidate

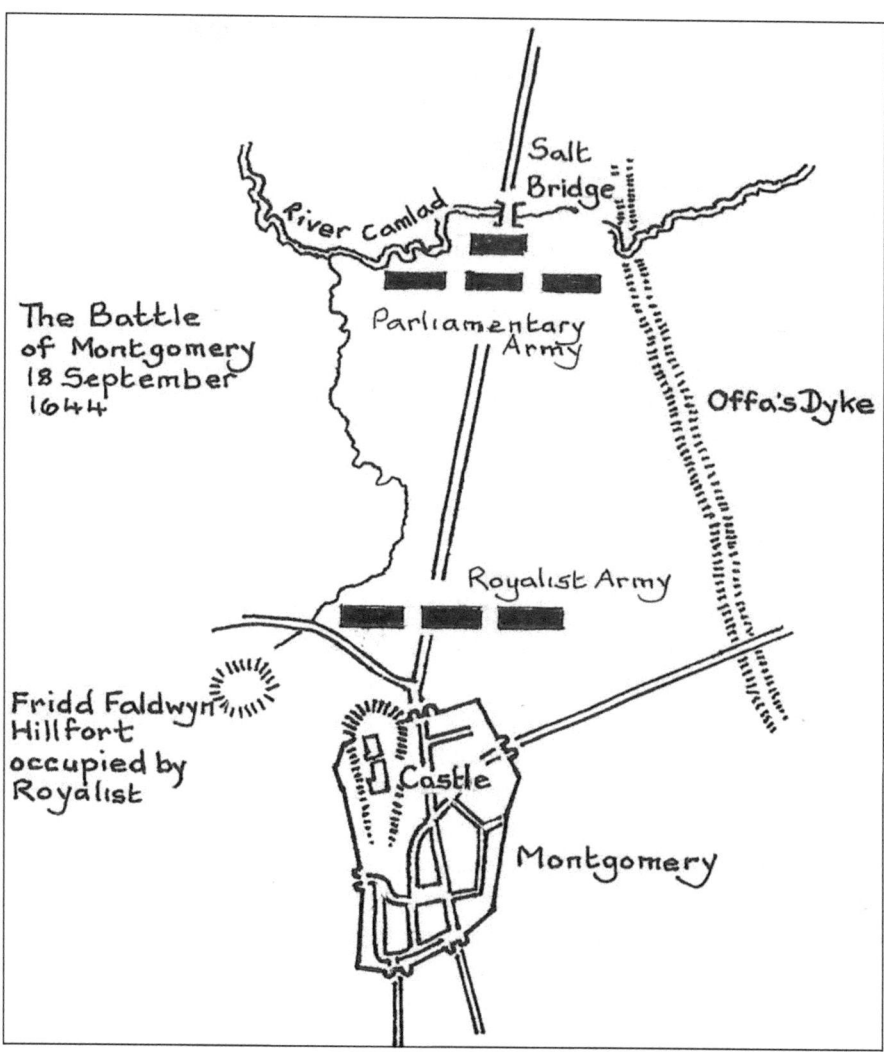

A map of the Battle of Montgomery

his hold on the town and castle. A force of up to 2,500 horse and foot was hastily assembled and, by Friday, 6 September, were within ten miles of Montgomery. Two days later, early in the morning, they began their attack, closing in on the town from two directions in a pincer movement.

There was a token resistance, but Myddelton, who had been taken by surprise whilst out on a foraging expedition, was forced to retreat northwards to Oswestry. He was almost captured when trying to cross a bridge which became a bottleneck because of the number of men trying to force a passage. Thirty of his mounted troops failed to do so and were taken back to Montgomery as prisoners.

Within Montgomery itself, many of the Parliamentary soldiers took refuge inside the castle, where they were besieged for the next ten days. Their situation seemed dire, as Myddelton had been unable to fully provision it and there was no certainty as to when, or if, help would come.

Montgomery Castle was now seen as a key stronghold by both sides. Whoever held it would control a large area of the Marches and the main routes in every direction. Sir Thomas Myddelton was determined to relieve the besieged garrison as swiftly as possible. He called for aid from William Brereton, then at Tarvin and from Sir John Meldrum and his regiment. In a period of a few short days, an army of about 3,000 men was heading towards Montgomery to rescue the 500 or so men occupying the castle. It was well supplied with munitions, as on 15 September, six barrels of gunpowder, six hundredweight of match and one thousand weight of musket balls had been issued from Myddelton's armoury at Oswestry.

The opponents now numbered about 4,500 soldiers, as the besieging force had been swollen by the arrival of Lord Byron, at the head of a mixed force of horse, dragoons and foot soldiers. Many of these were men who had served in Ireland.

At dawn on Wednesday, 18 September, these two armies were in place, ready for battle. The Parliamentarians stood to the open ground to the northwest of the town, where the River Camlad wound its way through farmland. The Royalists were still in possession of the town and the siege lines, with the bulk of their army camped on the high ground known as Fridd Faldwyn overlooking the streets and houses.

It must have been apparent to Byron that some of the Parliamentarian horse had been sent out to forage for supplies. Seizing the advantage, he launched a surprise attack. His troops moved down from the high ground to take up position on the outskirts of the town, advancing steadily towards the Parliamentary lines. Unusually, the cavalry was massed on one wing of the battlefield, rather than being placed on either side of the main block of infantrymen. In the confused melee of horsemen, hacking at one another with swords and firing off their pistols, Sir William Fairfax, Major-General of the Parliamentarian horse, was wounded, taken prisoner, rescued by his men and then, whilst leading another attack, mortally wounded. Colonel Marcus Trevor, commanding a regiment of Royalist horse, was almost lost when his favourite steed, a bay named Squire, was killed beneath him. He was lucky enough to be rescued by his men, who found him another mount.[32]

The two infantry blocks also came to close quarters. Sir John Meldrum's musketeers let loose what should have been a withering blast of fire, but at too great a distance from the enemy for it to have any real effect. The return fire from the Royalists forced Meldrum's men to retreat, until they rallied and came on again. Elsewhere on the battlefield, there was hand-to-hand fighting, with men slashing with their swords, or wielding their musket butts as clubs. Despite the undoubted courage of many of the Parliamentary soldiers, some of whom 'carried themselves more like Lions than men', the Royalists might have been victorious had it not been for the sudden, unexpected retreat of Byron's regiment which, with two other regiments, 'ran without a blow struck, which disheartened the foot so infinitely that being in disorder with the pursuit of the enemy they could not be persuaded to rally again; which the rebels did, and advanced and made good the place, relieved the castle, being the work they came for, and took some prisoners.'[33]

At this point in the fighting, the garrison of the castle emerged, perhaps having seen from the ramparts the disorganised flight of the Royalists. The remaining besiegers were driven from the entrenchments, back through the town and into the countryside beyond.

The battle had lasted for only about an hour, but the Parliamentarian horse are said to have continued their pursuit of the enemy for three or four miles, killing the fugitives wherever they found them. The foot soldiers, realising they had no chance of outrunning mounted men, quickly surrendered. In all there were over 1,200 of them, with even more weapons taken. The number of dead was estimated to be in excess of 400 on the Royalist side, with about 60 Parliamentarians lost.

The large number of prisoners was problematic. There were too many to be safely guarded and fed, so many of them were probably encouraged to enlist in Parliament's army. Persuading captured soldiers to switch allegiance was a practice common to both sides throughout the war. Four of the prisoners suffered a much harder fate. They were Parliamentary deserters, who had abandoned their comrades and joined the opposing side. They were tried by a council of war and executed on 25 September.[34]

One act of chivalry was noted in the aftermath of the battle. Sir William Fairfax, the Major-General of the Parliamentarian horse, was known to have been wearing a diamond ring and a gold bracelet, which disappeared from his corpse. Sir John Meldrum insisted on their return, even threatening to treat as enemies the surgeons and soldiers who claimed them as battlefield booty. The relics were sent to Fairfax's wife with a covering letter.

The Battle of Montgomery was a significant victory for Parliament. As Sir John Meldrum noted in the letter he wrote to the Committee of Safety on 19 September, '…so that by the blow delivered here the best of their foot are taken away. Shrewsbury, Chester and Liverpool, unfurnished with ammunition, and North Wales (which formerly hath been the nursery for the King's armies), in all likelihood will shake off that yoke of servitude which formerly did lie upon their necks, and will be reduced to the obedience of the King and Parliament by the example of Montgomery Castle… . The personal carriage and endeavours of Sir William Brereton and Sir Thomas Myddelton hath been exceeding great in the advancement of this service.'[35]

Arthur Trevor, the brother of Sir Marcus Trevor, the Royalist colonel who had been so nearly captured during the battle, was also in no doubt as to what the defeat meant. On 23 September, he addressed a letter to the Marquis of Ormonde. 'May it please Your Excellency, My last letter to your Excellency left the business before Montgomery in the balance and this will inform your Lordship that, both parties being weighed, we were found too light (of foot at least), for in plain English, our men ran shamefully when they had no cause of so great fear so we are ordained to be the mocking-stock of the War.'

Salt was rubbed into the wound in the early hours of 2 October, when Sir Thomas Myddelton attacked Powis Castle, then known as Red Castle, six or seven miles from Montgomery. Approaching the sleeping castle, he left 50 horsemen and 100 of the infantry to act as a rear guard whilst deploying the remainder of the infantry to surround the building. A fusillade of musket fire startled the garrison awake and, in the confusion, a petard was placed against the gate, the explosion of this small device blowing open the timbers. An assault party fought their way into the inner ward and the resistance of the garrison collapsed. Lord Powis and up to 100 soldiers were taken prisoner along with all their weapons and horses.[36]

In the months that followed, Myddelton raided Bishop's Castle, driving out its Royalist occupiers and then followed this with the storming of Abbey Cwm Hir in Radnorshire. He also concentrated his efforts into regaining two of his former properties, Ruthin Castle and Chirk, both of which had fallen into enemy hands some time before. The attempt upon Ruthin, in which he was joined by Colonel Mytton, was made in late October, but the streets had been barricaded. Breaking through these barriers allowed the cavalry to enter the town, where they pursued the Royalist horse through the streets and out into the open countryside. The castle, however, remained unchallenged, as Mytton's men were called away when news was received of a possible threat to Oswestry. Myddelton was forced to withdraw, breaking down the turnpikes and other fortifications as he retreated. The attack on Chirk Castle was made in December and, despite Sir Thomas' boast that he intended to spend Christmas in his own house, a three-day siege failed and the Parliamentarian troops were forced to withdraw.

Nevertheless, these failures were relatively minor blips in an otherwise successful campaign. Myddelton now held a large, if isolated, block of land in the Marches. His position was bolstered by the adherence of Sir John Price of Newtown, a former Royalist who had changed his allegiance. A man of great influence in Montgomeryshire, Price seemed the ideal candidate for the governorship of Montgomery Castle and by the end of the year had taken up the appointment.

There was now no real challenge from the Royalists, who seemed to have lost confidence after their defeat at Montgomery. Loyalty to their cause appeared to be draining away and there was a distinct unwillingness to support further military action. Attempts to pay extra military taxes were resisted across North Wales and Sir Michael Ernely was forced to write to Prince Rupert that there was a weakening of loyalty and that Parliamentary influence was growing.[37] This lack of cooperation was illustrated on 12 December, when the inhabitants of the Vale of Clwyd sent a letter to Lord Byron, complaining that Colonel Trevor's regiment of horse, which had been billeted in the area, was demanding contributions of cash and supplies beyond those normally expected in the monthly amounts. This was being done without the agreement of the local Commissioners of Array. People had been robbed on the highways and there was a resulting threat to the prosperity of Ruthin market. The petitioners begged that local people should no longer have troops quartered upon them, a plea which was sympathetically received by Byron, who ordered Colonel Trevor to put things to rights.

South Wales, June to December

On an unknown date in the early summer, Colonel Charles Gerard stepped ashore at Black Rock, near Chepstow. An experienced soldier who had seen action in the Netherlands, Gerard had raised his own regiment at the beginning of the war and was well thought of by King Charles. He had been sent into South Wales by Prince Rupert, to prevent the further advances of Rowland Laugharne and had brought with him a large group of about 1,000 foot soldiers 700 horse and 200 dragoons, some of whom who had crossed from Ireland to Bristol, probably during the previous November. Gerard's march westwards met with little resistance, because he was soon able to regain Cardiff for the king, displacing the garrison installed by Laugharne, and then pushing on, gathering recruits as he went.

In each of the counties he controlled, Gerard consolidated his position by ordering reports on the weapons and munitions available from the local armouries. He had also been given permission by the king to order local Commissioners of Array to press into service a large number of new soldiers, and to raise whatever taxes were needed to pay and feed them.[38] He did this, as we shall see, with such severity that it created a lasting hatred of him.

By 12 June, he had reached Carmarthenshire, where the castles of Cydweli, Carmarthen and Laugharne fell to him. He then struck northwards, attacking Newcastle Emlyn and then Cardigan, where he was reported to have killed or captured over 200 men. He next turned his attention to Pembrokeshire which, according to a report in *Mercurius Aulicus,* the Royalist broadsheet, was the 'most seditious county of all Wales, or rather of England, for the inhabitants live like English Corporations, very unlike the loyal Welsh men.'[39]

The news of this lightning-quick advance caused great alarm in Pembrokeshire. The County Committee summoned all able-bodied men to muster on 14 June, with arms, horses and enough provisions for six days. In all likelihood, very few answered the call, for there was no obvious attempt to block Gerard's line of march. He cut across Pembrokeshire towards Roch Castle, where he confiscated 300 head of cattle and 1,500 sheep. This was a serious blow to Laugharne, for these animals had been intended to feed his men.[40]

Soon Haverfordwest was in Gerard's grasp and the only towns holding out against him were Tenby and Pembroke. At some point in early July, Pembroke found itself surrounded by Royalist forces. It was the beginning of a long blockade of the town, during which neither side made a serious attempt to challenge the other. Gerard was possibly deterred by the stout walls of the town and castle, surrounded on three sides by muddy tidal creeks, but more likely he hoped to starve out the inhabitants. Laugharne may have been unwilling to pit his men against a numerically superior force, or he may have trusted that Parliamentary warships would come to his aid, as they had done in January.

He had already received an unexpected windfall thanks to the vigilance of Captain Moulton of the warship *Lyon,* still patrolling the Irish Sea from Milford Haven. Moulton had captured nine vessels laden with wine, tobacco and 100 pieces of ordnance, which he had appropriated for the use of the garrison of Pembroke. However, the captain recognised the gravity of the situation facing Laugharne. He sent an urgent letter to the Lord Admiral of the Parliamentary navy, warning him that 'unless there is a speedy sending of good commanders, a faithful committee and an enlarged commission to Colonel Rowland Laugharne, these parts are likely to be lost to Parliament.'[41]

Moulton must have known how unlikely it was that help would come by sea. Two of Swanley's principal warships, the *Leopard* and the *Swallow* were undergoing refits at Plymouth and three others were in a poor state of repair. The few vessels still remaining at Milford Haven were merchant ships on contract to the navy and their continued presence depended on the renewal of leases between their owners and Parliament.

At this juncture something entirely unexpected occurred. On 2 July, Prince Rupert was defeated at Marston Moor and the whole of northern England was lost to King Charles. By the end of the summer, Gerard was marching away, perhaps recalled to help his sovereign. He left behind him a legacy of bitter memories across South Wales. One account written at the time, described how 'the barbarous and cruel enemy drive away our cattle, rifle our houses to the bare walls. All provision of victuals, where they come, carried away or destroyed. Divers villages and county towns, being neither garrisons nor any annoyance to the enemy, burnt down to the ground. The standing corn they burn and destroy. All sexes and degrees stripped naked by the enemy – aged and unarmed. Persons inhumanly murdered in cold blood, and others half-hanged, and afterwards stigmatized, and their flesh burnt off their bodies to the bare bones, and yet suffered in great torture to live.'

Laugharne, buoyed up by the departure of his enemy, was further encouraged when Admiral Swanley was ordered back to Milford, where his fleet would be permanently based. In addition, 140 soldiers were sent to Pembroke by the Earl of Essex and the County Committee purchased food, iron, cloth and canvas to the value of £150 from the owners of the *Gillyflower* which, at a cost of £150 a month, was to serve as a guardship at Tenby.[42]

There was a further stroke of luck in August. Storms forced two Parliamentary ships into the calmer waters of Milford Haven. On board was a detachment of infantry commanded by Colonel Beale and Colonel Carter. Their original destination had been North Wales, to help Sir Thomas Myddelton to capture Anglesey, but now it was decided that they should remain in Pembrokeshire until plans could be made to march north to link up with Myddelton.

Events in Glamorganshire and Monmouthshire

In late September, Nicholas Mynne, who had been appointed as Colonel-General over much of South Wales, decided to attack the Parliamentary stronghold of Gloucester, but was intercepted by Colonel Massey at Redmarley and killed. Up to 500 of Mynne's men were slain alongside him, or taken prisoner.

In Herefordshire and Monmouthshire, tensions were rising between the Royalist garrisons and the local populace. In particular, the presence of the Sir Marmaduke Langdale's Northern Horse was much resented. As already noted, after the defeat at Marston Moor, Prince Rupert had retreated via Chester and Monmouth to Bristol. In his wake came the remnants of Langdale's command. Heavily defeated by their Parliamentary opponents during the battle, the survivors had made an epic march down through Lancashire and the Welsh borders, enduring further losses as they moved south. By September, they had established themselves in western Herefordshire, where they plundered cattle and supplies with impunity.

They eventually moved into Monmouthshire, where a group of them occupied the long, narrow peninsula at Beachley, between the rivers Wye and Severn, just outside Chepstow. From Beachley, it was hoped that the whole command would be able to cross the Severn and join Rupert at Bristol. Earthwork fortifications were hastily thrown up across the neck of the peninsula and, in each of the rivers, small frigates dropped anchor, their guns protecting the flanks of the entrenchments.

On 20 September, whilst plans for an evacuation were still being formed, Colonel Massey arrived from Gloucester with his regiment and four troops of cavalry. He waited until low tide, when the frigates were unable to move close inshore and sent a group of ten musketeers to draw fire from the earthworks. The main body of men then ran forward, drums beating, trumpets ringing out, and stormed the fortifications. Over one hundred prisoners were taken.[43]

Elsewhere in Monmouthshire, the remnants of the Northern Horse now found themselves isolated and facing increasing hostility. One of the officers, Samuel Tuke, wrote to Prince Rupert, asking for a 'swift passage' to Bristol, as many of his soldiers were in a poor state, some without horses. With no obvious signs of relief, Tuke was twice forced to move his men, once towards Chepstow and then to Llantarnam, near the river port of Caerleon. In another letter to Rupert, Tuke explained that he could not trust the country gentry, who he described as 'niggling traitors'. Even the tenant farmers had attacked the soldiers, wounding them and seizing their weapons.[44] The Royalist Commissioners of Array refused to intervene and many of the local people were beginning to look more favourably upon the Parliamentary cause.

In the meantime, Colonel Massey had not been idle. He had no sooner marched away from Beachley than he made another attack upon Monmouth. Amongst the Royalist officers in charge of the town was Major Robert Kyrle, a man of what can only be described as liquid loyalties. He had successfully trounced Lord Herbert at Pontrilas in November 1643 and later had formed part of the Parliamentary garrison of Bristol. Upon its capture by Prince Rupert in July 1643, he had sworn allegiance to the king and had been sent to Monmouth, close to his family home of Ross-on-Wye. He was clearly concerned by the mounting Parliamentary successes and by what that might mean for him as a turncoat. He made surreptitious advances to Massey, offering to betray Monmouth to him. A plan was concocted, by which Kyrle would ride out from the town with thirty men, apparently on a mission to ambush Massey, but he would himself be 'surprised' and taken prisoner. With his men safely captive, Kyrle would return to Monmouth in charge of a group of Massey's men masquerading as prisoners who, once inside the walls, would overpower the sentries and open the gates to the rest of Massey's force.

The plan almost fell flat when Kyrle's cornet evaded capture and fled back to raise the alarm. Colonel Marmaduke Holtby, the governor of Monmouth, was somewhat suspicious when Kyrle arrived at the town gates, but agreed to let down the drawbridge. From that point, the plan worked smoothly and Monmouth was swiftly taken. Governor Holtby escaped, but over sixty of the garrison were taken captive.

The loss of Monmouth was greeted with fury by the Royalist sympathisers, who regarded the town as a gateway into South Wales. Whoever held it could dominate the area. Accordingly, the Marquis of Worcester summoned as much help as he could find, and this makeshift force, bolstered by elements of the Northern Horse, were soon on the road to Monmouth. Massey was warned of their approach and, in a short, sharp engagement, drove them back. Those Welshmen who were taken prisoner were kindly treated by Massey, who did not wish to repeat the mistakes of his opponents. He allowed them to return to their homes, 'everyone with a little note directed to his master, or to the parish where he lived, to signify to them "That the intention of the Parliament, and of Massey in coming thither, was not to destroy or enslave their persons, to take away their good or livelihoods; but to preserve their lives and fortunes, to open the cause of justice, and free them of their heavy burthens under the forces of Rupert, a German." By which artifice, and free discharge of the prisoners, the Welsh people began to entertain better thoughts of the Parliament's party than formerly.'[45]

To prevent any further harassment of Monmouth, Massey set up a number of outposts in the large country houses in the neighbourhood. One of these was Wonastow House, into which he placed ten foot soldiers and sixty horse. On 28 September, this little garrison found itself surrounded by 500 of the Northern Horse under Sir William Blackiston, together with Sir Trevor Williams' regiment and soldiers drawn from Raglan Castle and Chepstow. The men of Wonastow House had insufficient ammunition to hold off such a large force. According to a tale which may or may not be true, they melted down the lead window frames and all the pewter pots they could find to make bullets, whilst a serving maid unearthed two six-pound bags of powder with which to fire them. Before their supply of makeshift ammunition ran out, help arrived from Monmouth. The attackers were driven off, losing so many weapons in their retreat that afterwards 'muskets were sold at sixpence a piece.' The maid was awarded two pieces of money for her bravery and received a kiss from the governor of Monmouth, who also took her into his service.[46]

There was now considerable trepidation in Monmouthshire about future events. Parliamentarian sympathisers feared the arrival of Colonel Gerard, who was known to be approaching from the west. Colonel Edward Harley, the son of the heroic Lady Brilliana Harley of Brampton Bryan, was resolved to raise a regiment of foot with which to hold Monmouthshire for Parliament. He sent officers to scour the villages of the Forest of Dean and the areas around Gloucester for recruits but, strangely, neither Colonel Massey or the Committee for South Wales offered any assistance.

The need for more men received an extra impetus when it was learned that Gerard was occupying Usk with 500 troops. Incredibly, the Parliamentarian leaders were squabbling amongst themselves, unable to agree as to where Harley's regiment should be stationed or who should command it. The officers of the regiment, already in place with few men to command, refused to serve under anyone but Harley, who was an MP in the House of Commons, or to garrison any town outside the county.

The king's supporters in Monmouthshire were at least united in their agreement that help was needed if they were not to be overrun. A few days after the failed attack on Wonastow House, they wrote to Prince Rupert, reminding him that infantry and ammunition were urgent necessities if the enemy was to be driven off.

Prince Rupert was already deep in plans to reoccupy Beachley. If a deep channel could be dug across the peninsula, effectively joining up the rivers Wye and Severn, the tip of the peninsula could be made into an unassailable stronghold, guarded by gunships. A garrison placed there could easily disrupt communication between the Parliamentary-held towns of Gloucester and Monmouth.

Sir John Wintour was sent by Rupert from Bristol with 500 men to oversee the work. Unfortunately, the same lack of communication that bedevilled relationships in Gloucester also resulted in a lack of cooperation between Gerard and Wintour. Although the fortification of Beachley was well in hand, it had not progressed as far as it might have done had they pooled their resources. Colonel Massey arrived on the evening of 13 October with about 100 musketeers and eight troops of horse. Just as in the earlier attack, warships lay at anchor offshore, their guns trained on the land and onshore, 'hammer-guns and murtherers' had been placed at either end of the earthworks.

Once again, Massey waited until dawn, when at low tide the guns of the warships were ineffective. His musketeers broke through the palisade easily enough, but then became trapped between a hedge and the palisade. Volleys of musket fire were poured upon them from the fence, but Massey forced his horse over the hedge and his helmet was knocked off by a blow from a gun butt.[47] He fell from his mount and could have been clubbed to death, but his soldiers leapt to his rescue and Edward Harley gave him a fresh horse. Captain Kyrle appeared with reinforcements and the Royalist lines collapsed. Thirty men had been killed and 220 taken prisoner, but Sir John Wintour managed to scramble down a cliff and escape by boat. Prince Rupert was a witness to all this. He was a passenger on one of the ships offshore and had planned to land at Beachley as soon as the tide allowed.

However jubilant Massey and his friends may have felt about their victory at Beachley, they were well aware that the defences of Monmouth required great improvement. On 15 November, Edward Harley wrote to Massey, advising him that more guns and ammunition, plus experienced gunners, were vitally needed. It was sage advice, but too late.

Massey had already been ordered by the authorities in London to prevent Colonel Gerard from linking up with the king, who had been at Worcester and was now heading for Oxford. Massey was soon on the road towards Evesham, hoping to intercept his line of march. He had left Monmouth in the charge of Major Throgmorton who, without Massey's knowledge, decided on 17 November to attack Chepstow Castle. His departure with a significant number of the garrison was reported to Lord Herbert by some of the townsfolk who happened to be his tenants. Herbert immediately sent for assistance from his brother, Lord Charles Somerset and from Sir Trevor Williams and Colonel Progers, the governor of Abergavenny. By dawn on 19 November, a mixed force of horse and infantry had assembled close to the town. Lord Charles Somerset and forty horse clambered up a bank and reached the Dixton Gate, driving away the guards. The chain across the gate was easily broken and the mounted troops galloped through the streets of the town to surprise the garrison, most of them still in bed. A large haul of 200 prisoners was made, including several members of the Committee for South Wales. The hammer-guns captured at Beachley were recovered and various other weapons and ammunition.

In the weeks that followed, Royalist garrisons across Monmouthshire were strengthened, some 1,800 men being stationed at Monmouth alone.

A tax of £1,600 was to be raised, half of it in provisions. Promises were made of no further exactions and the abolition of free quarter, but not always kept. In common with other areas of Wales, the money did not flow in as easily as expected.

Laugharne Moves North

At some point in October, the Parliamentary warship *Leopard* arrived in Milford Haven carrying £991 worth of arms and ammunition. Following the departure of Colonel Gerard, and strengthened by the addition of Colonel Beale's regiment and a detachment of seamen and a demi-culverin from the *Leopard*, Rowland Laugharne now felt confident enough to march out of Pembroke.

By Monday, 28 October, this army of 2,000 men was encamped about a mile outside the town of Laugharne, from which Rowland's ancestors had come during the Middle Ages. At dawn the next morning, he moved forward to the vicinity of Glan-y-Mor, where an ancient earthwork looked down upon the castle. A bombardment of the defences opened up, but to such little effect that on the following day Laugharne ordered yet another move, this time to Fern Hill to the west of the castle. From this vantage point, the guns could fire directly at the façade of the castle's outer gatehouse.

As darkness fell, Laugharne ordered forward a detachment of musketeers to storm the town gate, which was easily taken. Several of the Parliamentary guns were dragged forward and began a close bombardment of the castle. The firing lasted for two days, during which the gatehouse was reduced to rubble. At 11.00pm on the night of Saturday, 2 November, 200 men surged forward and after a brief exchange of fire captured what was left of the gatehouse.

The besiegers now faced the formidable task of storming the inner gatehouse. Its thick walls, several stories high, meant that a direct assault would result in a large number of casualties. Laugharne and his commanders must have been carefully considering their options when, at about 3.00am on the morning of Sunday, 3 November, voices were heard calling out of the windows of the castle, requesting a parley. By seven in the morning the castle had been surrendered. The garrison were allowed to march away to Carmarthen, leaving behind thirty-three dead. Laugharne had lost about ten men, with thirty wounded.

It was Colonel Beale's intention now to join up with Sir Thomas Myddelton who, feeling confident enough to leave Montgomeryshire in the capable hands of Sir John Price, was marching southwards to mop up any Royalist resistance in Cardiganshire and Radnorshire. The two forces eventually met at Llanbedr in Cardiganshire and on 27 November at Machynlleth they came across a Royalist troop led by Major Hookes. A firefight erupted, with Hookes' men falling back over the Dovey Bridge. On the far bank, they made a determined stand, only scattering when the last of their ammunition ran out. The Royalist broadsheets insisted that in the hours after the action, the people of Machynlleth had been plundered of cattle, sheep and household goods 'without mercy'. A day or two later, a detachment of Myddelton's men led by Captain Robert Farrar fell upon the ancient house of Mathafarn, the home of Rowland Pugh, the leading Commissioner of Array for Merioneth, killing two men and burning the mansion to the ground.[48]

Laugharne meanwhile was busy at Cardigan. A Royalist base on the borders of Pembrokeshire, it threatened the security of Pembroke itself. Shortly before Christmas, Laugharne sent a summons for its surrender, a demand with which the burgesses quickly complied. Major Slaughter, in charge of the garrison, was not so accommodating. As the Parliamentary press reported, he told Laugharne that 'he held that castle for the service of the King, and so long as he had life he would keep it for his Majesty (though thereon he was not a man of his word).'

Slaughter had managed to obtain guns from the frigate *Converse,* which had been wrecked shortly before on the nearby coast. These powerful weapons gave him an advantage over Laugharne's smaller pieces and he was able to hold off the attackers for several days. It was not until a large brass cannon had been hauled ashore from the *Leopard* that Laugharne was able to open up an accurate three-day bombardment that brought down a section of the castle walls. A storming party was ordered forward, but it was only as they struggled over the shattered masonry that they discovered beyond the breach a hastily erected crescent-shaped earthwork, bristling with guns loaded with case shot. One barrage would have torn apart Laugharne's men but, as Captain William Smith described in a letter written from the *Swallow* a few weeks later, 'the enemy, as men bereft of all sense, having not the power to give fire to their guns, although the linstocks were in their hands, ready lighted, cast down their arms and cried for quarter, the which was granted.'[49]

The prisoners taken at Cardigan included Major Slaughter and his wife, Captain Vaughan, a lieutenant and ensign, Doctor Taylor, one of the most eminent clergymen of the time, 100 common soldiers, six great guns, 150 arms and an impressive quantity of powder, bullets and provisions.

Having installed Rice Powell, his second in command as governor of Cardigan, Laugharne then set off from Cardigan to round up any last elements of Gerard's army that might be lurking in odd corners of Pembrokeshire. Most, but not all of these, were driven off early in January in an action at an unknown location somewhere on the borders of Pembrokeshire and Carmarthenshire. A significant number remained, however, and these would emerge early in the new year to trouble Laugharne again.

As 1644 faded into the past, on both sides of the conflict, there was a contemplation of what had been achieved and lost. Parliament had been successful in the campaigns in the north, the Midlands and in North Wales, whilst in South Wales the situation was more fluid. In southern England, the advantage lay a little more positively with the king's forces. Both sides were experiencing a war weariness, with growing resistance to military taxation, the constant demand for men and provisions and a revulsion against the cost in lives.

In Parliament, there was debate over the military performance of its armies and commanders, originating in the disappointing result of the second Battle of Newbury. This had been fought on 27 October 1644, when an army of 19,000 under the twin command of the Earl of Manchester and Sir William Waller, had faced a much smaller Royalist force of 9,000 which the king had led from the West Country. During the march, Charles had depleted his strength by leaving pockets of troops to garrison various strongholds and by sending 800 of his horse to relieve the besieged Banbury Castle.

It might have seemed to the Parliamentary commanders that a victory would be easily gained, but disagreements amongst the officers and the dilatory behaviour of Manchester, who failed to advance on time, ruined the strategic plan that had been drawn up. The fighting continued even after nightfall, but the darkness allowed the Royal army to slip away unobserved.

The debates in Parliament over the result of Newbury were indeed bitter and ended in the realisation that the only way to victory was to create a single, unified army with one coverall commander. The result was the formation of the New Model Army.

A second, equally decisive measure was the Self-Denying Ordinance, by which members of both Houses could no longer hold military commands. After the Ordinance's approval by the House of Lords on 3 April 1645, men like Sir Thomas Myddelton would have to decide where their preferences lay, to serve in the army or in Parliament as an MP. Myddelton gave up his military role in order to remain as member for Denbigh.

There was some hope for peace. In November 1643, Parliament had approved proposals for negotiations with the king. The Earl of Denbigh, Basil Feilding, was sent to Oxford with eight other commissioners with peace plans. Initially, Charles was dismissive in his attitude towards them, but later agreed that twenty-three representatives from Parliament should meet at Uxbridge in January 1645, with seventeen nominated by the king to discuss the terms of a treaty.

There was, on both sides, considerable disapproval of any kind of treaty, so it is not surprising that talks were abandoned early in the new year.

Chapter 5

1645

North Wales, January to June

Royalist hopes of maintaining and improving their position in North Wales now rested on the preservation of Chester. Since the previous autumn the city had been blockaded by units of the Parliamentary army, though the approaches from the west leading out of Wales were still open. It would prove difficult for William Brereton and his command to close off the western roads in the event of a siege because of the river and surrounding marshlands.[1] The city was also well garrisoned, with up to 3,000 foot soldiers and about 1,000 mounted troopers. During the course of the war, there had been regular improvements to the defences, the most recent having taken place the previous summer, when the surrounding earthworks had been repaired.

There were also two outlying royalist garrisons to take into account. Beeston Castle, towering up from a rocky crag a few miles to the south-east, and Hawarden, five miles to the west, were both strongly fortified and well-garrisoned. Beeston had been under siege for weeks before Christmas, but had defied all efforts to take it.

Within Chester, Lord Byron knew that the Parliamentary blockade and the frequent raids could at any time become a full-scale siege. At the beginning of the year, William Brereton had established his advance headquarters at Christleton, a small village almost within sight of Chester's outer defences. He had already set up outposts at Aldford, Trafford and Upton Hill, all within a three-mile radius of the city. These were challenges that could not be ignored, so in January, a series of retaliatory raids were launched, which disrupted the smooth operation of Brereton's plans.

The situation at Beeston Castle was becoming ominous, with dwindling stocks of provisions and ammunition. Byron knew that a relief was imperative, so on 18 January he emerged from Chester and attacked Christleton, hoping to destroy the earthworks protecting it and then go on to aid Beeston.

Preparations took so long, perhaps because of disagreements between Byron and William Legge, the governor of Chester, that Brereton became aware of what was planned. Byron played into his hands, because his advance from the city moved at a snail's pace and was so widely spaced that the musketeers at the front came under fire from Brereton's guns whilst the rearguard were still straggling out of Chester's gates. The vanguard attempted to establish a position in the hedges along their line of march until the rest of the column caught up, but were terrified into throwing away their weapons when charged by the Parliamentary cavalry. Some forty of them fell into the River Dee and were drowned, whilst others were rounded up and herded into captivity at Christleton.

Frantic attempts were made in Chester to gather together reinforcements, but before that could be done, Brereton had ordered a withdrawal to Christleton. It was a discouraging start to any defence of Chester, especially when it was rumoured that Prince Rupert's own regiment had been the first to flee, running off before even firing a shot and casting away their drums. Included in the 200 prisoners taken were two colonels, two lieutenant-colonels and, amongst the ordinary soldiers, a collection of cobblers, shoemakers, tailors and barbers, all Chester townsmen impressed into the Royalist army.[2]

Concern about the fate of Chester persuaded the king to appoint Prince Maurice to the command of North Wales, giving him full powers to grant honours, make awards and levy more troops as necessary. He was also to attempt the relief of Beeston and Chester. Sir William Brereton, alert to the dangers, decided to pre-empt the prince's arrival in the Marches by launching a night-time attack on Chester's outworks. As he approached the city in the dark hours of 26 January, the earth ramparts dimly visible against the starlit sky, he became aware of pinpoints of light fringing the top of the barricades and realised that he was looking at the lit match on the muskets of the garrison's musketeers. Somehow the enemy had learned of his plan and easily repulsed his storming party. Three days later, Brereton sent a force of horse and foot to capture and hold Holt Bridge, a move that would cut off any approach by the Royalist garrison of Holt Castle and from Wrexham. He also sent out squads of troops to march through Flintshire and Denbighshire to scatter any royalist forces gathered there which might join up with Maurice's army.

These were just a few of the many raids ordered by Brereton at this time, one of which succeeded in bringing back a good haul of cattle taken from enemy quarters which, Brereton noted with satisfaction, would now feed his own men. He may even have been hoping to starve out the garrison of Chester, because as early as March 1644, he had written to William Ashurst, MP for Newton in Lancashire, with the news that 'Wales is in so impoverished a condition as that there is no subsistence neither for the enemy nor us. Many of their men are there dead by eating unwholesome food and are in so much want as that they have craved and had supplies from Chester. This may conduce much to the recovery of Chester, which will be in a more distressed condition than ever, in case any assistance come unto us and no more force to them. Upon whom though we could do no great execution, yet the judgement of God hath fallen, for many are dead, others run away and those that remain distressed for want of provision.'[3]

Lord Byron, desperate for help, wrote an urgent letter to Sir John Owen, recently appointed to the governorship of Conwy Castle, asking him to secure Welsh troops to march to the relief of the city. He pleaded that he had written many such letters and had received in return empty promises. Sir John, deeply involved in quarrels with Archbishop Williams, who resented his presence in Conwy, did what he could. He ordered the Caernarfonshire Trained Bands to meet at Conwy where they were reinforced by trained bands from Denbighshire and Flintshire. Although they could not relieve Chester, they were able to march into Wrexham, where they formed a potent threat to any Parliamentary presence in the area.

Meanwhile, on 5 February, Prince Maurice arrived in Shrewsbury, as William Maurice recorded in his notebook: 'Prince Maurice came to Shrewsbury, and having stayed there nine days in ordering his forces, advanced towards Chester.' The Mayor's Account Book for 5 February shows that upon his entry into the town the prince was offered wine, sugar loaves and cakes to the value of £1 13s 4d.[4] Hopefully refreshed by these dainties, he set off again nine days later, passing through Ruthin and arriving in Chester on 19 February. His presence and the sight of the 2,000 men he brought with him, no doubt lifted the spirits of the people of Chester, but there was still no hope of relieving Beeston.

Many of the soldiers who accompanied Maurice had been drawn from the garrison of Shrewsbury, leaving the city fatally weakened.

Parliamentary sympathisers within Shrewsbury felt confident enough to open up communications with Sir William Brereton, who sent out a combined force led by Colonel Mytton and Colonel Reinking to seize the city.

Approaching Shrewsbury at about 3.00am on the morning of 22 February, they sent a team of carpenters across the River Severn to saw down the wooden palisades that lined the banks. With these disposed of, Colonel Reinking led his foot soldiers into the town and opened the gates to Colonel Mytton's horsemen. Shrewsbury fell quietly, with very few casualties, its citizens surprised in their beds. Sir Michael Ernley, the governor, was taken, as were the Commissioners of Array. A few escaped capture by fleeing into the castle, but that was surrendered on the following day. There was no plundering of the town because of the presence of so many Parliamentary sympathisers, and the garrison was allowed to march away with their personal arms.

This notable victory was soured by a quarrel that exploded between Mytton and Reinking. Both were eager to be awarded the credit for having taken the town and both saw themselves as possible governors. Reinking considered that a printed account of the action paid too much attention to Mytton's role, so he published his own 'more exact relation of the taking of Shrewsbury'. In retaliation, Mytton then went into print with 'Colonel Mytton's reply to Reinking's relation of the taking of Shrewsbury.' Parliament's opinion of this spat between two of its most prominent officers was made apparent when it was decided that neither man should be installed as governor. Authority over the city was instead vested in a committee.

Prince Maurice was still resident in Chester. On 4 March he imposed an oath of loyalty on all inhabitants of the city, who were to swear that they would do all in their power to defend the king's cause against rebels and those who had taken up arms without the king's consent. His doubts about the garrison's ability to defend itself is reflected in his decision to reduce the perimeter of the outworks. He allowed his men to roam beyond the walls at will and in the weeks that followed, tensions were ratcheted up in the city and its surrounding areas by a series of raids carried out by both sides. There is no doubt that homes were burned, property looted and resistance was punished by the unhesitating use of the sword.

Brereton, worried by the presence of so large a force, had retreated back to Middlewich and Nantwich, from where a report on the actions of the Royalist force was published in a broadsheet:

> 'Since the King's great army lay in these parts the country hath suffered much, and they have been as barbarous in their retreat; for they have not only plundered about Flintshire, Denbighshire and the borders of Shropshire and Cheshire but have committed so many murders and rapines…that the like has not been heard of. The Irish and Papists have been at Broughton…and burnt down all the houses in that town. From thence they went to Christleton and burnt down all that town, the minister's house and the church also.'[5]

Brereton was eager for a confrontation but realised that Maurice was unwilling to do anything until he had been joined by his brother, who was marching up from the south-east. On 17 March Maurice and Rupert were reunited at Ellesmere and, with a combined force of 7,000 moved back into Cheshire. At last Beeston was relieved.[6]

Prince Rupert also made a brief foray into Wales, perhaps hoping to bolster the flagging spirits of the king's supporters. At Holt, he ordered the hanging of twenty-four Welshmen, though for what reason is unclear. His main concern, however, was to obtain more reinforcements for the new campaign in England, which he knew would begin in the spring. He demanded another 1,000 men from an already exhausted North Wales and took 1,200 soldiers from the garrison at Chester. With his numbers much reduced, Lord Byron must again have had doubts about the future and the arrival of only 100 soldiers from Ireland cannot have done much to raise his spirits.

As Byron probably expected, Brereton wasted no time investing Chester once again. He established new garrisons to the south of the city, at Lache, Eccleston and Dodleston and on 3 April attempted to intercept the approach of a convoy of munitions destined for Byron's garrison. He was too late, for the convoy was forewarned and fled to the safety of Hawarden Castle, 'whither the country people drove in many carriages, and the malignants fled thither with their wives and children… .'[7] Brereton immediately ordered his engineers to begin mining beneath the walls of the castle, hoping to force a surrender of the garrison and to seize the munitions.

Leaving the engineers to continue their work, Brereton moved on to the ancestral home of the Davies family at Gwysaney, which he stormed, taking prisoner all within the building. Manly House, within sight of the walls of Chester, fell next, many of the defenders being killed. As Brereton approached the outer suburb of Handbridge, he would have seen columns of smoke billowing up from the huddled buildings, Byron having ordered its destruction for the second time, 'to prevent the enemy from nesting there, as were all the Glovers' houses under the walls by Dee Side and the houses without the Watergate.'[8]

Brereton soon discovered that the blockade of Chester was no easy business. Despite shutting off all the roads leading into the city, supplies were still being shipped in along the River Dee. His own men were also causing problems. There were desertions, with some soldiers anxious to return to their own homes because they had heard that their allies, troops from Yorkshire, were looting the towns and villages of Cheshire. There was also an epidemic of theft carried out by Brereton's own men, with stolen cattle being sold for profit.[9]

To add to his problems, Brereton was certain that Prince Rupert would soon make a re-appearance. The Commissioners of Array for the North Wales counties had been ordered to prepare troops to be ready at an hour's notice to join the prince's advance. On 24 April, Sir John Owen of Clenennau was similarly instructed to march with 1,000 men to Hereford.

Sir John Owen and the Archbishop

Brereton might have given a sigh of relief had he known that, at Conwy, Sir John was embroiled in a quarrel with Archbishop Williams. In an irate letter to Lord Digby, principal Secretary of State to King Charles, the Archbishop let fly:

> 'Sir John Owen is likewise governor of this place and intimateth a desire to have the Government of this castle...which his Majestie...had upon high and deare considerations passed over to me...and which from bare walles I have repayred, victuayled, and ammunicioned at myne own charges; and for which I am more likelye to give his Majestye a good accompt then this gentleman is,

who, without my costs and charges, was never able to have repayred the towne…nor hath any armes but what I lend him to defend it…. Valour will not doe the business; he must have prudence and experience with all that will governe a country, envireoned with enemies, and destitute of all money. And this man professeth openlye he will consult noe man, nor joyne with any his felowes and betters, the Commissioners of Arraye…as the two Princes have hitherto done.'[10]

There were equally vicious squabbles within the walls of Chester. Lord Byron was at odds not only with Colonel Richard Mostyn, commanding one of the regiments defending the city, but with William Legge. Well-regarded by Prince Rupert, Legge had been appointed by the prince to the governorship of Chester in May 1644 and from the first his presence grated upon Lord Byron. Legge was responsible for the maintenance of the garrison and inhabitants of the city, whilst Byron had military authority over the surrounding areas and North Wales. Inevitably there were times when both men found themselves in competition over limited resources, provisions and munitions. Byron was infuriated by Legge's habit of granting commissions without consultation and feared being blamed for any blunders that were committed. On a number of occasions, he fired off letters of complaint about Legge to Prince Rupert, with whom he also enjoyed a testy relationship, a practice that only deepened the rift between them.

The cause of the dispute between Byron and Colonel Mostyn is harder to discern, but there is no doubt that the two men did not get on. Perhaps Byron's natural aristocratic hauteur made him resent the energetic, assertive scion of a North Walian gentry family, who in turn chafed under his lordship's condescending attitude. It's also likely that the three men, Byron, Legge and Mostyn, had very differing ideas about the best way to prepare a meaningful defence of Chester.

On 26 April, Byron wrote a despairing letter to Lord Digby, informing him of 'the strong necessity there is of a speedy and powerful relief…. The two Princes, having united their forces and releaved Beeston Castle, were earnestly entreated by mee to cleare this country before they departed of those petty garrisons that infested Chester, but other considerations at that tyme hindred the effecting of it, and therefore with a promise that the army should continew in a distance till Chester were furnished both with victuall and ammunition, I was contented to returne and undertake the Government of that garrison, but the buysynesse of Hereford intervening, Prince Rupert was suddenly called away before either ammunition or victual could be brought into Chester, and together with his Highness marched away the remainder of the old Irish regiments, with some other horse and foot, to the number of at least 1,200, soe that I was left in the towne only with a garrison of citizens, and my own and Colonell Mostin's regiment, which both together made not up above 600 men, whereof the one half beinge Mostin's men, I was forced soone after to send out of towne, finding them by reason of their officers, who weare ignorant Welch gentlemen, and unwilling to undergoe any strickt duty, far more prejudiciall to use than useful.... . The Welch, though they have men for number, and armies sufficient to beat the rebels out of Wales, yet either will not or dare not stir, notwithstanding the many orders I have sent them. The truth is that soe long as that cursed Commission of Array...have any power there, the Kinge must expect noe good out of North Wales, and I am confident were it not for the castles which are well provided both with men, victual, and ammunition that country had long since taken part with Brereton and Midleton.' Byron went on to say that he had only about eighteen barrels of gunpowder left, few provisions and no money with which to buy more.[11]

These two letters reached Lord Digby at a time when discussions were taking place at Oxford over plans for the coming summer campaign. It was clear to the king and his commanders that if Chester fell to Parliament, the whole of the Midlands and the north of England would be under threat. The decision was taken to send the bulk of the king's army from Oxford to relieve Chester.

Back in the beleaguered city, the situation was growing ever more serious. Two of Lord Byron's brothers – there were seven, all serving the king – were captured on 15 April and the following day, Denbigh was attacked by Parliamentary forces, causing so much damage that, on the following week, the market had to be held at the other end of the town. On 23 April, Colonel Michael Jones, one of Parliament's most daring soldiers and a keen critic of Brereton's conduct of the war, led a raid into the heart of Denbighshire. It was an event that was never forgotten, as Jones' men pillaged without restraint. The mansion of Plas Ucha was put to the flames as was the house of Lady Hanmer, the entire garrison except two being slaughtered.

The target of another raid, this time led by Captain Coltham, was Rhual, the home of Evan Edwards, one of the Commissioners of Array for Flintshire, whose younger brother was a close friend of Sir William Brereton. During the raid, Lady Edwards was 'stripped out of her cloathes' and a box of jewels belonging to her was stolen. They were valued by Edwards at £7,000, though during a later investigation Colonel Jones said they were only worth £500.[12]

It's interesting to wonder if the investigation into the stolen jewels was as a result of Brereton's friendship with the Edwards family, but Sir William was not above a spot of looting himself. Over three days towards the end of April, he and Sir Thomas Myddelton, with their troops, thoroughly pillaged the parish of St Asaph, despoiling all the churches.

Not long afterwards, Sir Thomas Myddelton was forced to give up his military command because of the Self-Denying Ordinance, and returned to his role as MP at Westminster. His place as Major-General of Parliament's army in North Wales was taken by Colonel Thomas Mytton, who was married to the sister of Myddelton's second wife.

At Conwy, the private civil war between Sir John Owen and Archbishop Williams continued as hot as ever. At the centre of the conflict stood Conwy Castle, which Archbishop Williams had repaired and fortified and over which Sir John wanted control. Things came to a head on the evening of 9 May 1645, when Sir John entered the castle with a band of armed men and broke down the locks and doors, seizing all the powder, arms and victuals. The archbishop demanded that the 'rabble of grooms and beggarly people' should be prevented from stealing the store of goods, only to be told by Sir John that he would appropriate all Williams' plate and valuables for his own use. To add to the insult, the archbishop was expelled from the castle and had to seek refuge in his own house at Penrhyn.[13]

In a letter to the king, Sir John accused Williams of treachery, a charge that the monarch could not take seriously. He warned Owen to be careful with his words and to pay the archbishop the respect that his status deserved.

Meanwhile, the siege of Hawarden Castle continued. The engineers were mining close to the great Round Tower and five large guns had appeared in the Parliamentary lines, including a mortar. The governor of Hawarden, Sir William Neale, had been absent when the siege commenced, leaving his wife, Lady Helen, to conduct the defence. On 19 May, she wrote to her husband to tell him that they were in desperate straits, but that she would hold out 'as longe as there is meate for man for none of these eminent dangers shall ever frighten mee from my loyalty but in life and death I will be ye King's faithful subject and thy constant loving wife and humble servant.' [14]

A few days later, there was heartening news for Lady Neale. Her soldiers had dug a countermine and had broken into the enemy tunnel and blocked it. Within days, the besiegers were dismantling their camp and withdrawing, because news had been received that the king's army was fast approaching from Oxford and had reached Newport in Shropshire.

It was obvious that the siege of Chester must be abandoned. Brereton's troops retired in good order to Nantwich, withdrawing over a bridge of boats at Eccleston and wading through the shallows of the Dee at Shotwick. The Royalists were unable to harass them because they lacked the gunpowder, though Major Marcus Trevor managed to capture a group of naked Parliamentarians who were bathing in a tributary of the Dee. [15]

South Wales, January to June

On 4 January 1645, Cardigan suddenly found itself once more under siege. Many reports placed Colonel Gerard at the head of the besieging force, but he is known to have been at Worcester at this time. It is much more likely that Cardigan was attacked by those units of his regiment that still lingered in West Wales.

The attack was so unexpected that the enemy quickly gained possession of the town, but were unable to force an entry into the castle. As they had approached Cardigan along the banks of the River Teifi, they had intercepted boats taking provisions to the castle. It may have been from the crews of these boats that they learned the garrison was short of supplies. They therefore demanded the immediate surrender of the castle. Colonel Powell, who had been left in charge by Laugharne, refused point blank, but did manage to smuggle out a message calling for help.

The Royalists had partially broken down the bridge that spanned the river. Cannon were sited on the banks opposite the castle and began a steady barrage of fire against the ancient stonework. As the masonry tumbled down, raids were launched upon the weakest points, but losses were heavy. It was reported that over 150 men were killed in these attacks.

Laugharne was hastily gathering together an army of 300 foot soldiers, 600 horse, together with 120 seamen from Admiral Swanley's ships still at Milford Haven. As they drew near Cardigan, they came across a tired and probably very cold soldier from Powell's garrison, who had swum across the river during the night. He carried a second message from Powell, stating that the castle could not hold out for more than eight days, as they had very few provisions left. Powell, however, was certain that provisions and ammunition could be taken into the castle, 'if some seamen versed in managing a water fight and climbing up rocks were employed. So 120 seamen were sent, who, after a view had of the place, undertook it, which was performed in this wise... .'[16] A boat was found, to which were lashed eight other boats, four to each side. Musketeers were placed in two of these and the rest were loaded with supplies. Under heavy fire from the river banks, the precious cargo was rowed across the Teifi and brought ashore under the walls of the castle.

The besieging force, however, remained in place and it was clear that an effort must be made to dislodge it. On 22 January, an arrow was fired over the river into the castle by one of Laugharne's men. To it was attached a note warning Powell that an attempt would be made by Laugharne to gain a foothold on the north bank of the river, near the castle. As that sortie took place, Powell's men were to emerge from the castle in support.

There was no attempt to cross the river in boats. Instead, the ruined bridge was swiftly repaired with lengths of planking and the soldiers raced across it, the castle garrison issuing from the gate at the same time. The Royalists were driven out of their first and second barricades and then from the market place, falling back upon the church before fleeing the town and retreating towards Newcastle Emlyn, occupied by another royalist garrison.

There is no certainty of Colonel Gerard's whereabouts during this time. As already noted, he was not at Cardigan, though he is said to have been seen at Carmarthen on 21 February, where he took part in a recruiting drive. It is possible that he marched some of his troops into mid-Wales on the orders of the king, perhaps to counter any moves by Sir Thomas Myddelton, who was rumoured to be moving in that direction from North Wales. There was certainly a successful clash of arms between Gerard's forces and those of Sir John Price at Llanidloes. For a few weeks Gerard occupied parts of Montgomeryshire, where his ruthless exactions of money and supplies earned him the undying hatred of the population.

The gruesome story of the fate of one family who opposed him illustrates his brutal methods. When they refused to provide the supplies he demanded, he set fire to their home with the family still inside it. The father and two of the sons were killed jumping from an upstairs window and the others perished in the inferno.[17]

It is worth noting at this point that Sir John Price, who had abandoned his Royalist principles after the battle of Montgomery, turned his coat yet again after his defeat at Llanidloes and surrendered Montgomery Castle to the king's forces, though he kept the governorship of it.

Defeat at Newcastle Emlyn

Laugharne's victories in West Wales had earned him the gratitude of Parliament. Extra troops had been sent to Pembrokeshire in 1644, and he was appointed Commander-in-Chief of the Association of Pembroke, Cardigan and Carmarthen. On 15 January 1645, he was publicly thanked by the House of Commons for all his efforts and 1,100 more dragoons were sent to him, along with the necessary ammunition.

The arrival of these extra troops decided Laugharne to attempt the taking of Newcastle Emlyn. On 12 April, he set up camp before its gates and commenced a siege. He was unaware that his old nemesis, Charles Gerard, was closing in fast on his position. A parliamentary broadsheet reported that Gerard had been ordered back to Wales to deal specifically with Laugharne and there were tales that he had made a forced march of 100 miles from England in just a week.

Whatever the truth, on Sunday, 27 April, without warning, his men launched an attack on the camp of the leaguer outside the walls of Emlyn Castle. In the words of a contemporary pamphlet, Gerard 'suddenly and secretly fell upon our men, slew and took most of our foot companies, beside many horse... .'[18]

There was a complete rout of the besieging army. Anything between 150 and 400 men were killed, up to 490 taken prisoner and 700 weapons captured. Laugharne and the survivors fell back in disarray, finding refuge in Tenby and Pembroke. When news of the defeat reached Haverfordwest, its parliamentary garrison evacuated in such haste that they left behind stocks of provisions, ammunition and ordnance. The defenders of Cardigan Castle set fire to the buildings within the fortifications, boarded an armada of small boats and set sail for Pembroke.

With much of the county now open before him, Gerard quickly took Picton Castle and set up a garrison at Carew. He erected a battery above the river at Pembroke to prevent supplies and reinforcements reaching the castle and a group of Bristol merchants were invited to guard Milford Haven in the king's name. Supplies of food and other provisions were seized from the local population with no thought for their welfare. A report to the Committee of Both Kingdoms stated that the enemy did not hesitate to 'imprison, plunder and abuse the well-affected townsmen, range everywhere about the country, pillage and destroy that which should be the present and future livelihood of our army, and have given...a sure testimony that they will leave nothing undone that mischief and violence can invent against a distressed county.'[19]

John Poyer, who had done so much to prepare Pembroke for the war and who had worked consistently to support Laugharne, wrote to the Commons describing the sufferings inflicted on the people of Pembrokeshire. 'Colonel Gerard at the time he beleaguered the...town of Pembroke, caused divers of the dwelling houses, barns and reeks of corn to be fired...and their cattle and household goods did plunder for their utter undoing.'[20]

There is no record of an actual attack on the walls of Pembroke during this period. It's probable that Gerard preferred to starve out the garrison, as he had previously intended in 1644. Pembroke's walls were stout and the ridge of limestone on which the town stood was surrounded by tidal inlets, so a direct frontal assault might have cost him dear. As at Chester, houses lying beyond the walls had been destroyed lest they give shelter to the enemy. Thomas Powell, a local worthy, had sacrificed two of his outlying houses to be demolished 'for the better serving of the town of Pembroke'. His herds of cattle and flocks of sheep were taken for the garrison's cooking pots.[21] Another townsman who lost everything was William Adams, who 'voluntarily gave way for firing of divers of his houses in the suburbs of Pembroke...and the enemy then fired his houses and corn and drove away all his cattle.'[22]

The plight of Pembroke was the subject of considerable discussion in both Houses of Parliament. On 26 May 1645, the committee of Plymouth received the following instruction. 'We cannot send those [at Milford] any supplies which could reach them in time, we therefore earnestly recommend it to you to send thither 500 men if with any safety to your own town you can possibly do it; till we [are able] to provide for more.'[23]

A month later, the Committee for the Navy received an urgent dispatch from the Committee of Both Kingdoms. 'The garrisons of Pembroke and Tenby being in great want of ammunition, the Commons have appointed that 100 barrels of gunpowder, with match and bullets proportionable, should be delivered for their use... .'[24]

Sir Thomas Fairfax, at that point involved in relieving Taunton from its Royalist besiegers, was also handed a letter from Parliament, which had 'received diverse informations of the distressed state of Pembrokeshire, the whole county being reduced under the power of the enemy. If those be lost, Milford Haven would thereby be in the enemy's power, available for landing there the Irish forces and for all foreign correspondent hitherto by reason of the distance of those parts from all our forces. We have been unable to give them the relief they have desired. When you relieve Taunton, send to Pembroke 200 or 300 men with provisions that they preserve those places and the harvest there, till more effectual supplies can be sent them.'[25]

The garrisons of Pembroke and Tenby, isolated and encircled, may not have known of the efforts being made to send help, but at some point, news must have filtered through which raised their spirits. On 14 June 1645, the Royal army suffered an overwhelming defeat by Cromwell's New Model Army at Naseby. For many Royalists in England and Wales, there was the sickening realisation that very little now stood between them and defeat.

On board the guardship *Lyon* in Milford Haven, Captain Moulton addressed a jubilant letter to the Lord Admiral Warwick at Plymouth. 'The enemy is withdrawn about ten miles from Pembroke, that Colonel Gerard and all the strangers with 500 foot are gone out of the country.'[26]

Forcible Recruitment in South Wales

During the early months of 1645, there was a concerted drive in the south-eastern counties of Wales to raise more money, men and supplies for the war. The chief constables and receivers of each of the hundreds of Monmouthshire were ordered to ensure that everything was done to prevent any malicious acts by the enemy. Details were given of the exact amounts to be raised from each area and the time scale for collecting them. Some of the contributions were in cash, the rest in butter, bread, cheese and other foodstuffs.

In December 1644, the constables of the parishes within the Skenfrith hundred had been ordered to collect in £166 13s 4d within eleven days. The assessment was to apply to 'every tenant, inhabitant, occupier of land and tithes, clergy as well as laity'. The money was to be handed to Walter Powell of Llantilio Crossenny, one of the chief constables appointed to receive the contributions. It was the first of several payments. Skenfrith was expected to pay a monthly amount of £256 13s 4d for a four-month period beginning in January 1645. Half of the collection was to be in cash, the rest in food and supplies. Little leeway was given for delay. Skenfrith was soon £65 18s 4d in arrears and when Powell was late in handing over the payments, he received a letter from William Lawes, treasurer at war, threatening him with accusations of negligence. Any further delay would result in the quartering of troops on the various parishes, a possibility that must have horrified the inhabitants. It was no idle promise. At the end of March 1645, thirty-three troopers arrived in Skenfrith and within ten days, the missing amounts had been found. Obstructions continued, however, and on 15 April, orders were given for the arrest of those constables who were proving dilatory in their duty.[27]

It's not surprising, therefore, that some officials came to resent the tasks they were expected to carry out. One such was Sir Thomas Dabridgecourt, a nominee of Prince Rupert and wrote to the prince in March to tell him so:

'May it please your Highness,

I am very sorry that I should be so unfortunate, these being the first commands you were pleased to honour me withal, as not to be able to perform them with that speed you expected; if your Highness shall be pleased to command me to the Turk, or Jew, or Gentile, I will go on my bare feet to serve you; but from the Welsh, good Lord deliver me. And I shall beseech you to send me no more into this country, if you intend I shall do you any service, without a strong party to compel them, not to entreat them... . The ammunition hath been here these seven days for want of carriages, and I fear I shall stay seven more unless I have some power to force the people. They value neither Sir John Winter, his warrants, nor mine, nor any. Some say they will not come; the rest come not and say nothing. All generally disaffected... .'[28]

It was the same story in other parts of Monmouthshire. Contributions were expected towards the costs of building or repairing fortifications, the purchase of gunpowder and weapons and the feeding and accommodation of soldiers. What was not willingly given by the local people was taken from them by force. Cattle were rustled, houses looted, sometimes their contents stolen outright by soldiers for their own profit. Men were also needed for the king's army. When Sir Marmaduke Langdale marched through the Forest of Dean in April 1645, he carried away a number of pressed men and 3,000 head of cattle, plus leather and wheat for the garrison at Monmouth.[29]

The situation was much the same in mid-Wales. The expected contributions were only gathered in with much difficulty and local garrisons resorted to pillage and theft whenever necessary. The strongholds at Stokesay Castle, Lea Hall and Abbey Cwm Hir were famous for their ruthlessness, whilst Sir John Price gained a reputation for burning what he could not take.

One aspect of the resistance to the Royalist exactions was the growth of the Clubmen groups. In areas of England and Wales where the demands fell the hardest, people began to band together to resist them. In December 1644 a force of about 1,200 men had gathered in the Shropshire hundreds of Purslow and Clun, determined to oppose the pillaging of soldiers from Stokesay and Lea Hall. Another group was said to have formed at Leintwardine, whilst in Herefordshire a huge army of 15,000 marched on Hereford itself. Barnabas Scudamore, the city's governor, had attempted to collect supplies and cash from surrounding communities and his high-handed efforts to suppress opposition led to violence. Faced with the possibility of an attack on Hereford, Scudamore agreed to the demands of the Clubmen. Believing themselves to be successful the majority dispersed, whilst about 2,000 withdrew to Ledbury, where they were scattered by the approach of Prince Rupert's army. Some were imprisoned, others hanged and, as a punishment for disloyalty, Herefordshire's contributions were doubled.[30]

In Monmouthshire and Glamorgan, the Clubmen also made their presence felt. The garrisoning of Cardiff by Royalist troops was delayed by the opposition of the townsfolk who, whilst they never called themselves Clubmen, had many of the same aims. In the coming months, this growing band of anti-war rebels was to become known as 'The Peaceable Army' and was prepared to face down the king himself.

Meanwhile the fortifying of the border towns of South Wales was continuing. At Chepstow, the bridge was broken down to prevent a surprise attack and at Monmouth and Abergavenny improvements to the defences were carried out. Vulnerable points along the main routes of communication were also strengthened, even if only by increasing the numbers of soldiers on picket duty. A Royalist attempt to fortify the crossing point of the River Wye at Lancaut, just north of Chepstow, was challenged by a Parliamentary force from Sudeley Castle and routed, with over eighty casualties.[31]

As in 1643, a battle fought far to the east was to have a significant impact on events in Wales. On 15 June 1645, as already noted, King Charles' army was shattered at Naseby, driven from the field by Cromwell's New Model Army. In the aftermath, the victorious troops fell upon the Royalist baggage train, where they found dozens of unarmed women, who screamed out in a language the English soldiers could not understand. Believing them to be Irish, they slaughtered over one hundred in cold blood, slitting the noses and cheeks of others to brand them as whores. In fact, these unfortunate women may have been Welsh, accompanying their husbands to cook and wash and clean for them.

There were undoubtedly Welsh soldiers fighting in the king's army at Naseby. At least two, Robert Owen of Caerhun and John Williams of Pethkelert, were wounded and many years later were appealing for recompense from the authorities in North Wales. The names of others, the regiments in which they served and their ultimate fates, are not recorded.

King Charles had attempted to reverse the tide of battle by leading a charge against the enemy, but was urged away by his followers. He left behind his personal correspondence, which made clear his plans to bring into England an army of native Irish and to accept loans and mercenary troops from foreign rulers. Their discovery and publication by Parliament only confirmed to many that he was a slippery and deceitful character. In the weeks after Naseby, Charles made his way into Wales, where he hoped to regroup his army and recruit more men to his banner.

South Wales, July to December

During his retreat from Naseby, the king wandered westwards, staying briefly at Hereford. Discussions took place over the likelihood of raising another army of 10,000 men, most of whom would come from South Wales, with Herefordshire finding 2,000 men and 400 from Radnorshire. Many of the pressed men, however, slipped away at the first opportunity. There was more encouraging news from the gentry of the area, who presented him with £5,000 for use in the war effort. King Charles next moved on to Abergavenny, where he arrived on 1 July. He stayed at the Priory, the house of James Gunter, where he issued a proclamation for Prince Rupert to raise more troops. An expected 5,000 foot soldiers were to be found in Herefordshire and South Wales, with Glamorganshire providing 1,000 and Monmouthshire 800. A certain amount of juggling was needed with regard to the already existing forces in the area. Lord Herbert's mounted troops, depleted through losses in battle and by units being sent to serve elsewhere, was merged with Colonel Lingen's regiment. Later in July, the king issued instructions for a further 1,000 men to be levied in Glamorganshire, with a tax of £1,250 a month from the whole county.[32]

On 3 July, the king travelled to Raglan. He was greeted at the gatehouse by the aged Earl, now Marquis, of Worcester who, because of his age, had to be helped to his knees in order to kiss the king's hand. Charles remained at Raglan for a fortnight and though Worcester did his best to entertain his sovereign with games of bowls and walks in the gardens beside the lake, it was not always an easy time. The king at one point suggested yet another levy on the surrounding countryside, this time to provide food to feed his vast entourage. The Marquis is said to have replied, 'My castle will not stand long if it leans upon the country. I had rather be brought to a morsel of bread than any morsel of bread should be brought me to entertain your Majesty'.[33]

A number of important decisions were made during Charles' stay at Raglan. He was to remain in Wales or in the Marches, in order to raise more troops and in the hope that fresh levies would arrive from Ireland. The possibility that the Scots might attack Wales was dismissed with the comment, 'We should be able to starve a great army and beat a little one.'

On 16 July, the king went to Cardiff to meet the Commissioners of Array and to raise more men. He was back in Raglan two days later, remaining for two further weeks. On 24 July, the king departed for Black Rock, where boats were waiting to carry him over the River Wye. Something occurred to make him change his mind, because he headed instead for Cardiff. Perhaps it was the knowledge that Bridgwater had fallen to Parliament and the news that Hereford was threatened with siege by a Scots army. There were also rumours, never certainly verified, that the king had escaped capture at Black Rock by a hair's breadth and had been forced to flee. Whatever the truth, fresh orders were sent out for yet more troops to be found and brought to the king.

On the day following the incident at Black Rock, King Charles met the Commissioners of Array at Usk, where he inspected the men raised in the latest levy. He spent the next few days at Ruperra Castle as a guest of Philip Morgan, before returning to Cardiff. Whilst he was at Ruperra, the king was involved in a series of highly secret negotiations with the Scots, who were at that point encamped in the Forest of Dean, prior to besieging Hereford. The hope was to separate the more radical Presbyterian elements of the Scots army from its moderate sections and to use the moderates to further his aims. Secret meetings, often held at night, took place at a number of locations between the king's spokesmen and representatives of the Scots army. Nothing definite came of them, but Charles seems to have believed in assurances of the Scots' loyalty.

By 29 July, he had returned to Cardiff, where a gathering of gentlemen awaited him at Cefn On, just outside the town. If he imagined these to be the requested levies, he was mistaken. A massed body of 4,000 men were gathered in battle array, entitling themselves The Peaceable Army. Their leaders presented the king with a list of complaints about James Tyrell, the governor of Cardiff, who they wanted replaced. They refused to march to the relief of Hereford until all commanders in the area had been replaced by local men, and demanded the remission of tax arrears and a tax rate related to the ability to pay rather than an arbitrary figure. In return, they promised to find 1,000 men for the royal army and £800 to arm them. Charles agreed to replace Tyrell with the more moderate local figure of Sir Richard Bassett. Furthermore, Colonel Gerard was replaced as commander of the county by Sir Jacob Astley. To soothe Gerard's wounded pride, he was made a baronet.

Sir Jacob Astley did not trust the Peaceable Army. He wrote to Prince Rupert on 11 August, complaining that 'the County of Glamorganshire

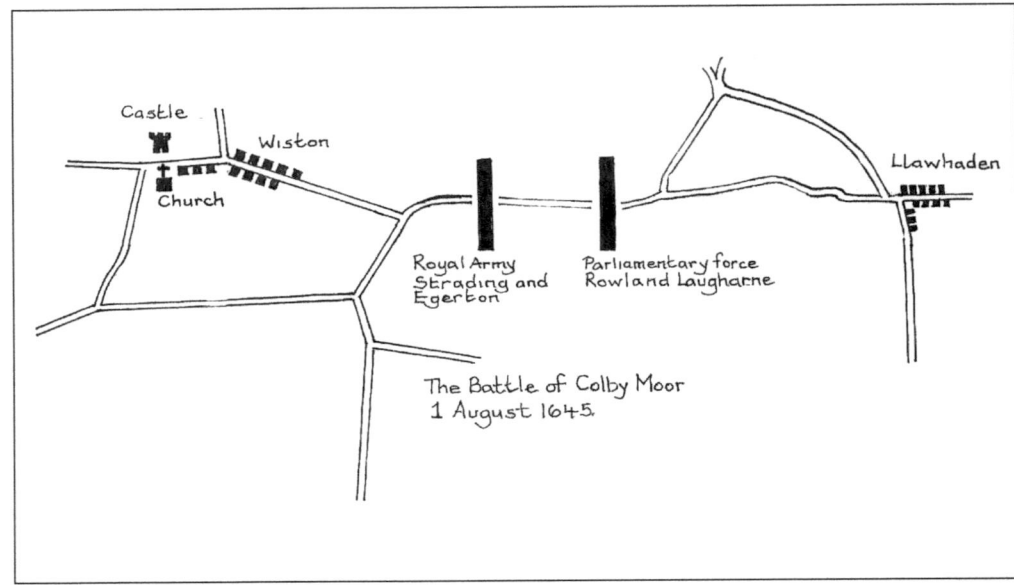

A map of the Battle of Colby Moor

is so unquiet as there is no good to be expected. Shall strive as far as I can to put things in order, which I despair of, because it is power to rule these people, and not entreaties with cap in hand to such as deserve the halter.'[34] To an extent, he was right, as The Peaceable Army was also in touch with Parliament. John Byrd, the Customs Controller for Cardiff, had received £404 worth of arms from Captain Robert Moulton, who had commanded the guardship *Lyon* at Milford Haven. Byrd smuggled them onto customs boats, eventually passing them on to a shadowy figure in Monmouthshire, possibly Sir Trevor Williams, who was in league with the Peaceable Army. These weapons, and the Army itself, were be used in the autumn to support a Parliamentary takeover in Glamorganshire.[35]

On 5 August, King Charles left Cardiff and reached Brecon by nightfall. He removed Herbert Price as governor before travelling on to Gwernyfed, the mansion of Sir Henry Williams, where he dined. Sir Henry escorted him to Glasbury, where he crossed the River Wye. Eventually, he passed into south-eastern Radnorshire and north-western Herefordshire before reaching Shropshire. There was a pause at Ludlow, before the journey resumed again.

In these wanderings King Charles was protected by a small force consisting of Gerard's horse, the King's Lifeguards and the regiments of Sir Marmaduke Langdale and Sir William Vaughan. It is likely that their route was decided by the whereabouts of the Scots army of Parliamentary allies besieging Hereford, and by its far-ranging its patrols, for they kept well to the north of the areas under Scottish control. Nevertheless, it was the king's intention to join up with the loyal Marquis of Montrose, who had recently defeated some Parliamentary opponents in Scotland. This plan came to nothing when it was learned that they were being pursued by elements of the Scots force around Hereford. There was no option but to head for Oxford, which was reached on 28 August.

A Battle in Pembrokeshire

The departure from Pembrokeshire of Colonel Gerard released the garrisons of Pembroke and Tenby from their isolation. In the weeks that followed, Rowland Laugharne was able to re-establish his authority in West Wales. The main stumbling block was the large Royalist garrison that Gerard had left in Haverfordwest. It became apparent that this force intended to move out in order to burn cornfields around Narberth, but it was also possible that it might move south to challenge Tenby or Pembroke.

Accordingly, on 29 July, Laugharne marched out of Pembroke at the head of a small army consisting of 550 infantry, 200 horse and dragoons and two small guns. At Canaston Bridge, where the road from Pembroke crossed the eastern arm of the River Daugleddau, they surprised a scouting party from Haverfordwest, killing one man and taking prisoner the remaining six. Near the same spot they also met up with about one hundred seamen from the Parliamentary frigate *Warwick*, which had recently entered Milford Haven. By 1 August, Laugharne's little force had crossed the river and occupied the village of Llawhaden before moving westwards towards Haverfordwest. In the late afternoon of that day, at Colby Moor, they came within sight of a Royalist army of 450 horse and 1,100 foot, backed by four large guns.

Colby Moor was then a stretch of open moorland, which had been used in the past for gatherings of the local militia, so it is likely that Laugharne knew the area well. There is no information as to how the two forces arranged their battle formations, but in a letter written afterwards to the Speaker of the Commons, Laugharne described how 'a small part of our horsemen, hoarded on both sides with 150 musketeers, charged their whole body.' The outcome of this bold action was for a time uncertain and the fighting was fierce, until the Royalist mounted troops began to buckle. A panic-stricken retreat resulted, with men casting away their weapons and deserting their cannon. Laugharne's cavalry chased them almost to the gates of Haverfordwest. Over 150 Royalists were killed to two Parliamentarians, 700 were taken prisoner, including more than thirty officers. Also seized were the four heavy guns, five barrels of powder, 800 arms and all the carriages and provisions.

That night, Laugharne and his men camped in the fields around Haverfordwest, whilst in the darkness, the Royalist horse left the town and headed for Carmarthen. The next day, Saturday, 2 August, Haverfordwest was occupied and the castle encircled. The following day was a Sunday, so it was not until Monday that a bombardment of the castle began. A full-scale assault was mounted later in the day, when the gatehouse was set alight and the walls were scaled. The ancient stronghold was taken with relative ease, its garrison of about 150 men quickly surrendering.

Over the next few weeks, Carew and Picton castles were given up and Newcastle Emlyn placed under siege, finally capitulating in December. Aberystwyth proved to be more stubborn, as we shall see, holding out into the early months of 1646.

Although there were no Royalist forces left in Pembrokeshire, Carmarthenshire still posed a threat. There were some 700 men at large, at least 400 of them bearing arms. Of these, 200 were mounted troops under Major-General Stradling, though the militia units carried only clubs and pitchforks.[36] The Commissioners and gentry of the county were well aware that this was not enough to resist a large-scale attack, so on 5 September 1645, they addressed a letter to Laugharne and the Committee of Pembrokeshire:

'Gentlemen, We, taking into consideration the unhappy effects that war...may produce between the County of Pembroke and the neighbouring Counties of Carmarthen and Cardigan...the unity whereof is requisite under many relations, to the preservation of which you and we equally pretend, namely, our religion, loyalty, and laws, though we have been hitherto so unhappy as to endeavour the preserving of these by destroying one another.

To prevent, therefor, the continuance of these miseries, we have formerly felt and the fears of worse that may ensue...and that we may move towards these ends, we severally profess to be the same, with better assurance of obtaining them, we conceive that...a treaty between a certain number commissioned out of these two counties and yours may produce a better effect to every of us than the hostility between us hath hitherto done, or...is like to do.'[37]

On 29 September, Laugharne indicated that he was willing to sign a treaty if full declarations of obedience were made to the King and Parliament. He expected the Royalist horse to be detained or delivered to him and also desired that four representatives from Carmarthen should attend him at Haverfordwest to agree the terms of the treaty and to sign it.

On 2 October, the Carmarthen Committee sent Laugharne another letter, which signalled an unexpected change of attitude. 'Expecting this day to have understood the full sense of the inhabitants of this county, that thereby we might have been armed with power to have treated as was in your letter mentioned, you may understand the country met not (as we expected). Therefore, we consider ourselves not in condition to send unto you according to our undertakings. This we thought fit to intimate you.'

Laugharne, writing to the Speaker of the House of Commons on 12 October, explained that the proposed treaty had been sent to the king for approval by Colonel Lovelace, the Royalist governor of Carmarthen and his officers, 'which breeds my doubt they have rotten cores; and I shall try before I overmuch trust them.' He went on to describe how the Carmarthen Commissioners, in defiance of the governor, had brought 1,500 clubmen into the town who, with the townsmen, dismissed the governor and his soldiers, pledging to defend it themselves.

Laugharne had advanced with 600 horse and 2,000 infantry as far as St Clears, about eleven miles away, and there awaited some gun carriages. The next day, he placed his men in several bodies around Carmarthen and spent the evening in exchanging parleys. Overawed by the sight of such a force, clearly prepared for battle, many of the 'criminous' enemy fled. The 1,500 clubmen, their job done, marched out of one gate, whilst Laugharne entered by another. Some of the enemy joined Parliament's service, whilst in Cardiganshire opposition was mopped up by Colonel Lewes.

The town of Carmarthen was described by Laugharne as very spacious, though he thought that it would need about 1,000 men to protect it. 'If we could give pay we should not want men, and these we have, with a little encouragement, would deem no enterprise too hard. If it would please the state to afford some supply for money and clothing, I doubt not they should speedily reap the fruit of them. I restrain plunder, and use the country with all lenity.'[38]

With Carmarthen settled, Laugharne headed for Glamorganshire. Here, there was every hope that the Royalist influence had been overthrown. Sir Jacob Astley had been left in charge of South Wales by the king. On 8 August, at Abergavenny, Astley called a meeting of the gentry to plan the relief of Hereford, but most were unwilling to attend. Another meeting was arranged at Crickhowell, but only people from Monmouthshire bothered to turn up. Articles of Association had been prepared, but those at the meeting had refused to sign them in the absence of anyone from Glamorgan. Astley, in despair, was convinced some of them were in contact with Parliament. He was to be proved right and even the return of the king to South Wales did not alter the situation

King Charles Returns to Raglan

The king had barely settled back in Oxford before he decided that he should attempt the relief of Hereford. At his approach, the besieging Scottish army withdrew. There was no thought of pursuing them and bringing them to battle. Bristol, under the command of Prince Rupert, was under heavy siege and was desperate for help. For four days, Charles remained in Hereford, trying to decide what to do. It seemed to the king that his presence in Wales might encourage more men to join him, so he set off for Raglan, where he arrived on Sunday, 7 September. Once again, the aged Marquis of Worcester had to bend his creaky knees to his sovereign, but this visit was less amicable than the first one.

The Marquis had fallen out with his son, Lord Herbert, who had been raised to the status of Earl of Glamorgan. The problem between them was

Glamorgan's demand for more money for the raising of troops, which Worcester was unwilling to give him. Not long afterwards, Glamorgan had been sent to Ireland by the king, ostensibly to help the Marquis of Ormonde, the king's lieutenant there, in the raising of more troops but he had also been given a commission to supersede Ormonde's authority in certain circumstances. Glamorgan's interpretation of these instructions, as we shall see, was to lead to trouble. If Worcester knew anything of the commission, it can only have added to the unease pervading the atmosphere at Raglan.

Soon after his arrival at the castle, King Charles dispatched Sir Marmaduke Langdale and Sir Jacob Astley to persuade the Peaceable Army to put aside its weapons and to supply more cash for the war effort. The Army readily agreed to this proposal, but in fact, did nothing about it.

On 11 September, the king left Raglan for Abergavenny. He intended to deal with five prominent citizens who he believed had not been active enough in his cause, or who had deliberately hindered it. They were a Mr Morgan, Mr Herbert of Colbrooke, Mr Barker, one unknown gentleman and Sir Trevor Williams of Llangibby, who had been somewhat elastic in his loyalties. All five were imprisoned, a move that earned the disapproval of Lord Worcester, who told the king to his face, 'To prison, what to do, to poison the garrison?' Sir Trevor, for some reason, was granted bail, a mercy that would later be regretted.

On 14 September, having returned to Raglan, King Charles received sensational news from Bristol. On 10 September the city, under siege by Parliamentary troops since late August, had surrendered after a fierce assault. The decision to capitulate had been taken by Prince Rupert, sent by the king to improve the defences and to prepare for a possible siege. On 11 September, having agreed terms, he marched his men away from Bristol, heading for Oxford. It was a humiliation for which his uncle never forgave him. He ordered the prince to leave England and seek his fortune abroad.

There was no point in Charles remaining any longer at Raglan. On the same day that he learned of the fate of Bristol, he set off for Hereford. From there, he decided to go to Worcester, but a Parliamentary troop lay between him and his destination, so he moved north-west to Presteigne, then to Newtown. His journey took him next to Llanfyllin and Chirk, where he is said to have received news that Chester was on the point of collapse. The besieging Parliamentarians had captured the outworks, possibly through the treachery of some of the garrison, and there was little hope that the city could hold out. Urgent messages were sent to Lord Byron, promising aid within twenty-four hours. Early next morning, the king took the road to Chester.

The Peaceable Army Seizes Control of South Wales

On 17 September the Peaceable Army, equipped with the guns smuggled to them by John Byrd, took over Cardiff Castle. Within a month they had given way to a committee of gentlemen devoted to radical Protestant views. Both these groups may have been spurred on by news of the capture of Bristol

Laugharne, meanwhile, had marched upon Brecon. Royalism had been particularly strong there, but enthusiasm seemed to have waned. The castle soon surrendered and on 23 November, thirty-four of the most influential gentlemen signed a declaration promising to submit themselves, their lives and fortunes to the service of Parliament. This pledge was forwarded to Parliament, where it was formally read out to the members on 5 December.

Despite the fact that the war was dragging to a close, Chepstow had seen further military action. It was still held in the king's name when early in October it found itself challenged by Sir Trevor Williams who, after breaking the terms of the bail granted by the king, captured the town after a short, four-day siege. The defenders took refuge in the castle and refused a summons to surrender. Colonel Morgan arrived from Gloucester with 300 horse and 400 foot. A gun battery was thrown up less than a hundred yards from the walls and two brass culverins and an iron cannon opened up a lethal fire. A breach was soon punched through the wall and the garrison sent out a drummer with an offer to capitulate. On Saturday, 11 October, the great fortress was handed over to Parliament.[39]

It was only just in time. A Royalist relief force had been raised which included troops from Hereford, Monmouth, Raglan and Worcester and was marching towards Chepstow. They were dispersed by an ad hoc army consisting of Glamorganshire clubmen, soldiers led by Sir Trevor Williams and a troop of horse commanded by Colonel Kyrle. It was Williams and Kyrle who, a short while later, re-joined Colonel Morgan

132

and set off for Monmouth. Their numbers were swollen by the addition of more clubmen from Glamorgan and Monmouthshire and some sappers from the mines in the Forest of Dean.

When they arrived at Monmouth, the town lay open to them, the garrison having withdrawn into the castle. A request for surrender was turned down by the castle governor, Captain Price, but a summons from Sir Trevor to the local people for assistance met with a ready response. Dozens turned up, armed with shovels, spades and pickaxes. The sappers from the Forest of Dean dug under the castle walls and, after six days, prepared to blow the mines. The threat of destruction was enough to ensure compliance. On 24 October, the castle was surrendered.[41]

The victors then fell out amongst themselves. Colonel Morgan returned to Gloucester, leaving the castle in the hands of a subordinate, Captain Forster, with a hundred men. The town of Monmouth became the responsibility of Sir Trevor Williams, but his men, all local levies, declared that they did not wish to serve in a garrison and went home. Williams suspected that they had been subverted by Royalists so, with Monmouth undefended, made frantic appeals to Gloucester for help. Within twenty-four hours Kyrle returned at the head of 700 men and a few days later, 200 troops marched in from Gloucester. Feeling suitably confident, Williams issued an order for all suspect persons to leave the town upon pain of death, leading to an exodus of Royalist sympathisers.[40]

There were two remaining Royalist strongholds that posed a danger. Raglan Castle and Hereford were still held for the king and cooperated in the seizure of Abergavenny in November. On 18 December Hereford was taken by a Parliamentary army led by Colonel Morgan and Colonel John Birch. The garrison offered only a token resistance and the governor, Sir Barnabas Scudamore, escaped over the frozen water of the River Wye. As news of this victory spread through South Wales, many Royalists began to abandon their cause.

North Wales and Chester, July to December

In North Wales, the efforts of both sides were concentrated on Chester, the Royalists hoping to supply and then relieve it, the Parliamentarians to capture it. To some extent, the advantage now lay with Lord Byron, as

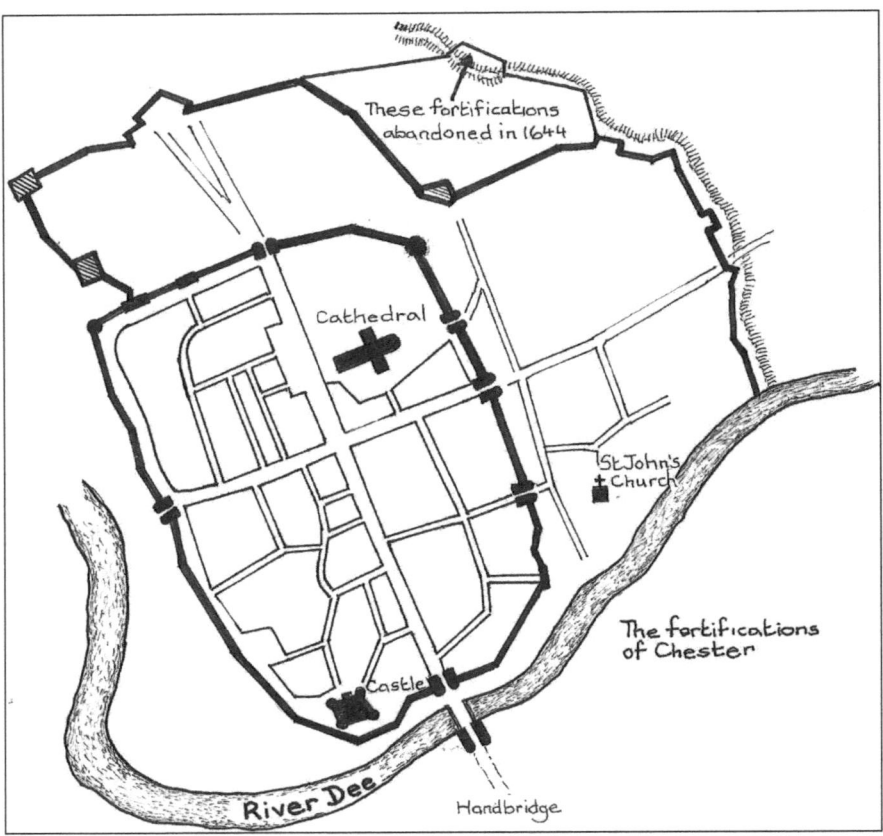

These fortifications abandoned in 1644

Cathedral

St John's Church

The fortifications of Chester

Castle

River Dee

Handbridge

A map of the defences of Chester

his chief opponent, William Brereton, had been summoned to London to answer charges of looting levelled against his troops and to resume his role as member for Cheshire. The command held by Brereton was administered by a committee of five, of which he was one, albeit an absentee. Most of the military decisions were, however, left to his subordinate, Colonel Michael Jones. Brereton did not return to the Marches until mid-October.

Byron was still busy trying to improve the defences of the city. He planned to build a sconce, a star-shaped earthwork fortification, as an addition to the outworks, but as money was scarce, he went to Denbigh in the hope of raising funds there. The sconce never seems to have been completed, so perhaps sufficient funds didn't materialise. He also travelled into North Wales in a failed effort to defuse the ongoing quarrel between Archbishop Williams and Sir John Owen. Then he made his way to Flintshire to discuss with the Commissioners of Array the poor response to further levies of troops and cash. To add to his woes, Beeston Castle was again under siege by the enemy.

During his stay in Flintshire, Byron learned that suspiciously large numbers of Parliamentary troops were gathering at Tarvin. As this might well be the prelude to a move against Chester, messages were sent to the garrison to expect an attack. A strike against Chester was imminent, but it did not come from Tarvin.

On 19 October, a force of 500 horse, 200 dragoons and 700 foot were quietly withdrawn from the leaguer around Beeston Castle. Using back roads and country lanes, the Parliamentarians, led by Colonel Jones, marched through the night hours, arriving at Chester well before daybreak. A group of soldiers made their way in the darkness to one of the outworks known as the Gun Mount and placed the scaling ladders they carried against the earth walls. The first man up one of the ladders found that it was too short to reach the top, but pulled up the man behind him, enabling him to scramble over the rampart. This second man reached down and hauled up the others, completely surprising the half a dozen guards, most of whom fled.[41]

In a few minutes, Jones' men were racing through the streets of the suburbs, sweeping aside any resistance, whilst the panic-stricken citizens, alarmed from their beds, fled towards the safety of the city walls which formed the inner ring of defences. Some were still in their nightclothes, others had managed to grab their most precious possessions, but others abandoned everything. In the panic, the Mayor, Charles Walley, became separated from his wife, who was left behind. The garrison managed to slam shut the massive Eastgate but the suburbs outside it were lost.

The stout medieval walls of Chester held fast against any attempt to breach them and Jones was forced to hold back, consolidating his grip on what he already held. Knowing that the king was marching northwards from Raglan, urgent pleas were sent by Jones requesting assistance from surrounding Parliamentary strongholds. In London, the Committee of Both Kingdoms sent instructions to Staffordshire to provide as much assistance as possible to the besiegers. Colonel Sydenham Poyntz, who had been shadowing the king's movements since his departure from Raglan, was ordered to do everything he could to impede the royal progress towards Chester.

Byron came back hotfoot from Flint and managed to enter the city. He ordered supplies of spades, shovels, lanterns, ropes and other necessities to be gathered together, weapons to be stockpiled, and the Eastgate to be barricaded with earth and dung. In an attempt to deny cover to enemy snipers, fire arrows were launched into the thatched roofs of the houses in the suburbs which stood nearest to the walls.[42] The destruction of these buildings did not deter snipers from climbing up the tower of St John's church outside the Newgate, bringing with them a small gun, and firing at anything that moved inside the city.

A battery of guns was also set up near the church and these bombarded the walls. By Monday, 22 October, they had opened up a breach in the masonry. At about 8.00pm that night, in brilliant moonlight, two companies of Parliamentary troops moved forward, attempting to storm the walls near the breach. Three times they reached the top of the walls and each time were driven back. Several of the attackers were taken prisoner and it was discovered that they were drunk, apparently having been given a mixture of brandy and gunpowder to fortify them.[43]

Colonel Jones must have been bitterly disappointed by the failure of this attack, but he now faced considerable danger. King Charles was fast approaching Chester, having left Chirk on 22 September. He had split his army into two parts, one moving directly to the city along the Welsh bank of the Dee, the other crossing the river at Holt, hoping to trap Jones' force in the suburbs. This second formation, commanded by Sir Marmaduke Langdale, camped overnight on 23 September on Hatton Heath, about five miles south-east of Chester, whilst the king entered Chester over the Dee Bridge that same evening.

The plan to trap the Parliamentarians between a force attacking from their rear and the garrison of Chester issuing out of the gates might have worked had it not been for one unforeseen circumstance. The redoubtably named Sydenham Poyntz with an army of 3,000 horse, was fast approaching from the south. Langdale only received warning in the early hours of 24 September and hastily drew up his men in formation on nearby heathland. Poyntz, too, didn't receive information about Langdale's position until the last minute, so neither side was completely prepared to meet the other. It was only when his vanguard came under fire from Langdale's musketeers hidden in the hedgerows that Poyntz could be absolutely sure of where the enemy lay.

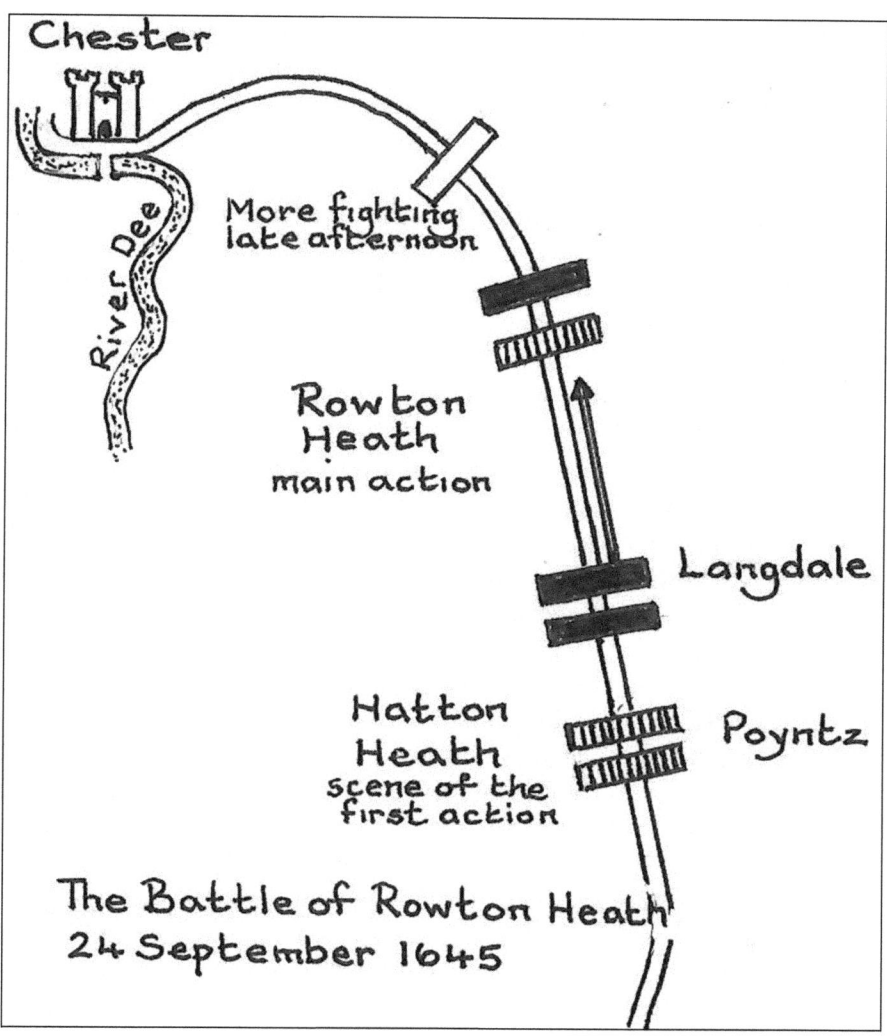

A map of the Battle of Rowton Heath

Langdale hoped to drive off the Parliamentarians before Jones could attack his rear flank and sent forward his mounted troops, who fiercely engaged Poyntz's men, inflicting casualties and taking prisoners. A messenger was sent into Chester for reinforcements, as Langdale knew that he had no hope of complete success without help. There was also the possibility of another, unsuspected group of Roundheads attacking from a different direction.

In fact, both sides were trying to send out reinforcements, Jones from the suburbs, and Byron and the king from Chester itself. There seems to have been some sort of delay in getting troops out of the city, not entirely caused by clearing the gates of barricades. Perhaps exhaustion played its part after the previous days of fighting, or maybe extra troops were awaited from outlying posts, but whatever the reason, it was at least 3.00pm in the afternoon before the garrison was able to send out help. By then, Colonel Jones had galloped up to Hatton Heath with 350 horse, with 400 musketeers following.

Aware of this new threat, Langdale moved on to Rowton Heath, another stretch of open ground and there he faced the combined forces of Poyntz and Jones. The next stage of fighting opened with a fusillade of musket shots from the Roundheads, whilst their horse moved forwards. Again, fighting was hard and bitter, but volleys of fire dispersed the Royalist cavalry. A headlong flight followed, as men attempted to reach the walls of Chester. Many became hopelessly entangled with the troops emerging from the city and in the chaos that resulted, dozens were cut down by the pursuing Parliamentarian horsemen.

The destruction of the Royalist army was clearly visible from the walls of Chester. King Charles had earlier in the day climbed up into the cathedral tower to watch events, but a cannonball struck off the head of the officer standing next to him. The king took up a less exposed vantage point in the Phoenix Tower on the city walls. As he watched the destruction of his army, he is said the have muttered, 'O Lord, O Lord, what have I done that I should cause my people to deal with me thus.'[44]

As darkness fell, the bodies of about 600 men, English and Welsh alike, lay scattered across the battlefield. There were probably a similar number of wounded and a few hundred prisoners had been taken by Colonel Jones' soldiers. The gates of Chester were firmly closed again and the suburbs re-occupied by Parliament. In the cold night hours, after much discussion, the decision was taken that the king should leave the city as swiftly as possible. To remain would risk capture should the enemy renew the siege, as they were most likely to do. Early the next morning, with screens of animal hides erected by the roadside to preserve secrecy, Charles rode away from Chester for the last time.

He reached Denbigh on 28 September, where he rested for a few days. He had scarcely arrived before more bad news reached him. The Marquis of Montrose, who had fought hard for him in Scotland, had been comprehensively defeated at the Battle of Philiphaugh. In the aftermath of the fighting over 300 camp followers, men, women and children, had been murdered by the victorious Covenanters. Burdened with so much disaster, the king left for Oxford but, according to William Maurice, 'the king retreated to Denbigh Castle and having laid there two or three nights, returned to Chirk Castle. The next morning...he advanced from thence with his army through Llansilin, and quartered that night in Halchdyn and so passed through Montgomeryshire towards Ludlow, taking a route to Chirk and Ludlow.'[45]

Within days of Rowton Heath, the blockade of Chester had resumed. In succeeding weeks, new batteries were set up and the guns were steadily bombarding the walls. Fresh breaches were opened up, which the defenders worked furiously to fill in, using timber, lumps of stone, even pieces of furniture. Prominent in this work, and in dousing blazes caused by mortar fire, were many of the townswomen, at least three of whom were killed by enemy fire.

Mortar fire was particularly terrifying. Randle Holmes, mayor of Chester, gave a vivid description in his diary of a mortar bombardment that took place on 10 December:

> 'Eleven huge granadoes like so many tumbling demi-phaetons threaten to set the city, if not the world, on fire. This was a terrible night indeed, our houses like so many splitt vessels crush their supporters and burst themselves in sunder through the very violence of these descending firebrands...another Thunder-cracke invites our eyes to the most miserable spectacle that spite could possibly present us with – two houses in the Watergate slippes joynt from joynt and creates an earthquake, the main posts josell each other, whilst the frighted casements fly for feare, in a word the whole fabric is a perfect chaos lively set forth in this metamorphosis. The grandmother, mother and three children are struck stark dead and buried in the ruins of this humble edifice, a sepulchre well worth the enemeye's remembrance... .'[46]

There were also plans to undermine and blow up sections of the defences, though these seem not to have come to fruition.

On 8 October, Colonel Poyntz issued a summons to surrender. An exchange of notes went back and forth during a lull in the hostilities, but Lord Byron did not intend to capitulate. A fierce cannonade heralded the resumption of activities and on the late afternoon of 9 October, storming parties began to scale the walls. After two hours of hard struggle, the Roundheads were driven back.

Despite the tightness of the blockade, communications with the outside world were still possible by river and along the roads leading to Flint and Denbigh. The garrison also managed to launch a number of surprise raids and sorties against the enemy. They met with varying degrees of success, but the very fact that they were hitting back raised the morale of those within the defences.

Lord Byron knew that strenuous efforts were being made to help his stricken city. Archbishop Williams was at Beaumaris, hoping to fill a ship with as many provisions as possible. He also arranged for a company of foot soldiers to join with a troop of horse and march on Denbigh. Meanwhile, Sir William Vaughan was rallying troops from the garrisons along the Marches, intending a relief of Chester. Sir John Owen was hoping to raise a troop of cavalry and Colonel Mostyn had slipped out of Chester, crossing to Dublin with the aim of recruiting more soldiers.[47] Another who escaped undetected from the city was Lord St Pol, General-of-Horse, who arrived at Rhuddlan to discuss with Gilbert Byron, his lordship's brother, future plans for the relief of Chester. It was hoped to bring about a general muster of these forces at Denbigh Green, then a large open area, and move towards Chester.

Sir William Brereton, now back in command, got wind of these preparations and ordered Colonel Michael Jones to take 1,550 horse and 1,000 foot to disrupt the muster. By 31 October, this force was at Ruthin, where it was joined by Thomas Mytton who, as the senior officer, took command and the march towards Denbigh continued.

Sir William Vaughan was ready for them. On 1 November, he assembled a force of 1,700 horse and 400 infantry on Denbigh Green, near St Marcella's Church at Whitchurch, just outside the town. The hedges lining the road concealed Vaughan's musketeers and dragoons, who opened fire as Mytton's men approached. The fighting spilled out of the lane into the open country beyond, with the Royalist soldiers being driven back towards Denbigh. Vaughan's mounted troops fled to Llanrwst, whilst the infantry took refuge in Denbigh Castle. William Maurice noted in his diary that '…Sir William Vaughan was overthrown with all his army; whereof many weare slain in the pursuit, which continued six miles, even to Llangerniw.'[48]

Mytton and Jones did not linger in the vicinity of Denbigh. They considered that they had achieved their aim, so returned swiftly to the leaguer at Chester. The Royalists, undaunted, were soon on the move again and on 4 November marched out of Denbigh to reunite with their cavalry at Llanrwst. They began making plans to relieve Chester.

The city had now become something of a vortex, around which swirled a flood of patrols, raids, counter-raids, and troop movements. Towards the end of November, Beeston Castle finally surrendered, its garrison permitted to march away, heading for Denbigh and Beaumaris. At about the same time, Brereton issued a summons to surrender, which Byron defiantly spurned. On 25 November the garrison made an unsuccessful attempt to burn a bridge of boats which the Parliamentarians had been constructing across the Dee in order to move with ease from one side of the river to the other. A night attack took place, with two boats stuffed full of combustible materials, gunpowder and bullets drifting up the river on an incoming tide. Unfortunately, both exploded short of their target. The horse and foot sent out of the city skirmished with the besiegers, then retreated back behind the walls, leaving several men dead.[49]

On Christmas Day, knowing Chester to be short of food, a group of Welsh Royalists attempted to drive a hundred head of cattle into the city. As they neared Holywell, they realised that they had been spotted by the enemy and scattered the animals through the surrounding hills for safety. A few days later, a band of a hundred Cavaliers evaded patrols to gallop in through the city gates. Every rider carried behind him seven stone of meat, some oatmeal and gunpowder.

On 30 December, Brereton took his mounted troops across the river at Blacon Point and raided up towards Mold, Northop and Denbigh. Units of the infantry were ferried across the river on boats to strengthen the leaguer on the Welsh bank. Mytton established himself at Wrexham, which now became the headquarters for the Parliamentary committee for Flintshire. And in Chester itself, the poorer citizens rioted because of the lack of fresh meat, asking to be allowed to leave the city, and there were daily gatherings of women demanding food for their families.

There were food shortages too in the leaguer and Brereton had to deal with a mutiny of his own men who, in November, had rioted, demanding arrears of pay. As much of Cheshire had been stripped of food, supplies had to be brought in from elsewhere and were slow to arrive.

As the new year of 1646 approached, it was clear to most people, except perhaps King Charles, that the end of hostilities was not far off. The king had made overtures to Parliament, hoping to find some sort of common ground by which a peace could be agreed, but his efforts were rebuffed. Fresh elections had been held in the autumn of 1645 and most of the newly elected members were strong supporters of the Parliamentary cause. It was rumoured that the Committee of the Two Kingdoms was in possession of an explosive piece of information which would ruin the king's already tattered reputation if it was made public – as it was early in the New Year.

On 26 October 1645, Malachy O'Queely, Archbishop of Tuam in Ireland, was killed in a skirmish between Irish Confederate forces and Scottish troops. The Archbishop was a leading figure in the Catholic Confederation, which aimed to re-establish the Catholic religion in Ireland. Amongst his papers was discovered a copy of a treaty between the Earl of Glamorgan and the Confederation, by which 10,000 Irish troops would be sent to England, provided that there was complete toleration for all Irish Catholics, over whom the Protestant clergy would have no authority, and the restoration of all church lands. Glamorgan had assured the Confederates that the king and Parliament would approve the treaty.[50]

Whether or not the king knew of, and accepted, the terms of the treaty was immaterial. He certainly denied all knowledge of the affair as soon as it became public. In actuality, Glamorgan's actions in signing the treaty probably far outstripped his original instructions, but he was in Ireland on the king's behalf, and his written commission from Charles allowed him, under certain circumstances, to supersede the authority of the Marquis of Ormonde. It was also well-known that he was in Ireland to raise more troops, so the king's complicity seemed at first glance to be obvious. It made no difference to public opinion that Glamorgan was arrested for treason as soon as the contents of the treaty became known.

Charles' peace offers were thus tossed aside, but he still clung blindly to the hope of victory. There were only two significant bodies of troops still at his disposal, one in Cornwall under Lord Hopton, whilst the other, under Sir Jacob Astley, still hovered near the Welsh Marches in the hope of relieving Chester. A few isolated garrisons still held out, but already some Royalist families were reconciling with Parliament, whilst others took refuge on the Continent.

Chapter 6

1646

Mid and South Wales, January to June

During the first few months of 1646, the southern half of Wales was still in a state of turbulence. Aberystwyth Castle, held for the king, had been under siege since the previous November and the besieging Parliamentary forces raided the surrounding countryside without mercy. On 2 January a group of them headed north into Merionethshire and on the following day plundered the village of Barmouth before departing by boat.

This was only one of a similar number of attacks and the local inhabitants were driven to protest to Major-General Rowland Laugharne, whose troops were responsible. He issued the following apology:

> 'These are to certify, whom it may concern, that what inroads were by my soldiers made into Montgomery and Merioneddshire (sic) were without orders and command from me, and was done in my absence. Therefore, I desire a free and usual intercourse and correspondence to be carried on between the counties of my association and the said Counties of Montgomery and Merionedd; promising that if hereafter any of my men commit the like offences they shall be exactly punished according to the law of war.'[1]

Raids were also taking place in Glamorgan and Monmouthshire as Royalist adherents attempted to push back into areas seized by the Roundheads. At Caerleon on 22 January, a troop of horse from Raglan under Lord Charles Somerset ambushed a party of 200 infantry and eighty foot commanded by Captain Bowen, killing forty and taking 140 prisoners. It was afterwards claimed that some of the prisoners were thrown into the River Usk to drown.

There were also raids on Newport and Abergavenny, but the most serious incident came when the Royalists tried to recapture Monmouth. The ancient gateway on the Monnow Bridge was seized by soldiers from Raglan and when Captain Kyrle of the defending garrison attempted to drive them off, another group of Royalists waded across the shallows of the river and attacked from the rear. A confused struggle raged through the streets as Kyrle fought his way back to the marketplace where, reinforced by a hundred men from the castle, he managed to route the attackers. In the aftermath of the battle, officers who were regarded as suspect were arrested and some townspeople expelled.[2]

The flames of rebellion crackled up again in February, when Edward Carne of Ewenni, High Sheriff of Glamorgan, suddenly declared for the king. He was probably motivated by fears that the clique of radical Puritans holding power in Cardiff were about to impose the Solemn League and Covenant upon Glamorgan. Linking up with Sir Charles Kemeys of Cefn Mably, he marched to Cardiff and drove the Puritans to seek refuge in the castle. Edward Pritchard, who had succeeded Sir Richard Bassett as governor at the further insistence of the Peaceable Army, refused to give up the stronghold and sent frantic messages to Rowland Laugharne asking for help. There was little ammunition in the castle to withstand a siege, though the situation improved when the Parliamentarian Vice-Admiral, John Crowther, managed to provide powder and guns by sailing them up the River Taff, which then flowed under the walls of the castle.[3]

By Monday, 16 February, Laugharne, with 250 horse and foot and 'some others of the country that rose and joined him', was approaching Cardiff.[4] Crowther sailed his vessel close inshore and fired off his cannons as a signal to Pritchard that relief was at hand, 'at the sight of which ship, and the hearing of which pieces, our men (in the castle) gave a great shout and were very glad.'[5]

As Laugharne drew near, Carne withdrew his men from Cardiff and occupied a stretch of moorland a mile to the north of the town, where he was joined by the soldiers of Sir Charles Kemeys. The battle began almost at once, the Parliamentary troops fighting with such determination that Carne's men fled in so much disarray that, as a pamphlet later stated, 'Carne himself stayed not to keep them together, but like a vagabond ran up and down, bemoaning himself, and glad he was he had a nimble horse, not to charge, but to fly with.'[6]

As it happened, Carne had not fled, but was taken prisoner and negotiated the articles of surrender, which allowed many of his followers to escape harsh punishment. The ordinary soldiers were allowed to return to their homes, their officers could withdraw to nearby Royalist garrisons, though Carne suffered imprisonment and was fined. Kemeys too escaped rigorous punishment and in future he would cause more trouble.

This leniency was all the more extraordinary because, the day after the agreement was signed, some sort of quarrel erupted between the withdrawing Royalists and the Parliamentarians. A vicious struggle resulted, with Laugharne's cavalry pursuing the enemy across seven miles of countryside and killing many of them.

It remained now to mop up the remaining centres of Royalist resistance. Raglan still held out, and in the west, Aberystwyth was under siege. Surrounded by a Parliamentary leaguer commanded by Colonel Rice Powell since the previous November, Aberystwyth was proving to be the proverbial thorn in the side. Powell was assisted by Colonel John Jones of Nanteos and John Vaughan of Trawscoed. The latter, who had Royalist sympathies, was said to have offered his assistance with the siege in order to win favour. Most of Powell's soldiers came from Cardiganshire and, as we have seen, they were not above a bit of pillage on their own account. This may well have been because food supplies were scarce, but when they resorted to kidnap and ransom as well as theft, they completely lost the favour of the country people.

It was not until 12 April that terms of surrender were agreed. The Royalist officers were allowed to march away with their swords, though the foot soldiers had to give up their arms. Many of them headed for Harlech, still held for the king, eventually moving on to Denbigh. Colonel Whitley and five of his officers were given safe conducts that allowed them to go wherever the king might be.[7]

A letter from Laugharne's headquarters stated that, with the siege over, 'now we are ready to be put into a capacity for further service, either for Carnarvon, or to assist against Raglan, or what other service shall be thought meet, if the soldiers have but money.'[8] The lack of pay was to prove a problem when, at Abergavenny in June, Laugharne's troops became mutinous and demanded to go home. The Usk Committee had to find £200 to pay them off.[9]

The Fall of Raglan Castle, May to August 1646

It was clear to the Marquis of Worcester and his 800 strong garrison that Raglan must prepare for a siege. Accordingly, stocks of provisions were collected and tenants were pressed to supply oats, wheat, barley and other food supplies. Nearby houses, which might afford cover to the enemy, were demolished and trees were cut down to provide timber. The horses of the mounted troops were brought into the castle and, according to tradition, were stabled in a large underground chamber near the Fountain Court.[10]

The Parliamentarians were no less busy. Until their dispersal in June, Rowland Laugharne based his men at Abergavenny and Llanarth, whilst Captain Kyrle was stationed close to Raglan. Another camp was set up at Llandenny, two and a half miles from Raglan, and became the Parliamentary headquarters.

Both sides did what they could to disrupt the activities of the other. A party of Roundheads stole into the village of Raglan on the night of 20 May and seized a number of horses, but were themselves surprised and driven off by soldiers from the castle. A few nights later, another group of Roundheads were drinking in a nearby house when they came under attack and had to hide in a cornfield. Another raid the next day resulted in the burning of the village.[11]

By late May, over 1,500 Parliamentary troops were surrounding Raglan Castle. Most of them encamped to the south and the east, close to twenty acres of ponds well stocked with freshwater fish.[12] Commanding the leaguer was Colonel Thomas Morgan, described as short in stature and temper. He was a man who led from the front and whenever the garrison of the castle made a sortie, he rode out to meet them in person.

The siege began with the usual invitation to surrender, to which Lord Worcester replied that he must seek the permission of the king. A second demand, presented on 20 June, threatened no favours if the castle had to be stormed. The Marquis replied that he served '…a Master that is of more might than all the armies of the world; and to His holy will and pleasure I submit myself… .' A few days later he narrowly escaped death when a musket ball ricocheted off a pillar and, its force spent, struck him on the head.[13]

After the surrender of Oxford on 24 June, a fresh batch of 2,000 Parliamentary troops arrived at Raglan, followed by more over the next few weeks. The net was drawn tight around the castle and the garrison, which had not hesitated to issue forth and challenge their enemies, could not stir beyond the walls. The heavy guns, situated on high ground to the east of the castle, were steadily battering at the ramparts, eventually opening up a breach in the east wall. Four great mortars were set up closer to the walls. Galleries and trenches were dug to within sixty yards of the castle, with the intention of springing mines to bring down the foundations.

On 7 August Sir Thomas Fairfax arrived to take control of the siege and immediately sent a third demand for surrender. This met with a 'dilatory' answer, but a day later, the Marquis asked to have propositions sent in to him. Fairfax replied at once; the Marquis must place himself at the disposal of Parliament, but fair terms were offered to the rest of the garrison. On reading these, Worcester agreed to a truce while further discussions took place. During the intervening period, the soldiers of both sides met outside the fortifications and talked together.

The surrender finally took place on 19 August, when the garrison marched out with colours flying, drums beating, trumpets blaring and every soldier armed with sword, and musket, their match lighted at either end, bullets in their mouths and carrying twelve charges of powder. They were to go to any place within a radius of ten miles, there to be disbanded after handing over their weapons. The officers and gentlemen were given passes to go to their homes and had three months to make their peace with Parliament or travel overseas if they wished.[14]

The Marquis, who had remained in the castle, was taken up to London in October, where he was imprisoned. He was by now seriously ill and died on Christmas Day 1646. He was buried in the Beaufort Chapel at Windsor Castle. When he was told where his resting place would be, he remarked 'God bless my soul! Why then, I shall take a better Castle when I am dead than they took from me whilst I was alive.'[15] His own castle, of which he had been so proud, was partially demolished, the country people roundabout summoned to a meeting armed with shovels, spades and pickaxes and made to drain the moat in the hope of finding treasure. The fishponds were also drained, but the worst damage was done to the Great Tower, which was undermined on two of its six sides until they collapsed. The castle was never occupied again.

South Wales had now fallen to Parliament, though there was still some trouble in Radnorshire and the adjacent Marches. Sir William Vaughan, an unflinching Royalist who had escorted King Charles from Cardiff towards North Wales in August 1645, had remained active at Knighton and later in the Leominster-Pembridge area. He was determined not to give up the struggle and in February 1646 raided towards Clun, Knighton and Presteigne. Brought to bay by a Parliamentary force near Stokesay, his men were scattered. Undaunted, he launched another raid from Ludlow, penetrating into Radnorshire and Breconshire, plundering houses and taking prisoners for ransom. It was only after the capture of Ludlow in late April, and the capitulation of the Royalist garrisons of Worcester and Goodrich Castle in July, that the situation in the Marches was stabilised.[16]

What may have sapped Royalist determination across England and Wales was the news that King Charles was no longer at liberty. When it became obvious that his headquarters at Oxford would soon be invested by a Parliamentary army led by Fairfax, he made the decision to leave. In the early hours of 27 April, disguised as a groom with his face hidden by a cap, he crossed the Magdalene Bridge and disappeared into the darkness. He headed towards Newark, then under siege by the Scottish army, appearing at their camp at Southwell on 5 May. He had established prior contact with the army's leaders and clearly hoped that they would declare their support for him if Parliament refused to acknowledge his rights. In reality, he became the Scots' prisoner, until they handed him over to Parliamentary representatives in January 1647.

Chester, January and February

As the New Year dawned, the Chester garrison still hoped to receive reinforcements. Early in January, Lord St Pol managed to make his way undetected out of the city, hoping to take charge of any troops that might have been gathered for relief operations. Both Lord Digby and Colonel Mostyn had arrived in Ireland to recruit more men, but the response had been disappointing. Mostyn had only been able to find about 160 soldiers and returned with them to North Wales, where he expected to raise another 200 or so. His failure in Ireland caused Archbishop Williams to remark, 'There is no relying on these Irish forces for this service'.

Other Royalist troops were gathering. Colonel Gilbert Byron was in Caernarfonshire with about 600 soldiers, and at High Ercal in Shropshire, Sir William Vaughan had drawn together a mixed band of 1,500 horse and foot. He hoped that his numbers would be swollen by the arrival of Sir Jacob Astley, then at Lichfield, or that secret negotiation between Lord Glamorgan and the Confederates would bring the promised 10,000 strong army from Ireland.

Both sides were aware that conditions within Chester were grim. The city was packed with soldiers and with civilians, many of them refugees from the burnt-out suburbs. Food was at a premium, though limited supplies were being brought into the city by men who knew their way through the network of marshes and lanes in the area.[17] This in itself caused problems, as the wealthier citizens could pay the smugglers for whatever they wanted.

Food was so scarce that some Welsh soldiers died of starvation, whilst others were so weakened that they were unable to perform their duties. At a military parade one evening, 300 Welshmen cast aside their arms and told Byron that, unless they were offered more meat, they would not do their duty. It was not just the soldiers who caused disturbances. Groups of women congregated outside Lord Byron's house every day, demanding to know if they should eat their own children as there was nothing left in their larders.[18]

On 14 January, Byron ordered a survey of all the food left within the city. Teams of searchers visited every house and noted down what provisions were left. The results were shocking. In the Eastgate and St Bridget wards, where about 900 civilians and 150 soldiers lived, over a hundred families had no corn. Elsewhere, some families were reduced to just one large loaf for their sustenance.[19]

The situation was so desperate that the city's mayor, Charles Walley, was in secret negotiations with Brereton, possibly to discuss terms of surrender. Contact was enabled by the mayor's wife, Mrs Walley, who had been left behind by her husband on the autumn night that the outer suburbs had been captured.

On 3 January, Brereton had addressed a letter to the inhabitants of Chester, copies of which were smuggled into the town. It reminded them that they owed their present sufferings to those who commanded the garrison. Their miseries would only increase the longer the siege dragged on. On 6 January, another letter invited Lord Byron to surrender the city, but received a contemptuous reply. Brereton was undisturbed by this rejection, as he knew that the fall of Chester was only a matter of time.

He was right. At a meeting with the city's councillors, Byron admitted that he was ready to discuss terms, but asked them to leave him to decide the matter further. Their angry response and the shouts of a large crowd gathered outside, left him no option but to agree to immediate discussions with Brereton.

Negotiation began on 15 January, with a message sent from Byron to Brereton, and lasted for two weeks. Byron was stalling for time, hoping to hear that Sir Jacob Astley had joined up with Lord St Pol and was marching to Chester. On 29 January, he learned that Astley had in fact retreated to Bridgnorth. The news caused a further outbreak of anger amongst the city's aldermen and forced Byron to accept whatever terms were on offer.

The treaty for the capitulation of Chester was signed on 3 February. Lord Byron, his officers and soldiers were to march away to Conwy, under protection for five days. Their eventual destination was Caernarfon. Welsh officers and soldiers could return to their homes. Some officers could take with them their horses, servants and even a sum of money. The city and all its arms and ammunition, was to be delivered up to Parliament. As a result of this condition over 2,000 weapons and 520 helmets were piled up in the castle courtyard. Most important of all, Chester and its people were to be preserved from plunder.[20]

North Wales, January to December

Despite the fall of Chester, there was to be no peace for North Wales. When Sir William Brereton learned that Colonel Gilbert Byron and Lord St Pol were likely to join with Colonel Mostyn and his Irishmen to relieve Chester, he sent Colonel Mytton to disperse them. The Royalists fled towards Denbigh and Ruthin, Lord St Pol finding refuge at Flint. Mytton turned his attention to Chirk Castle, which was given up at the end of February. The leader of the garrison there, John Watts, abandoned the castle before Mytton even appeared, leaving the care of it to Sir Thomas Myddelton's daughter.

There were still a number of formidable strongholds offering resistance to Parliament. Some were dealt with more easily than others. Hawarden surrendered on 16 March, having received permission to do so from the king. Ruthin came under siege in March and finally fell on 12 April, after holding out for six weeks. The day before the surrender was finalised, a party of Royalists left Denbigh Castle to attack the headquarters of Captain Richard Price, commanding the leaguer. Their approach was observed and Price rode out to surprise them, killing some and capturing others. Not surprisingly, Denbigh became the next target.

Denbigh

The castle was under the command of Colonel Salesbury, with a garrison of some 500 men. Some of the local gentry were also said to have taken refuge within the walls. Two wells supplied water to the defenders, though one of these sometimes dried up in the summer months. The other was in the Goblin Tower, a part of the town walls, and this became a target for the Parliamentary artillery. Heavy siege guns had been dragged to Denbigh from Chester and it was hoped that they would soon breach the ancient walls.

The siege actually lasted until the following October and was marked by a courteous exchange of letter between Colonel Mytton and Colonel Salesbury. Mytton was at first anxious to emphasise that he did not wish to shed blood if it could be avoided and, in his first letter written on 17 April, suggested that a surrender would result in beneficial terms for the garrison. Salesbury replied that he would defend Denbigh until otherwise instructed by the king. As letters were sent back and forth with no result, the townspeople of Denbigh became concerned about the effects of the siege upon themselves and their homes. On 8 May, a group of forty-seven residents signed a petition and sent it to Salesbury. It became known as the Bumpkin's Petition and begged the governor to avoid the shedding of Christian blood and the ruination of rich and poor alike.[21] Salesbury still stood fast in his loyalty to the king.

On 24 June, Mytton again requested a surrender, and told Salesbury that Caernarfon and Beaumaris had both fallen to Parliament. The governor loftily replied that whatever Caernarfon and Anglesey did was no business of his. He did, however, ask if two gentlemen could be allowed to go to the king and request his opinion. Mytton told him that, on the orders of Parliament, no such concession could be made.

Despite the polite exchanges, this was still a war. The defenders of the castle made regular sorties out from the walls, attacking the Parliamentary entrenchments and ambushing their foraging parties. Both sides lost men in these incidents and there were outbreaks of disease within the castle, no doubt caused by the insanitary conditions.

The exchange of letters continued. Salesbury professed himself unworried by the increase in the ranks of the besiegers, as more troops marched into the leaguer. He signed off one epistle with the words '... the addition of a new force, bee the consequence what it will, will but add to my honour which is all I have now left to care for.'[22] He had, however, managed to smuggle out a message to the king informing him that the castle had held out for several months and praying for the sovereign's health and happiness. It is certain that the messenger also carried a verbal description of the sufferings of the garrison. The reply from the king included an authorisation for the capitulation of the castle upon honourable terms.

The articles of surrender were signed on 14 October. As at Chester, the terms were generous. The garrison was to march out with drums beating, colours flying, all soldiers bearing weapons and at a place ten miles distant, chosen by the governor, there to be disarmed. Salesbury was allowed to take as much of his own property from the castle as was necessary for his subsistence.

Denbigh was one of the last of the Royalist strongholds in North Wales to capitulate. Others had fallen earlier in the year and their stories were just as dramatic.

Caernarfon

Lord Byron, having marched away from Chester, eventually made his way to Caernarfon, where he placed himself in charge of the garrison. The castle had been held for the king since the outbreak of the war, and had been attacked at least twice before by Parliamentary troops, but the third occasion became a long drawn out siege. When General Mytton first brought his troops into the town in May, they were ambushed by Byron's forces, who lay in wait on the approach road. Fortunately, he managed to drive them back towards the castle, clearing the suburbs as he went, with very few casualties amongst his men. Over the next four weeks, the defenders made several sorties out of the castle. On the second occasion, Mytton himself narrowly evaded death, but seventeen of the enemy were taken.

Supplies were brought into the castle by sea, but once the Parliamentary warships had increased their patrols, there could be no more relief. There was a shortage of fresh water, which it was hoped would soon force a surrender. The garrison's position became even harder when Mytton sent commissioners to Anglesey to demand a surrender, sweetened by the promise of £2,000 when the treaty was signed. The authorities on the island agreed to negotiate, perhaps wary of two armed Parliamentary vessels that dropped anchor off Beaumaris, requesting passes to proceed to Caernarfon. Some of the seamen from one of the boats were said to have landed at night to convey supplies and ammunition to a Parliamentary outpost at Aberleiniog.

With no prospect of either supplies or reinforcements, Byron accepted terms of capitulation on 4 June. He, his officers, and the gentlemen with their servants, were allowed to go home, or depart for foreign shores if they preferred. Within ten days, Beaumaris Castle and Anglesey also submitted to Parliament.

The Fate of Holt, Flint and Rhuddlan

Holt Castle, a short distance from Wrexham, had been placed under siege at about the same time as Ruthin. Although the castle was a strong one, the garrison was quite small and might not have been able to withstand an attack by a large force of Roundheads. For some reason, part of the besieging force was withdrawn, leaving the remainder in a weakened position. They were now outnumbered by the garrison.

In a letter to the Speaker of the House of Commons, Mytton described how the Royalists were able to issue out of the castle and burn down one of his guardhouses as well as about forty dwellings in the town. In April, there was another attack, when the enemy attempted to capture a building where troops were quartered. Five of Mytton's men were killed and fifteen wounded. The number of sorties made by the garrison increased until they were occurring on an almost daily basis. The besiegers were in great need of muskets and powder if they were to beat off the attacks. These must have been provided, because the siege continued until the final surrender on 13 January 1647. Only Harlech held out for longer.

Flint castle had been placed under the command of Colonel Roger Mostyn, who had retreated there after the fall of Cheshire. His garrison may have been low in morale, because on 22 May, forty-six cavalrymen left the castle at midnight and either joined the Parliamentarians or fled for home. The final surrender came towards the end of August.[23] By then, Rhuddlan too had given in, its governor, Gilbert Byron, signing the articles of surrender at the end of July.

Conwy

Conwy had been the headquarters of John Williams, Archbishop of York, until shoved aside by Sir John Owen. Williams had spent a small fortune on refurbishing the walls of the town and castle and had done everything in his power to advance the king's cause. With the collapse of Chester, and the submission to Parliament of large parts of North Wales, the Archbishop reconsidered his position. Perhaps it was his treatment by Sir John Owen, or his fears for the future of the town where he had been born, but at some point in the summer of 1646, he made overtures to General Mytton, offering advice on a planned attack on the town and castle.

On 8 August, Williams and Mytton attended a council of war, at which a feasible plan for the storming of Conwy was developed. An attack would be made on the northern side of the town, designed to draw off the defenders from other sections of the walls. Another assault would be launched on the south side and in two other places along the defences. Three companies of 'resolute men', were selected for this task and acquitted themselves well. Throwing up scaling ladders, they attempted to clamber over the battlements, but discovered that the ladders were at least four feet too short. Even so, they were successful in entering the town, racing through the streets, killing and wounding any who resisted and capturing many more, including at least fifty armed townsmen. Amongst the prisoners were some of the Irish soldiers sent over by the Marquis of Ormonde. These were tied back-to-back and thrown into the sea to drown.[24]

With the capture of the town complete, Mytton sent a message to Sir John Owen in the castle, demanding surrender, with an answer expected in two hours. Owen replied that he would not give up the castle, but was prepared to treat with Mytton if the general accepted certain conditions. Mytton signified his willingness to examine the proposals, but when none had been received by 12 August, he resumed his attacks.

To encourage the Parliamentary troops, Archbishop Williams preached a sermon in the parish church, taking as his text the first verse of Psalm 144: 'Blessed be the Lord my Strength, which teacheth my hands to war and my fingers to fight.'[25] His words might equally well have been aimed at the defenders of the castle, for they endured weeks of bombardment. The three drawbridges of the castle were shattered by cannon fire, and sections of the curtain wall were similarly damaged. It was not until 18 November that Sir John Owen finally surrendered. This stalwart defender of the royal cause was allowed to retire to his home at Clenennau, though he was heavily fined.

Aftermath

The presence of military forces had a profound effect on the people of Wales long after the last actions had been fought. Parliament considered it necessary to retain troops of soldiers in key locations across the land, much to the discomfort of the inhabitants. Throughout the summer and autumn of 1646, soldiers stationed in the Vale of Clwyd caused such trouble that many people were afraid to leave their homes. In Mid and South Wales, the continued monthly assessments towards the upkeep of the military was deeply resented, especially the billeting of troops on civilian households. In some areas, the men appointed as local collectors and treasurers were found to be fraudulent. When the accounts of Lieutenant-Colonel Howell Jones of Nantmel were examined, he was found to have pocketed some of the money raised by the sequestration of Royalist estates and to have paid soldiers in the Worcester garrison £60 less than he had accounted for.[26]

There was considerable opposition in Glamorgan to the levying of contributions for the upkeep of Laugharne's forces, still present at several locations. Even amongst the soldiers there was discontent, as many had not received their full pay. On 4 August, in a bid to forestall possible trouble, the Commons suggested the disbandment of all the Glamorgan troops, except one. Five companies of foot would be stationed at Cardiff and Swansea. The disbanded men would be offered service in Ireland on the promise of a month's pay or they could return to their homes, having received some of what they were owed.[27] A troop of 200 horse were to be sent to South-West Wales, enough, it was hoped, to ensure quiet.

In fact, Pembrokeshire refused to remain quiet. When, in September, the Commissioners of Excise visited Haverfordwest to consider further exactions, sending out warrants summoning the inhabitants, 'there came to the town hall a company of the poorest sort of women…who made a mutiny and forced the Commissioners thence to their lodgings.' The commissioners complained to the town authorities, who they hoped would suppress any trouble, but at the next meeting, 'the women came again and would have forced into the town hall.' Some of the women were arrested, 'but they fell again into such a mutiny that for safeguard of the commissioners lives they were forced to leave the hall and repair to the latter's lodgings with an intent to see the commissioners safe out of town.' The women would have forced entry into the lodgings and for the next six hours behaved in a threatening manner. The town council appealed to Rowland Laugharne 'for the pacifying of these idle women'.[28] Promises of support were made but, in Pembrokeshire as across Wales, public unrest continued to grow.

Chapter 7

1647–49

On 16 March 1647, Harlech Castle, the last stronghold in England and Wales to be held in the king's name, finally surrendered. Its garrison was commanded by Colonel William Owen, the brother of Sir John Owen, who had signed the surrender of Conwy. The first Civil War was finally over, but the seeds of the second were already germinating.

With the war over, sharp religious disagreements surfaced within the ranks of the victors. Two distinct and opposing points of view emerged. The Presbyterians were focussed on the overthrow of the Anglican church and of episcopacy, and sought to replace it with their own brand of worship, based on the parish system, where someone's place of birth decided to which congregation they belonged, within the framework of a unified national church. In defiance of this, the so-called Independents insisted that it was the right of every person and every congregation to worship as they liked. The Presbyterians held the upper hand in the Houses of Parliament, and had banned the *Book of Common Prayer* in 1645, as well as the expulsion of Anglican parish clergymen from their churches. The Independents were particularly strong within the army.

A month earlier Parliament, concerned about the political stance of the New Model Army, decided upon the disbandment of its troops. The standing army numbered about 22,000 men, and of these, 10,000 foot soldiers and 6,000 mounted troops were to be dismissed and a fresh army of 12,600 men were to be formed for service in Ireland. A small field army was to be stationed at key locations across England and Wales to quell any possible risings. Disbanded men would receive no more than six weeks arrears of pay, a proposal greeted with howls of dismay by infantrymen, who were owed eighteen weeks of back pay, whilst some mounted troops were forty-three weeks in arrears.[1]

Negotiations between the military and Parliament led nowhere, so on 14 June 1647, the army issued a declaration that asserted its right to oppose Parliament if its demands were ignored. These demands included full payment of arrears, pensions for war widows and disabled soldiers and guarantees against future conscription. Parliament refused to acknowledge the declaration and issued further instructions for disbandment. The army, gathered at Newmarket, would not give in, its members believing that they had been betrayed. They were determined to put pressure on Parliament to grant their aims.

The army already held a trump card. Since May 1646, the king had been a prisoner in the keeping of the Scots army at Newcastle. Parliament had sent him proposals for a possible peace treaty, which included terms for his restoration to the throne, but he had refused to consider them unless he was allowed to come to London to discuss matters in person. This was unacceptable to MPs, who were also anxious to see the Scots army back in its own country. The Scots were equally eager to leave the north of England and had become disenchanted with the slipperiness of the king. At first hoping that he would support Presbyterianism, they had come to realise that his real intention was to use them in driving a wedge between them, the army and Parliament. In January 1647, they accepted a sum of £400,000 as recompense for their part in the war and King Charles was handed over to a group of English commissioners sent to escort him south.

By 16 February he had been installed under guard at Holdenby House in Northamptonshire. Recognising the leverage that possession of the king's person would give them, some of the more radical members of the New Model Army, including Oliver Cromwell, decided to remove him from Holdenby. On 3 June 1647, he was taken to Newmarket, where he was met by Cromwell and Fairfax. He was persuaded to write to both Houses, instructing them to accept the terms presented earlier by the army. Parliament ignored his letter and continued with its plans for disbandment.

In London a group opposed to the army was plotting ways in which it could regain control of the king. On 26 July, it organised a mob of apprentices and disbanded soldiers to riot in the streets and invade Parliament. The Speaker of the Commons was ordered by them to put to the House a vote to invite the king to return to the capitol to agree a treaty. Under a barrage of threats, the MPs had no other choice.[2]

Charles was probably encouraged by news of these disturbances and by the tidings that the Scots were now sympathetic to the idea of his restoration, but the New Model Army did not hesitate to impose its authority. On 6 August, General Fairfax led a 14,000 strong force through the streets of London, occupying the city. Opponents were arrested, or fled. The king was moved to Hampton Court Palace, still under guard, where he was to reside until it was decided what to do with him.

There were ever louder demands for his trial on charges of shedding the blood of his subjects. Both Oliver Cromwell and Charles himself received warnings of assassination plots against him. He knew that a Royalist group were close to signing a secret treaty with the Scots to restore him to power. To avoid any possibility of murder, he fixed upon a plan of escape. On 11 November 1647, in the winter darkness, he crept from his apartments and fled through Hampshire to the Isle of Wight with a small group of supporters. There, he approached the governor of the island, Colonel Robert Hammond, hoping for a sympathetic response and, possibly, help to escape to France. Instead, Hammond advised the king's companions that it would be wiser for Charles to give himself up, rather than risk capture by others who might do him harm. Hammond, if not the king, realised that by breaking his given word not to escape, he had placed himself in even graver peril.

The king was imprisoned in Carisbrooke Castle where his own servants were replaced by men chosen by Parliament. He was now negotiating not only with Parliament, but with the Scots, with whom he signed a secret treaty allowing a Scottish invasion of England with the proviso that he would in turn establish Presbyterianism across his realm. He was encouraged in his manoeuvrings by news of ant-Parliamentarian riots in Canterbury, Oxford, Norwich and Ipswich.

There was an unsuccessful attempt to spring him from prison on 29 December and in March 1648, he made his own, failed, effort to escape. In November he was removed to Hurst Castle on the mainland and within a month he was locked up at Windsor. It was the beginning of the path to the scaffold, for the radicals in both Parliament and the army were determined to bring him to trial.

A Rising in Glamorgan

Rumours abounded that the king and the New Model Army were seeking the overthrow of the Presbyterians and these tales encouraged a group of Glamorgan Royalists to stir up a rebellion. Its leaders included names already familiar to us; John Stradling, the son of Sir Edward Stradling of

St Donats, who had fought under the royal banner at Edgehill and been captured; Sir Charles Kemeys of Cefn Mably, who had been involved in the Carne rebellion the previous year; and Sir Richard Bassett who, at the request of the Peaceable Army, had been appointed governor of Cardiff by King Charles in place of the widely disliked Tyrell. Arrayed with them were Sir Thomas Knott and Sir Edward Thomas, both leading members of the local gentry.

The rebels announced their support for the king and sent warrants to the constables of the hundreds of Glamorgan, calling on them to assemble with armed men at Cowbridge where the county armoury was sited. On Sunday, 15 June, a force of 1,000 foot and 300 horse had gathered and its leaders issued a proclamation known as 'The Heads of the Present Grievances'. It accused the members of the Committee for South Wales of continuing to demand contributions, ostensibly for the upkeep of armed forces, but which actually went into committee members' pockets; of accepting bribes; and of imprisoning anyone who opposed them.

On 17 June, they marched towards Cardiff, pausing at Llandaff. Messages were sent to the governor of Cardiff, Colonel Pritchard, demanding the surrender of the castle. Another letter was dispatched to Rowland Laugharne, then at Carmarthen, assuring him that they were for the king and offering him a monthly amount of £1,300 to pay his men. Laugharne imprisoned the messenger and set off for Cardiff.

Colonel Pritchard likewise refused their demands and sent for help to Monmouthshire, where the local committee convened a meeting at Usk to discuss ways of meeting the new threat. Colonel Birch was summoned with his men from Hereford and Robert Kyrle was instructed to defend Monmouth against possible trouble there.

By 21 June it was all over. The rebels had drawn up on St Lythans Down, near Cardiff, but the sight of Laugharne's approaching army caused panic. Men fled in all directions and the leaders had galloped off, some to Brecon, others further afield. The County Committee for Monmouthshire ordered all Papists and delinquents to be disarmed or arrested, their houses searched and castles and magazines to be secured. The area was now temporarily at peace, though some of the rebels would soon cause more trouble.[3]

Complaints about the level of taxation and the cost of maintaining local garrisons did not abate. At the beginning of March, the Commons issued instructions for the disbandment of the garrisons at Monmouth and

Abergavenny and the levelling of fortifications. On 30 March, Captain Kyrle arrived at Monmouth and, with the help of soldiers and townspeople, began the demolition work. The task took until December and was not sweetened by the £100 demanded from the town for paying off the soldiers.

The occasional quartering in the area of soldiers in transit between Wales and England also caused resentment. In October and November of 1647, troops of mounted men were billeted on households in and around Monmouth and it must have been a welcome sight when, on 27 December, the garrison of Monmouth marched away for the last time.[4]

North Wales

The situation was much the same in North Wales. Archbishop Williams, in his new guise as a Parliamentary supporter, was still concerned about the unruly behaviour of the troops based in Caernarfonshire. He wrote to Parliament suggesting a swift disbandment of troops who had no useful function to perform, and a reduction in the number of men in certain garrisons. In January 1648 Fairfax, by now Lord General of the New Model Army, gave orders for disbandment of forces in North Wales. Garrisons were to be maintained at Conwy, Beaumaris, Caernarfon, Denbigh and Red Castle (Powys Castle). At the last three locations, a marshal, a gunner and two assistant gunners known as matrosses were to be on duty. The marshals were to be paid 10d a day, the gunners 1s 4d and the matrosses 4d each a day. In Caernarfon, fifty men were to be stationed in the castle, with only forty at Conwy.[5]

The unfortunate men at Conwy soon became the target of local resentment. When they emerged from the castle to assist the constables responsible for collecting the contributions for the maintenance of the garrison, they found themselves manhandled by the country people and imprisoned, their weapons taken from them. It took some persuasion for them to be released.

Problems in Pembrokeshire

In the summer of 1647, John Poyer, the governor of Pembroke, found himself enmeshed in a net of his own making. A self-made man, before the war he was a merchant dealing in wool, coin, skins, butter and tallow. His family background is something of a mystery, though there are Poyers recorded as bailiffs to the mayor of Pembroke in 1604, 1616 and 1617. John Poyer is recorded as a bailiff in 1633, and in the same year was appointed as commander of the trained bands in Pembroke.[6] He served as the town's mayor in 1641.

A supporter of Parliament from the outbreak of hostilities, Poyer had seized the castle and repaired the defences at his own cost. Parliament seems to have accepted him as governor of Pembroke quite early on in the war, but he soon found himself at odds with some of the local gentry families, particularly the Lorts of Stackpole and the Elliotts of Earwere. Perhaps they resented a man of humble origins holding so much responsibility, but Poyer's own character may have played a part in the quarrels that marred their relationships. Confident, assertive and perhaps more aggressive in his convictions than was necessary, it is not surprising that he was twice called up to London to account for his activities. Amongst the charges laid against him were accusation of embezzlement, the most serious relating to Picton Castle. The lease to Picton was held by Sir Richard Philipps, but Poyer was said to be guilty of using for his own purposes the stock and profits of the demesne lands of the castle to the value of £300, and that he had despoiled the timber from the estate.

The two visits to London, in April and December of 1645, resulted in a long drawn out investigation, the second detaining Poyer in London until 1647, but eventually it seems he was cleared of all charges. He was back in Pembroke by June 1647, though there is some confusion about the conditions under which he left London. John Elliott accused Poyer of running off to Pembrokeshire after being served with a warrant by the Committee of Accounts. The warrant stated that more than £6,000 remained unaccounted for by Poyer and demanded an explanation. If the accusation is true, is difficult to understand why the Committee did not issue a summons for his immediate arrest, or why he was allowed to resume the governorship of Pembroke, which he did as soon as he was home.

Poyer quickly resumed his feud with the Lorts and Elliotts. Accusations continued to pile up against him, including one from an anonymous writer that Poyer had imprisoned Roger, Sampson and John Lort in an attempt to extort money from them. They had apparently been left in an open space of ground for forty-eight hours, with no straw to lie on and had been denied bread and water. Poyer claimed that he had acted in self-defence, as the Lorts had attacked him on the highway and had even attempted to assassinate him during a church service.

How true all this was is uncertain, but in September Poyer received a direct order from his military superior, Sir Thomas Fairfax, instructing him to release the three men. He ignored it and it was only when Poyer was summoned to Haverfordwest by the Assize judges and kept in custody that the Lorts achieved their freedom.

Things went from bad to worse when, in December 1647 or early January 1648, Colonel Fleming, an officer of the New Model Army, arrived in Pembroke. He had been appointed by Fairfax to replace Poyer as governor of Pembroke. Poyer refused to cooperate and banned Fleming from the castle. It is hard to understand his intransigence, unless he feared further investigations into his conduct and Rowland Laugharne, who might have advised a more moderate course of action, was absent at Windsor.

Laugharne was also finding that his own position was being undermined. On 8 April 1647, a vote was taken in Parliament, which decided that only a hundred horse and the same number of dragoons should be kept in South Wales for the safety of the area. These were to be under Laugharne's command, but when the motion was put to the vote in the House, fifty-five members were for it, but fifty-three were against. The closeness of the result clearly forced a re-think and it was further resolved that command of the dragoons was to be vested in Colonel Okey, a well-regarded New Model Army officer. Laugharne's reactions to what was effectively a demotion are unknown, but he may have realised that Parliament now intended to give all posts of command to professional soldiers rather than provincial leaders.[7]

Laugharne was at this moment still at Windsor, but he was soon summoned to London to face the Derby House Committee. This had been created in 1646 to draw up proposals for the reorganisation of the army. On 25 January 1648, Parliament issued an order that 'Major General Langhorne (sic) be desired to pass his word that he will not go out of the town without leave of this Committee, there being divers things under examination of great concernment wherein he is named. Accordingly, he passed his word and saith his lodging is the Spread Eagle in the Strand.'[8]

There were clearly concerns that Laugharne might be closely involved in a recently uncovered Royalist plot to seize Gloucester and restore the king to power. Some eighty officers were said to be involved, one of whom was supposedly Laugharne himself.

On 25 December 1647, Fairfax had written to seven of his commanders, ordering them to dismiss as speedily as possible all soldiers and officers under their command who had been in service since the previous March. Two months pay in cash was to be made to members of disbanded units, with bonds for the remainder of their arrears. Any soldier who had joined the army after 6 August that year was to receive bonds only. An indemnity against all actions perpetrated during the war was granted to all soldiers. Any outstanding claims were to be submitted to the Commissioners for Monthly Assessments in each county, The Commissioners for Pembroke happened to include the now freed Lort brothers Roger and Sampson, and John Elliot, the mortal enemies of Poyer. It was Elliot who wrote to the Derby House Committee, informing it that Poyer had refused to hand over Pembroke Castle to the authority of Parliament.

Tidings of the stand-off between Poyer and Fleming had spread swiftly across Wales and England and led to further reports that Poyer had arrested influential men in Pembroke, hoping to extort money from them, and that he was stockpiling food and other provisions in the castle. All cattle in the locality had been gathered in and were corralled near the town.

Fairfax, upon receiving news of Poyer's actions, immediately instructed Sir William Constable, commander of the Gloucester garrison, to send 200 foot to Pembroke to reinforce Fleming's troop. The Commons wrote directly to Poyer, reminding him of Fairfax's orders transferring the castle to the authority of Parliament. When the letter arrived in Pembroke, Poyer refused to receive it. It was eventually handed to him by Fleming, who was allowed to meet Poyer in person, under a safe conduct. Poyer accepted the letter, but explained that he was unable to answer it before 10.00am the next morning, due to 'illiterateness.' Fleming went back to his headquarters to await a reply, but it was not until 22 February that he received one.

In his letter to Fleming, Poyer promised that his garrison would willingly march out if their demands for arrears of pay were met. The money offered to Poyer for his arrears he regarded as insufficient and, though he desired no man's possessions, he knew his own life was 'thirsted after by men of bloude'. In fact, some arrears of pay had already been guaranteed by Parliament, so it is more likely that Poyer was stalling, in order to avoid an enquiry into his actions. It was already being rumoured that he was in touch with Royalist agents.

The wider effects of Poyer's stand became apparent in March, when a large crowd of disbanded troops gathered in Glamorgan, together with known malcontents, some of whom wished to make contact with the Pembroke garrison. This was opposed by Laugharne's officers, who instead addressed a petition to Sir Thomas Fairfax. This document was written 'for the clearing of ourselves and the rest of the Commanders, Officers and soldiers under the command of Major-General Laugharne, from such false reports and scandals as are raised upon us; and for the satisfying of the public, we have thought fit to declare that our intentions are really to submit and yield obedience to the Ordinance of Parliament... .'[9]

They also declared themselves to be entirely innocent of the actions of John Poyer and emphasised their willingness to disband on the conditions laid down by Parliament. They accused John Elliot of defrauding the army of provisions and begged that he should not be given custody of the arms gathered in from disbanded troops.

No action seems to have been taken by Parliament in response to this petition, which was passed on to the Commons by Fairfax. Fleming now wrote to the Speaker, advising him that Poyer was still frantically victualling the castle and warning that another troop of musketeers was urgently needed in Pembroke, because in the present confusion, Milford Haven lay open to invasion by foreign forces.

Parliament swiftly issued another ordinance that Poyer should surrender the castle within twelve hours after receiving the latest notification, together with all arms and ammunition, or be declared a traitor and a rebel. Troops were put on standby and shipping in Milford Haven and the River Severn were ordered to deliver guns, ammunition and men to Fleming to ensure the capture of Pembroke.

At the beginning of March, the 200 musketeers ordered from Gloucester arrived in Pembroke. Fleming was now able to occupy the town, though the gates of the castle remained closed. The ordinance issued by Parliament was conveyed to Poyer by a drummer with a twelve-hour deadline to return a reply. It arrived long after the deadline expired.

> 'Sir,
> The order and letter I read before your drum to the soldiers; they return this answer. That the officers and soldiers be paid part of their arrears according to the proportion of others, and sufficient security for the rest. Second. That £1,000 be paid unto me, which I have disbursed; and my arrears as other officers according to my place and time of service. This granted, we are ready to surrender the Castle and all that we have in our possession; if not we are resolved with the assistance of the Almighty to hold the Castle for King and Parliament, according to the Covenant by us taken... . Our trust is not in the arm of the flesh, but our hope standeth in the name of the Lord, and if bloud be spilt, judge ye who shall answer it at the dreadful day of judgment... . But what yourself and those mercenaries desires, that you have brought to murther us, and take the bread out of the mouths of our wives and children... . The Lord be judge between us whose heavenly protection I am assured of, knowing his cause to be just. I have not else to trouble you but rest.
>
> Your humble servant
John Poyer'[10]

Fleming made one last attempt at negotiation. He offered Poyer £200 in cash, with the promise that he and his men would be paid upon disbanding on the same terms as had been offered to all supernumeraries. Those gentlemen with whom Poyer had quarrelled would cease all actions at law against him, a clause that would have ensured freedom from further investigation. Poyer's answer came within a day or two. Without warning, his cannon opened fire on Fleming's headquarters, wounding at least fourteen men, though Royalist broadsheets claimed sixteen fatalities.

Within days, the garrison at Tenby abandoned the castle. During the absence of Rice Powell, the governor, they captured the commissioners who had been sent to the town to oversee the disbanding of troops and slipped away by boat, sailing round to Pembroke to join Poyer in the castle. It was reported that five troops of Laugharne's disbanded soldiers were marching from Lampeter to Pembroke. The companies of Captain Agborow and Captain Addis in Glamorgan were also promising to come to his aid.

Poyer now contacted the Glamorgan force, warning them that he planned a surprise raid on Fleming's men and asking them to attack the Parliamentary force from the rear. When the action took place on 23 March, Fleming's men were completely taken by surprise. There were many casualties, whilst those who fled were pursued far out into the countryside. Fleming himself managed to escape from Pembroke and took refuge in a nearby country house.

Parliament had already ordered more troops to Pembrokeshire. On 28 March, 350 men of Colonel Overton's regiment came ashore at Pwllcrochan, about four miles west of Pembroke. They occupied the church of St Mary, but the next day found themselves surrounded by a hundred foot and two companies of horse hastily assembled by Poyer. A fierce firefight followed, but eventually Overton's men had no option but to capitulate. They were allowed to sail away with their weapons on condition that they did not return to Pembrokeshire. Amongst them was Colonel Fleming, who had managed to reach the church from his hiding place.

An ominous lull now followed. Tensions in the Pembroke garrison must have been high, because it was obvious that retaliation would not be long in coming. Poyer and his associates drew up a declaration which justified their actions, which was published on 10 April. Amongst its ringing phrases was an assurance that '…wee do still continue to our first principles, to bring the King to a personal treaty with his Parliament with Honour, Freedome, and Safety so that the just Privileges of Parliament, Lawes of the Land and Liberties of the People may be established in their proper bounds.

That wee will as much as in us lyes protect the people from injury and maintaine the Protestant religion, and the Common Prayer as it is established by Law in this Land, and therefore crave the assistance of the whole Kingdom therein.'[11] The declaration had already been sent to the Prince of Wales in France, asking him to confirm Poyer and Powell in their present positions. The prince replied with an assurance of help and confirmed the appointment of Poyer as governor of Pembroke.[12]

All roads now converged on Pembroke. So many discontented Royalists were heading westwards that the number of men making up the garrison was soon reckoned to be 2,000 at least. Parliamentary troops were on the move, too. Fairfax had ordered soldiers from the garrisons of Brecon and Cardiff to rendezvous at Neath. The Derby House Committee sent instruction to Captain Crowther, Vice-Admiral of the Irish Sea, to take his ships to Tenby as soon as favourable winds allowed. A Captain Jordan set sail from Bristol to Milford Haven, the holds of his vessel stuffed with round shot, powder and bullets.

On 15 April a skirmish took place at Llanelli, where a detachment of Rice Powell's men was surprised by a troop led by Colonel Fleming, now back in action for Parliament. The combined force from Brecon and Cardiff, under the command of Colonel Horton, found its route into Pembrokeshire blocked at Carmarthen by a much larger group made up of English, Scottish and Welsh troops, reinforced by 'diverse porters, butchers and rascally fellows come from London.' Horton swung eastwards but was again brought to a halt at Pont-ar-gothi, a few miles from Carmarthen where, on the far bank of the River Towy, Powell had positioned a numerically superior force. After a two-day standoff, Horton was informed by some local sympathisers of a ford across the river and was able to advance on Carmarthen from the east and north.

Powell retreated with his men to the top of a nearby hill. Horton sent Colonel Fleming to take control of a pass some seven miles off, but their advance was challenged by the enemy, who were driven back by fierce volleys of musketry. Fleming was eager to follow up this advantage, but to his horror blundered into a block of Powell's troops that had been held in reserve. Within minutes, Fleming was in retreat, some of his men abandoning their horses and fleeing on foot.

Fleming and 119 of his men took refuge in a nearby church. There is no clear evidence as to which church this was, but Llandeilo Fawr or Llangathen have both been suggested as the site of what now became a scene of bloodshed. About one hundred of Fleming's soldiers were granted quarter, but Fleming himself was found dead clutching a pistol. It has never been established if he was killed in the storming of the church or whether he committed suicide to avoid being taken by the enemy. Horton fell back on Brecon, where he could re-supply his soldiers.

On 30 April the London broadsheets reported that Rowland Laugharne was back in Pembrokeshire. He had either been released by the Derby House Committee or had broken his parole. He had obviously changed his allegiances, because in a letter dated 19 April, the Prince of Wales promised Laugharne that his loyalty would be rewarded. He granted

Laugharne the power to issue general pardons in the king's name and gave an assurance that arms and money would be sent to him.

Exactly what prompted this about-turn has never been established. The rise to prominence in Westminster of the radicals, with talk of the execution of the king and the creation of a republic, had encouraged many middle-of-the-road Parliamentarians to reassess their ideas of what they had fought for. Perhaps Laugharne was amongst their number. Whatever his reasons, on 30 April, he left Haverfordwest and a day or two later joined Rice Powell on his advance into Glamorganshire.

The Battle of St Fagans

After his defeat of Fleming, Rice Powell had moved south to seize Swansea and Neath and was intent on capturing Cardiff. To counter this, Horton left Brecon and, in a series of forced marches in drenching rain, had reached St Fagans, a few miles to the west of Cardiff. He set up guard posts at the crossings of the Taff and Ely rivers, hoping to block Powell's approach from Neath. He did not realise at first that Laugharne and Powell were actually only a few miles away and over the next two days the scouting parties of both armies exchanged shots in the fields and lanes of the surrounding countryside.

On 4 May, Laugharne wrote a stiff note to Horton:

'Sir,

I desire you would let me know by what power you first came and still remain in these counties of my association, I being commissioned Commander-in-Chief of these parts by an Ordinance of Parliament...and upon what grounds the injury of seizing on some of my troops was offered...I should gladly be satisfied in these particulars, otherwise your perseverance in these affronts to myself and the soldiery, and the country, will not be without difficulty. Sir, if you please to withdraw your forces out of this country, it may be a special means to prevent several inconveniences, besides the necessary resolutions which otherwise must be forced upon, Sir,

Your servant
Row. Laugharne.'[12]

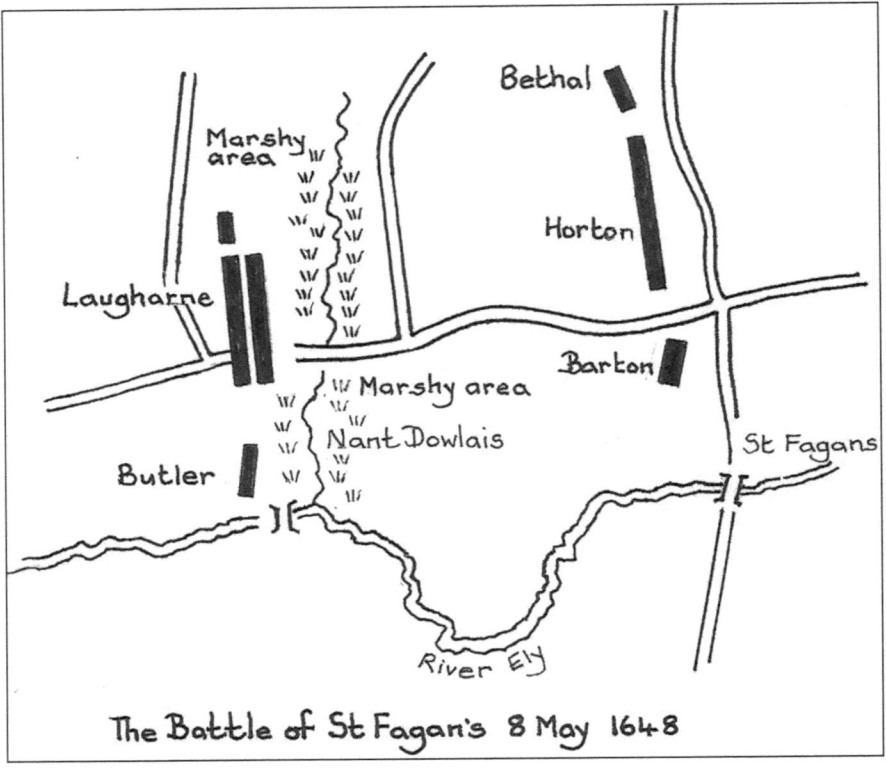

The Battle of St Fagan's 8 May 1648

A map of the Battle of St Fagans

On the following day, Horton returned an equally stiff reply, reminding Laugharne that it was Lord Fairfax, by Ordinance of Parliament, who decided what official posts were held in the army. He also recounted all the steps by which Poyer and Powell had encouraged rebellion and finished by adding that '...considering the former trust the Parliament reposed in you and your late obligations to them, I would rather have believed you came with an intention to join with us for the suppressing of that tumultuous assembly with you, than to appear amongst and own those who have manifestly violated the authority of Parliament, which you seem to maintain and insist upon in your letter to me.'[13]

There was little left now but to prepare for battle. Laugharne's army numbered about 8,000 men, of whom 2,500 were musketeers. About 1,000 were pikemen with some 4,000 clubmen carrying a variety of weapons.[14] Amongst the officers were Rice Powell, Major-General Stradling, who had commanded the defeated Royalist army at Colby

Moor and Laugharne's brother Thomas. John Poyer was probably not present, as several sources stated that he had remained at Pembroke.

Horton had mustered a force of about 1,200 horse, 1,400 foot and 700 dragoons. All were experienced, well equipped veterans of previous battles. His officers included other hardened campaigners such as Colonel John Okey and Major Nathaniel Barton. Nevertheless, he knew he was in a vulnerable position. Not only was he facing a numerically superior force, many of whom knew the lie of the land, he was also aware that Chepstow Castle, with its arsenal of thirty cannon and 20 barrels of gunpowder, had been seized by Sir Nicholas Kemeys at the head of 140 adherents. There was now an enemy stronghold to his rear. There must have been cold comfort in the knowledge that Oliver Cromwell had left Windsor on 3 May at the head of several thousand soldiers and was making a forced march towards Wales. He would not arrive in time to assist Horton.

The news of Cromwell's advance may have been the final factor that decided Laugharne to make his next move. During the night of 7–8 May, he moved his army forward, closer to Horton's position, crossing the River Ely and approaching St Fagans from the west. Horton may have been caught by surprise because, as he noted in his letter of 13 May to the Speaker of the Commons, his scouts discovered the enemy when they were within a mile and a half of the Parliamentary camp. Horton described how '…we drew out and took best ground we could. Major Bethel commanded the horse on the right wing, Major Barton on the left, and Colonel Okey and his Major with the Dragoons on both wings with the horse.'[15]

Laugharne sent forth his Forlorn Hope, a body consisting of infantry and dragoons, widely used in warfare to advance ahead of the main army and seek out weak spots in an opponent's front line. Horton advanced his own Forlorn Hope, a group of 30 horse and 20 dragoons, which 'charged and routed them, doing good execution, which gave us the advantage of a new ground; so we advanced with horse and foot upon them… .'[16] The men of both armies found themselves hampered by ground still waterlogged after days of rain and by hedgerows which were fiercely disputed by their foes. Running down the middle of the battlefield were the waters of the Nant Dowlais, a narrow stream bordered on both sides by marshy ground. It may have been somewhere along this watercourse that Horton's troops came to a bridge where the majority of Laugharne's troops were placed.

Horton's men were held up here, under continuous fire, waiting for the foot to join them. When it did, 'the first division of foot...fell close up to the enemy's front; Major Wade with the second division got over the little brook on the left flank of the enemy; Major Barton, likewise, with the left wing of the horse, with much celerity passed over a boggy place and the little brook to second those foot; and some of the enemy's horse coming on to charge the foot, were gallantly resisted and beaten back by Captain Hughes. By this time the horse and dragoons on the right wing were gotten over also, the enemy's foot standing very stoutly to it, until out horse began to surround them, and then they presently all ran, and we cleared the field, out horse and dragoons pursuing them for eight or ten miles.'[17]

About 200 of Laugharne's men had been killed in the fighting, including his brother Thomas. More than 3,000 were taken prisoner, a large number of them being imprisoned temporarily in Llandaff Cathedral a few miles away. Most were released after swearing an oath not to take up arms against Parliament, though some 240 unmarried men were shipped off to help in the colonisation of Barbados.[18] Of the captured officers, Major-General Stradling was imprisoned in Windsor Castle, where he later died.

Rowland Laugharne and Rice Powell had both escaped from the battlefield and were fleeing westwards towards Pembrokeshire. As they passed through Carmarthen, they withdrew some guns from the castle. They may at some point have agreed to split up, as Laugharne headed towards Pembroke and Powell to Tenby, anxious now to prepare for the military actions that were bound to follow.

Cromwell at Monmouth and Chepstow

Cromwell had reached Gloucester by 9 May, where he was informed of Horton's victory at St Fagans. Within a day or two he was at Monmouth, where two Parliamentary soldiers awaited him, hoping to secure his help in restoring order in their native county of Somerset. There was overwhelming evidence that revolt was spreading across Wales and England, with disturbances in North Wales, Herefordshire, Shropshire and Worcestershire.[19]

On 11 May, Cromwell's army approached Chepstow, finding that the town walls were lined with musketeers. An attack was launched on the town gate, which was taken after a vicious exchange of fire. The town was occupied in a short time, but the majority of the garrison fell back upon the castle. Cromwell sent a summons to surrender, but pot-shots were taken at the drummer carrying it, and a firefight broke out. During the night, in heavy rain, an attempt was made to storm the gatehouse, but was driven off. One of Cromwell's officers, Major Grigson, was killed when a heavy stone was dropped on his head from the battlements.

Cromwell was soon on the march westwards, eager to deal with Pembroke and Tenby. He left the siege of Chepstow to Colonel Ewer, who sent to Gloucester for two heavy guns. Two more were brought ashore from a ship and all were placed facing the south wall of the castle. The fire from these cannon shattered the battlements of the castle, whilst mortars lobbed shells into the interior. One fell into the governor's chamber, which forced a hasty retreat to accommodation at the other end of the building. By the end of the first morning's bombardment, a section of the curtain wall had been brought down.

There was an attempt by some of the garrison to submit, men calling out from the battlements that they were willing to surrender. A few of them appear to have sneaked out of the castle but Ewer, determined to achieve a complete capitulation, ordered them to be fired upon.[20] The governor of the castle sought to speak with Ewer at the drawbridge but his request was initially turned down, as he had previously ignored the summons to surrender. Ewer changed his mind after being persuaded to do so by some local gentlemen. A parley took place at the drawbridge. The governor asked for an assurance that the garrison could march out unharmed, but Ewer demanded that they yield at mercy. Negotiations came to an abrupt end when some of the garrison scrambled over the ruined curtain wall and surrendered. Ewer's troops entered the castle at the same spot, bringing the siege to an end.

The abject surrender of Kemeys' men may have been prompted by the realisation that a carefully prepared means of escape had vanished. A boat had been moored on the river in a small cove below the castle. It was spotted by a Parliamentary soldier, who swam across the river with a knife clenched between his teeth. He sliced through the mooring rope and, gripping the rope in his teeth, swam back to the far bank.

Nicholas Kemeys was shot out of hand by the victors, the site of his death marked today by a plaque. The captured soldiers were locked up in the church. Amongst the booty taken at the castle was a cache of letters which implicated Sir Trevor Williams and others in Kemeys' plot to take the castle. As soon as he learned of this, Cromwell ordered the immediate arrest of Williams, who he regarded as one of the most dangerous malignants in Wales. Incredibly, despite detention, Williams survived well into the reign of Charles II, when he was still causing trouble.

There was one last spasm of Royalist resistance. In August 1648, the Herefordshire gentleman Sir Henry Lingen stirred up a brief rebellion. Monmouthshire and its neighbouring counties were ordered to call out whatever troops they could muster, but the rising collapsed almost before it could have any real effect. The authorities remained nervous however and, in the wake of events at Pembroke, decided to impose more war taxes towards the cost of subduing the troubles. Monmouth was to pay an extra £192 9s and a year later was fined £3,000 for its delinquency.[21]

The Sieges of Tenby and Pembroke

Colonel Horton had hurried on ahead of Cromwell, his advance guard reaching Tenby on 14 May. An attempt to storm the walls was driven back and no further effort was made until the arrival of Horton with the main force a few days later. There were now at Horton's command some 1,230 of Colonel Overton's regiment, with two additional companies of Colonel William Constable's men from Gloucester. Offshore, two warships, the *Bonaventure* and the *Expedition*, were ready to bombard the town.

On 23 May, Cromwell marched into the camp of the leaguer before Tenby. He stayed only a day before moving on to Pembroke, but he was confident in Horton's ability to bring about a surrender. Horton ordered a sortie to be made against a 'certain work' in the suburbs, which was taken with the capture of up to thirty of the defenders. Powell sent out an appeal for surrender on terms. Horton refused to consider it, 'knowing the serpentine malevolency of their natures, especially of that proud and insolent Colonel Powell, that shameful apostate who indeed deserves no mercy at all, but that he should be cast into that current of the floodgate of Justice, and be made exemplary to Posterity and to all perfidious villains. This nest of vermin did not desist from creeping and crawling until they were not able to subsist no longer and then they were forced to strike sayle and submit to mercy and out pleasures.'[22]

A bombardment of the walls tore a breach in the ancient stonework, after which terms were offered to Powell on the understanding that if they were not accepted, the defenders could expect no mercy. There was immediate agreement, the acceptance perhaps urged on by Tenby's inhabitants.

Rice Powell and thirty-five of his officers were taken into custody. The common soldiers were allowed to return to their homes, having sworn the usual oath never again to fight against Parliament. A few days later, Powell was taken up to Carmarthen, where he was imprisoned. He seems to have been popular with some of the townsfolk, because the bailiff's account shows that upon leaving Tenby, he was given a bottle of sack and a bottle of white wine to the value of four shillings.

Pembroke would prove a harder nut to crack. Situated on a limestone ridge with tidal inlets protecting it on three sides, it was further defended by stout walls pierced by three main gates. The mighty castle stood at the extreme west end of the town, topping formidable rocky cliffs. Several small suburbs stood outside the walls, the largest of which, Monkton, was located opposite the castle on the other side of the south-western creek.

Cromwell set up his camp, which became known as the Camp of the Leaguer, on St Daniel's Hill, a rising crest of ground to the south of the town. Here were encamped most of the 6,000 men at his disposal, though some formed subsidiary camps at Monkton and at The Green, to the north of the town. Another 2,000 soldiers were stationed at Tenby, Haverfordwest, Carmarthen and Cardiff as a precaution against further risings and to keep open routes of communication.

Crammed into the town were some 2,000 Royalists, in addition to the townspeople. The castle must have been crowded with men, whilst others were perhaps housed in the two churches or billeted in private houses. Almost from the beginning of the siege, there were quarrels amongst the defenders. Poyer and Laugharne are said to have fallen out, though the reason is unknown. What is clear is that Poyer was distancing himself from Laugharne, later claiming that he had not been party to Laugharne's rebellion.

Cromwell suffered a setback at the beginning of the siege, when the heavy guns he had ordered from Gloucester were lost in a shipwreck in the River Severn. Some smaller guns, described as two drakes, two culverins and two demi-culverins were obtained from the guardship *Lyon*. Two of these were placed in the churchyard at Monkton, whilst

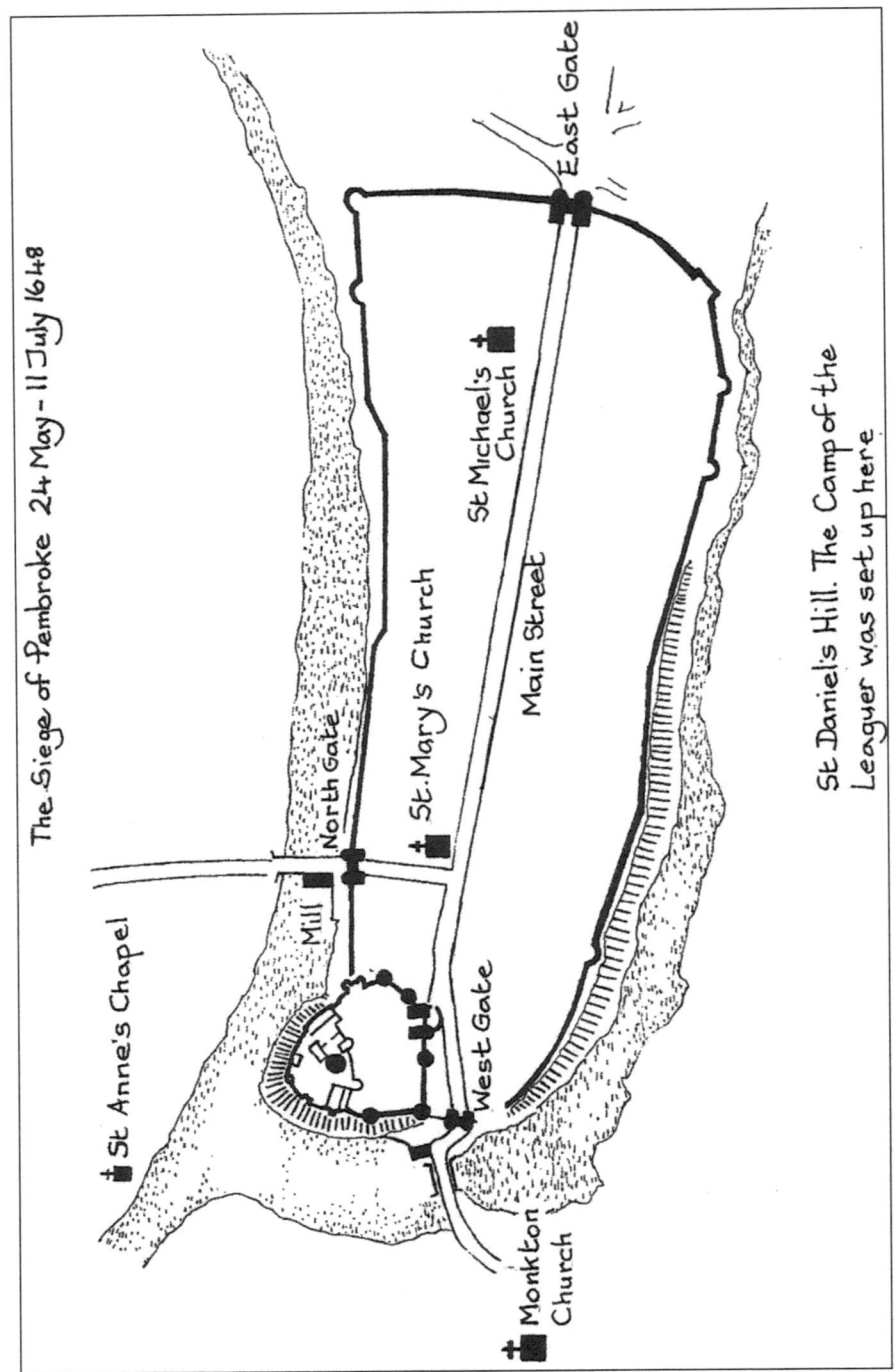

The Siege of Pembroke 24 May – 11 July 1648

St Anne's Chapel

Mill

North Gate

St. Mary's Church

West Gate

Monkton Church

St Michael's Church

East Gate

Main Street

St Daniel's Hill. The Camp of the Leaguer was set up here

A map of the Siege of Pembroke

others were sited on Golden Hill, overlooking the town from the north. It was these latter guns which, on about 13 June, battered the houses in Main Street, Pembroke's principal thoroughfare, setting many ablaze.

At least two attempts were made to storm the town. On 4 June, in the early hours of the morning, a party of Parliamentary soldiers carrying scaling ladders drew close under the walls near the eastern end of the town. When the ladders were put in place, they were found to be too short. The sentries on the battlements realised what was happening and opened fire, killing twenty-three of the attackers and wounding many more.

A far more serious attack took place not long after, when cannon fire had brought down a section of walling. Colonels Horton and Okey led a charge through the gap and fought their way up Main Street almost to the castle, before being driven out. Casualties were heavy on both sides.

There were also retaliatory strikes by the garrison. On one of these occasions, Laugharne himself led a raid out through one of the town gates towards the camp of the leaguer. He was driven back with the loss of nine dead and twenty captured. He must have recovered from the wound received at St Fagans, perhaps due to the tender ministrations of his wife Anne. She had not been present in Pembroke at the beginning of the siege, but her entry into the castle during hostilities illustrates a chivalrous side to Cromwell's character. He allowed her to pass through the siege lines to see her husband, bringing a doctor with her, and also restored to her some cattle taken from the family estates early in June.

As the siege dragged on, morale within the town began to ebb away. There were desertions, with men lowering themselves from the town walls during the night hours. Some were captured by Parliamentary patrols, and told tales of food shortages, mutinous behaviour, even that horses were being fed with thatch torn from the roofs of houses. Although Poyer is said to have ensured a good stock of provisions in the castle before the siege, the feeding of over 2,000 men and the townspeople must have quickly depleted the stores.

Cromwell was also experiencing difficulties in providing for his men. In a letter to Lord Fairfax written on 28 June, he described some of the problems he faced. 'The Country, since we sat down before this place, have made two or three insurrections; and are ready to do it every day; so that, – what with looking to them, and disposing out horse to that end, and to get us in provisions, without which we should starve, this country being so miserably exhausted and so poor, and we no money to buy victuals, – indeed, whatever may be thought, it's a mercy we have been able to keep our men together in the midst of such necessity, the sustenance of the foot being but bread and water.'[23]

Towards the end of June, some heavy siege guns and mortars finally arrived at Pembroke. These opened up a devastating fire against the town and gaps were soon knocked through the walls. It must have become obvious to both sides that Pembroke could not hold out for much longer and, with no hope of help coming from another quarter, Laugharne and Poyer decided to ask for terms.

Cromwell was initially inclined to demand an absolute surrender, with no conditions at all, but knew that this might lead to the siege lasting weeks if not months longer. He was under pressure from Parliament to end things as quickly as possible, because a Scots army had crossed the border and on 28 April had seized Berwick for the king. The Marquis of Hamilton was rumoured to be collecting extra arms and ammunition for the army and, after urgent appeals from the Commons, on 25 June Cromwell had dispatched some of his troops northwards to block a further invasion.

Nevertheless, the terms of surrender Cromwell offered were much stricter than either Laugharne or Poyer had anticipated. All the principal officers of the garrison were to surrender unconditionally to the mercy of Parliament. To accept, as everyone realised, might result in execution. A plea for easier terms was made but, apart from some minor alterations, the conditions remained the same. They were sent into the castle on 10 July, accompanied by the following letter:

'Sir

I have (together with my Council of War) renewed my propositions [and] I thought fit to send them to you with these alterations, which if submitted unto I shall make good. I have considered your condition, and my own duty; and (without threatening) must tell you that if (for the sake of some) this offer be refused, and thereby misery and ruin befall the poor soldiers and people with you, I know where to charge the blood you spill. I expect your answer within these two hours. In case this offer be refused, send no more to me about this subject.

I rest your servant, Ol. Cromwell'[24]

However dismayed Laugharne and Poyer may have been by the tone of Cromwell's letter, they knew there were few other options. As well as a responsibility towards their soldiers, they also owed a duty to the civilians of Pembroke, dozens of whom might perish if the town was taken by storm. Acceptance of the terms were agreed by a majority of the officers, though Poyer and Laugharne had to be persuaded to capitulate and their signatures do not appear on the final document. The main signatory for the garrison was Poyer's brother David.

On 11 July, commissioners arrived at the town gates to accept the final surrender of the castle and all the garrison's armaments. Poyer, Laugharne and their principal officers were taken into custody. Other officers were to leave for their homes, where they were expected to live quietly. All the ordinary soldiers were given passes to leave and were guaranteed safe conduct. The townspeople of Pembroke were not to be plundered and were to enjoy their liberties as they had previously done.

Five days later, Cromwell marched out of Pembroke, having given instructions for sections of the town walls to be demolished and for parts of the castle to be brought down with gunpowder. He headed north, ready to meet the Scottish invasion. He took with him Laugharne, Poyer and Powell, leaving them in custody at Nottingham as he passed through the town. They remained there until the autumn, when they were brought to London for trial.

All three were accused of high treason and tried by Court Martial. They were found guilty and sentenced to death but Parliament, perhaps swayed by memories of the sterling work carried out by the three during the first Civil War, and by the public campaign for clemency mounted by the men's families, decided on a show of leniency. Three pieces of paper were placed in a bag, two of which bore the message 'Life given by God', the third being blank. A small child drew the lots, handing one to each of the prisoners. Poyer received the blank piece and was shot by a firing squad at Covent Garden on Wednesday, 25 April 1649, three months after the execution of the king. He was reported to have died bravely and with every sign of penitence for past misdemeanours.

North Wales

As news of the rebellion in Pembrokeshire spread into North Wales, Sir John Owen of Clenennau gathered together a band of Royalist sympathisers. He was soon at the head of a band of about one hundred volunteers, many of them men who had been in positions of command during the first Civil War. This troop of die-hards rode into Caernarfonshire before retreating towards Dyffryn Ardudwy. They were pursued by a company of mounted Parliamentarians from Denbigh. At Llwyngwril, the horsemen came across a party of Owen's footsoldiers who, assuming that the riders were some of their own men, offered no resistance and were soon taken prisoner. One of the captives was a relative of the Earl of Carbery. By midnight, the Parliamentarians were herding their captives back towards Denbigh.

Sir John Owen was informed that the Parliamentarians were resting at Dolgellau and headed off from Ardudwy to intercept them. He was too late, so instead marched towards Caernarfon, hoping to surprise that town. Meanwhile, General Mytton was making every effort to nip in the bud this Royalist resurgence. He sent instructions to his commander in Denbigh, Colonel Twisleton, to send as large a force as possible to defend Caernarfon, following a route from Denbigh via the bridge at Llanrwst. Mytton also decided to challenge Owen's force himself and organised several raiding parties. One of these was led by William Lloyd, the High Sheriff of Caernarfon, assisted by Captain Thomas Madryn.

On Saturday, 3 June, Lloyd, at the head of twenty horse, suddenly found himself facing the advance guard of Owen's troop. A sharp, confused engagement followed and Lloyd, wounded seven times, was taken captive. General Mytton, following behind with sixty foot, was unable to prevent the enemy withdrawal and retired swiftly to Caernarfon, dispatching a message to Twisleton asking for urgent help. Unfortunately, Twisleton was busy reinforcing his Denbigh garrison with seventy soldiers summoned hastily from Chester, and this enlarged force now set off for Conwy, hoping to unite with men from the garrison there before moving on to Caernarfon.

Owen had been warned of Twisleton's approach and left Caernarfon to challenge him. The two sides met on 5 June on the flat plains bordering the eastern mouth of the Menai Straits, at a place known as Dalar Hir. The fight that followed, like the whole campaign leading up to it, was confused and disorderly. None of the men involved wore uniforms or any distinctive badges or sashes by which friend and foe could be identified. The Forlorn Hope of each force advanced towards one another and fought with courage, until Twisleton's men were forced back towards their reserves. A long hard-pressed encounter followed, but at last Owen's men broke and ran. In the resulting chaos, Owen was wounded and taken prisoner. About thirty of his soldiers were killed and another fifty-eight taken prisoner.

In the aftermath of the battle William Lloyd was discovered to be in a critical condition. He had been forced along on Owen's march to Caernarfon. His wounds had not been cleaned or tended and when he became too weak to sit on his horse, he was carried on some kind of bier, which offered no protection from the wind and rain. At one point, he was deliberately thrown off the bier, suffering further serious injuries. A plea from General Mytton for him to be brought into Caernarfon for his wounds to be dressed had been refused. The surgeon who examined the body stated that his injuries, had they been quickly attended to, would not have proved mortal. The circumstances of Lloyd's death and the shooting of three surrendered and helpless Parliamentary soldiers were regarded as unforgivable atrocities.

Sir John Owen was imprisoned in Denbigh Castle, but his presence there was still troublesome. One evening in July 1648, a group of determined Royalists crossed the Menai Straits from Anglesey and surprised a company of Roundhead troops near Aber. Forty were taken prisoner and the Royalists then moved on towards Caernarfon, capturing more men and horses on the way. This may have been part of a plot to distract the attention of the Denbigh garrison, and facilitate the escape of Sir John Owen.

At the end of June, a party of some sixty men scaled the walls of Denbigh Castle under cover of darkness and seized the inner ward. Two members of the garrison had apparently helped them, and were ready to open one of the sally ports to let in more men. The garrison was only saved because the captain of the guard, unable to sleep and troubled, 'though he knew not for what' walked about the battlements and spotted the invaders.[25] The alarm was sounded and they were driven out, but not before they had plundered what they could.

Within the month, Sir John Owen was removed to a stricter confinement in Windsor Castle. Even that did not deter his followers, because about 16 July, a group of them appeared before Denbigh Castle and defiantly fired their pistols before galloping away.

The attempted rescue of Sir John Owen was not the last action to take place in North Wales. Lord Byron, who had retreated into Lancashire and Cheshire after the fall of Chester, was encouraged by reports of the disturbed state of the six northern counties of Wales, particularly after the invasion into England of the Scots army. At some point in late June or early July he made his way secretly to Anglesey. On 14 July, probably at his instigation, the leading figures of the island published a manifesto declaring loyalty to the king. A party of them marched down to Llanrwst to seize the all-important bridge crossing the River Conwy. Here they were joined by more Royalist sympathisers, but when news came that Cromwell had shattered the Scots army at the battle of Preston, they withdrew to Anglesey.

The defence of the island was placed in the hands of Colonel Richard Bulkeley, the eldest son of Viscount Bulkeley. How experienced a soldier Bulkeley was is unclear, but it was probably felt that, as a familiar figure in the area, he would appeal more to the loyalties of the local people than an outsider. Lord Byron, who clearly considered that the command should have been offered to him, made an angry withdrawal to the Isle of Man.

Meanwhile, Thomas Mytton and Sir Thomas Myddelton rapidly pulled together a force of about 1,000 horse and foot and, from Ruthin, marched into the Conwy Valley via Llanrwst. As they moved towards Conwy, they continued to recruit more men, so that by the time they arrived within sight of the town walls they numbered hundreds more. This force was now divided, with 1,500 marching along the coast to Bangor and the rest travelling by sea.

At Bangor, there was a delay of four or five days, as further preparations were made. At dusk on 15 September, the whole force crossed the Menai Straits on a fleet of small boats, coming ashore near Cadnant. As they waded onto the beach, a Royalist major, Hugh Pennant appeared with his troops, but was driven away by heavy fire from Mytton's musketeers sheltering behind the hedgerows and rocky outcrops along the shoreline. With the opposition scattered, Mytton moved on towards Porthaethwy, a short distance away, where a detachment of Royalist foot had been stationed under the command of two officers. These also melted away, probably because Mytton was said to have bribed at least one of the officers to offer no resistance.

The main target of the Parliamentary advance was Beaumaris, where Mytton suspected the main body of the enemy was to be found. He moved his troops to a position just to the west of Beaumaris, where his left flank was situated near a row of still extant almshouses bearing the date 1613. Facing them were Bulkeley's men, spread across the road close to Gallows Point. At about 3.00pm in the afternoon of 1 October, Mytton gave the signal to advance.

From behind the hedges of the Harp Field, Bulkeley's musketeers let loose volleys of fire, which sent Mytton's foot reeling back. Elsewhere, it was the Royalist foot that lost heart and fled in disorder. Major Pennant charged forward with his mounted soldiers, causing some casualties amongst Mytton's troops. Bulkeley did the same with his men, but was driven back behind a set of barricades, where fierce fighting took place, during which the Reverend Price, Royalist vicar of Bettws Abergele, was mortally wounded. Some of the Parliamentary soldiers were killed or wounded by snipers placed on the roof and steeple of the nearby church. A Captain Lloyd of Penhwnllys had been instructed to guard the church, but he locked his men into it and ran away with the key.

However hard Bulkeley's men fought, they were soon driven back in confusion and disorder, many officers and soldiers taking refuge with the walls of Beaumaris Castle. One of their detachments, consisting of men from Talybolion and Llison, two of the most remote communities on Anglesey, were still on the way to the battlefield when they heard that the conflict was over, so turned about and went home.[26]

Mytton's forces occupied Beaumaris and a message demanding surrender was sent into the castle. Bulkeley and his associates were left in no doubt about what would happen should they refuse; all prisoners taken that day would be executed. Terms were straightaway accepted and Bulkeley was held prisoner upon payment of a ransom. The inhabitants of Anglesey agreed to pay a sum of £7,000 within two weeks, the money to be used to pay the wages of the officers and soldiers of Mytton's army.

The capture of Beaumaris was the last large military action of the Civil Wars in Wales. A peace of sorts had been achieved, but the country played no major part in the third Civil War, which broke out in 1651, when Charles II made an effort to regain the throne. Nevertheless, there could be no sense of tranquillity whilst there were minor insurrections and riots in various areas of Wales, all quickly suppressed as the increasingly militarist and Puritan government in London strengthened its grip across the country. The main concern of most people, however, was to rebuild their shattered lives and broken communities.

Chapter 8

After the War

The effects of the Civil Wars on Wales lasted well into the eighteenth century and were felt in a variety of ways. One of the most obvious and far-reaching was the economic aftermath. Formerly prosperous towns struggled to regain their prominence, the trades on which they had relied having withered away. So many herds of cattle and flocks of sheep had been appropriated by the warring armies that it took years for numbers to reach the pre-war levels. The lack of ready materials affected the trades on which so many people had relied for their livelihood. When John Taylor, the Water Poet, passed through Flint at the end of July 1652, he noted, 'surely war hath made it miserable, the sometimes famous castle there…is now almost buried in its own ruins, and the town is so spoiled…they have no sadler, taylor, weaver, brewer, baker, botcher or button maker; they have not so much as a signe of an ale-house.'

The story was the same at Harlech, which he reached on 6 August. The town had 'neither hay, grass, oats, or any relief for a horse: there stands a strong castle, but the town is all spoild, and almost [uninhabitable] by the late lamentable troubles.' Pembroke was no better, with 'some houses down, some standing, and many without inhabitants.'[1]

At Caernarfon, trade was much reduced because the quay and the shire hall were in a ruinous state. Tenby, which had enjoyed a thriving, pre-war maritime trade, was affected by such poverty that, when in 1649 Oliver Cromwell passed through on his way to Ireland, he donated £10 for the relief of the poor.

It was often the suburbs outside a town's walls that suffered most. The outlying areas of Chester had been burned down, the houses of Handbridge being destroyed, rebuilt, then destroyed again. The same story could be told at Caernarfon and Denbigh, a part of Bangor was deliberately destroyed by its defenders, whilst at Wrexham an accidental fire in 1643 reduced 143 houses to ashes. Oswestry suffered the loss of St Oswalds church, which stood outside the walls, as well as houses adjacent to it, all cleared to prevent enemy occupation.[2]

It was often the building of defences intended to protect a town that caused destruction. The raising of earthwork ramparts involved the loss of hedges, fields, gardens, orchards, cottages and anything else that stood in the way of a clear field of fire. Carmarthen suffered the ruination of valuable agricultural land just outside the town when its mud ramparts were built.

Even the strongest of defences could not prevent destruction of property within the walls of a town. At Pembroke, as we have seen, the houses of Main Street were deliberately targeted in the bombardment of June 1648. In Chester, dwellings had been brought down in many streets by the explosion of grenades, particularly close to the Eastgate.

Most towns showed an astonishing degree of resilience, beginning the task of rebuilding as soon as possible. Some of this reconstruction was spurred on by a committee of the House of Commons, set up in January 1648 to consider how buildings destroyed in the fighting might be repaired. It became known as the Committee for Burning and examined petitions for help from communities across England and Wales. Qualified assessors were sent to examine damage and recommended what could be done. During the Commonwealth, towns which had supported the king in the wars received no help, so presumably it must have been up to the citizens to find funds where they could.[3]

In 1648, a collection was organised for those whose homes had been destroyed in the fire at Wrexham five years before, and at Denbigh seven acres of land close to the castle were built over to provide much-needed housing. At Chester, a considerable amount of rebuilding was taking place by the mid-1650s, some of it on plots of land not used before the siege, but other built-up areas wrecked during the conflict were left empty. An apparent slump in Chester's economy, which may have affected the speed its recovery, was due to a recession and an outbreak of disease.

A number of castles were deliberately dismantled in the aftermath of the wars. At Pembroke, and Raglan, sections of the walls were demolished, rendering the ruins uninhabitable. Beaumaris was maintained as a garrison until the 1650s when it was slighted, a fate which also befell Conwy and Denbigh. Montgomery Castle, the home of Lord Edward Herbert of Cherbury, was inherited in 1648 by his son Richard, the second Baron Cherbury. As Richard had actively supported King Charles, he was fined by Parliament and ordered to destroy the castle. The demolition work was thorough, even the new mansion within the walls being erased. The sale of materials salvaged from the ruins helped to pay off Richard's fine.

With the loss of these strongholds, a considerable economic benefit to the communities around them was lost. Castles offered employment to maidservants, grooms, blacksmiths, masons, carpenters, stewards, porters, washerwomen, gardeners and a host of other occupations. Farmers, traders and merchants had a ready market for their goods, but demolition forced all these people to look elsewhere for their livelihoods.

Poverty even affected the once-prosperous members of the gentry and the merchant classes. Rowland Laugharne, once the owner of numerous tracts of land in Pembrokeshire, was encumbered with debts of £4,000 when he was finally released from imprisonment on 7 May 1649. He had lost an income of £1,000 a year, had been forced to sell off much of his land, and had been fined £712 for making war against Parliament. He spent much of the rest of his life trying to recoup his fortune, but when he died in 1676, he wife Anne was so much in debt that she had to move from house to house to avoid arrest. Sir John Owen of Clenennau was heavily fined by Parliament for his Royalism, but did not lose his beloved family home.

Owen was lucky. During the Commonwealth, many of the king's supporters had their lands sequestrated by Parliament. Both sides had taken the assets of their opponents during the war in order to finance their campaigns. The practice was continued during the 1650s and the money raised was used to fund the new regime. However, as early as 1645, Parliament allowed Royalists to regain their lost estates by paying a fine for delinquency of anything between a sixth and a half of the value of their lands. As time went by, fines varied according to the level of someone's delinquency and how long they had delayed in coming to terms with Parliament.[4] Fines were fixed by the Committee for Compounding, but the actual process of sequestration was carried out by local committees, who forwarded the balance of the proceeds to London. The system was open to fraud. The less honest members of the local committees soon learned how to operate things to their advantage. The profits of a sequestrated estate were paid to a committee until half the value had been collected. After that, it was no longer their concern, responsibility passing to the Committee for Compounding. It was therefore advantageous to allow sequestration hearings to drag on for as long as possible.

The system also encouraged people to denounce their neighbours. Clerks and lawyers were in a good position to know exactly how much their clients had in the way of land or other possessions. A quiet word to the local committee about undeclared lands often resulted in a payout for the informant.[5]

Catholics, because of their religion, could expect little consideration from the Committee for Compounding. It was almost automatic to regard them as malignant and a danger to the state. They could expect most of their estate to be sequestrated. A typical example was that of William Jones, owner of a small estate near Abergavenny, worth no more than £300 in cattle and other good. He was forced to flee his house in January 1646, when Rowland Laugharne's men came raiding. He eventually took refuge in Raglan Castle, but witnesses attested that he had left before the siege began. That did not protect him from accusations of being a Papist-in-Arms and most of his possessions were taken from him. He was eventually allowed to compound for £172 17s and his sequestration was discharged not long after.[6]

The more prominent the person, the more was likely to be taken from them. Sir Thomas Myddelton briefly lost Chirk Castle during the Commonwealth, after declaring support for Charles II, but it was restored to him following the Restoration. The Marquis of Worcester's estates were broken up after the fall of Raglan, some of the lands being offered to major figures on the Parliamentary side. Oliver Cromwell is said to have been enriched to the tune of £2,500, all of it raised from the Marquis's possessions.[7] Sir Thomas Eyton of Shropshire, apparently a prisoner at Conwy, compounded to the tune of £976, a large amount that must have left his pockets empty. Twelve of the most notable of the defenders of Denbigh Castle were fined for delinquency, paying amounts of between £28 and £172.[8]

Hardship must have been a common factor in many people's lives at this time. Certainly, the demands of the military continued to weigh heavily on communities across Wales, especially where garrisons were stationed. Towns and villages everywhere had taxes levied on them for the upkeep of troops and had to provide quarters for them, in addition to what other difficulties they might be experiencing. The plight of Tenby was such that in October 1648, a Captain Beale had received a written order from his superior officer; 'In regard to the poverty of Tinby, you are to march to Haverfordwest and to quarter your soldiers there until further notice.'[9]

This did not please the councillors of Haverfordwest. The town had already provided care for soldiers wounded in the siege of Pembroke and was paying a heavy rate of assessment and a tax for the relief of Ireland.[10] Their complaints did them no good. In 1649, a new tax of £45 a month was levied for the support of troops, three times what had been paid before. A petition was sent to Parliament, reminding members that Haverfordwest was a stopping point for soldiers en route to Ireland, all of whom had to be quartered in and around the town. 'And by reason hereof, your petitioners are brought very poor and most of the inhabitants of this town not able to maintain themselves and families, and many of them forced to leave this town by reason of the heavy said assessment will be to your petitioners utter undoing'.[11]

By November 1649 the council was seeking compensation for the £500 it had spent on the quartering of troops. Within four years the unpaid arrears owed by Haverfordwest amounted to £1,260. Further petitions at last succeeded in reducing the monthly rate to £25 and the arrears were remitted on the payment of £120.[12]

The situation was the same in Monmouthshire. During the winter of 1646–7 a man named Richard Fitzgerald was sent to South Wales to collect taxes for the upkeep of the army in Ireland. Four of the counties he visited paid up, but Monmouthshire delayed, as the Usk Committee made no effort to discuss the matter and the High Sheriff proved unhelpful, dithering over signing the necessary warrants. When he did pick up his quill, the money trickled in so slowly that only £390 was collected and Fitzgerald had to find his way back to Ireland at his own expense.[13]

The behaviour of the troops continued to cause offence. In 1648, a man named Robert ap William ap Robert of Llanllechid was murdered at Llandegai by Captain Oakes and his men. The killing prompted a grand jury in Caernarfonshire to protest that the troop of horse quartered on the area was a useless and unnecessary charge.[14] In December of the same year, Colonel Horton issued a warning to his men in South-West Wales:

'Whereas I have been informed that divers soldiers both dragoons and foot under my command within this county of Pembrock have by disorderly carriage and misbehaviour in their quarters forced their landlords to quarter them in inns and alehouses, the dragoons at 3s 6d per diem, and the foot at 1s per diem, as well as for the punishment of the said offence as the prevention of the same and others for the future I do declare that if any soldiers or soldiers have or shall commit the said offence or any other contrary to the articles of war...the party offended shall have due reparation and the offender undergo the judgement of a court-martial.'[15]

Perhaps the most serious and heartbreaking result of the civil wars was the human cost. It is difficult to assess how many lives were lost during the eleven years of conflict, as record-keeping in the seventeenth century was far from exact and not all records have survived to the present day. After a battle, for example, there was often no time to accurately count the number of dead, so estimates were made. Both sides might give widely varying numbers of the men they had killed, especially if the fighting had resulted in a draw and each army wanted to claim the victory. After Edgehill, the Parliamentarian Lord Wharton gave figures of 3,000 killed in the king's forces and only 300 on his own side. Lord Clarendon, for the opposing army, was sure that the king had lost 1,600 dead, whilst inflicting 3,400 casualties on the Army of Parliament. Other authorities at the time gave figures varying between 1,500 and 8,000.[16] Men were also killed in small skirmishes, when no numbers were noted at all. Similarly, there are no totals for the numbers of civilians killed in sieges, in the storming of towns and castles, in random atrocities or as a result of disease and famine. Both were problematical at that time, but were given a greater impetus by wartime conditions. Occasionally there are glimpses of how horrifying the fighting could be. In the immediate aftermath of the storming of Leicester in May 1645, by Prince Rupert's forces, the parish register record 709 burials, many of them civilians cut down by the victorious Royalists. At Bolton, when the Royalists ran wild in the taking of the town, anything between 200 and 1,800 people died. The parish registers record seventy-eight burials, including two women. At Pembroke in 1648, when Cromwell ordered a bombardment of Main Street, some thirty people were killed, some of whom were probably townsfolk. Fortunately, no Welsh town seems to have suffered a storm such as those inflicted on Leicester and Bolton.

The numbers become even more speculative when trying to reach a total for the Civil Wars as a whole. All four nations of the British Isles were caught up in the fighting and all experienced bloodshed on a sickening scale. It is estimated that between the years 1642 to 1652, a total of perhaps 868,000 people perished, out of a population of 7,500,000. By far the biggest percentage of this was suffered in Ireland, with 618,000 dead, a total which may or may not include those men brought from Ireland to fight in the king's army. There is no suggested total for Wales, but a figure of 190,000 for England may include casualties for Wales.[17] Many Welsh soldiers undoubtedly died on English soil during the battles that took place, but no one at the time bothered to identify how many Welsh bodies were being tossed into the burial pits. There was no time to differentiate between the nations.

Another unrecorded aspect of the wars that received little mention was the psychological trauma that must have been inflicted on those involved. As already noted, many Welshmen were pressed into service in the king's army. They were completely untrained and were unprepared to witness the sight of their companions being torn apart by cannon fire, or decimated by musket volleys. It's hardly surprising that some of them ran away.

The records are also silent about the sufferings of the women and children caught up in the wars. For those women who chose to remain at home when their men were called away, there were months, if not years, of separation, often with no news of the fate of husband, father, brother or son. A woman who chose to accompany her man as a camp follower had to live by her wits, as often no provision for females was made by a regiment in regard to food or shelter. At the worst, she might suffer the fate of the unfortunate women at Naseby, at best endure any number of hardships as she followed her husband from place to place.

For many women, the fear of death was outweighed by the fear of rape. Most females who died as a result of violence would seem to have been killed during the sacking of towns or the storming of garrisons, without molestation, but there are occasional stories of sexual violence. Sometimes these tales are propaganda, used to blacken one side or the other, but a few have a core of truth. In 1645, as Sir Marmaduke Langdale marched his men through Northamptonshire they indulged in widespread rape and plunder.[18] In September of the same year, as King Charles made his way from Raglan towards Chester, he was pursued by a group of Parliamentary soldiers. When these troopers came to Willey Court near Presteigne, they found only the female servants in the house and several of the women were molested by them. When the owner of the house, Edward Legge, discovered what had happened, he and his men set off in pursuit, catching up with the group at Knighton, where they killed one soldier and wounded several others.[19] Tales such as this spread quickly and can only have added to the terrors of women watching the passage of armed men through their communities, or who were trapped in towns under siege.

The threat of violation was terrifying enough. When Lord Carbery made his infamous promise to plunder the town of Pembroke in 1643, threatening to 'kill the dogs and ravish the bitches...' a group of local gentlewomen went to meet him in Tenby. They were led by Elizabeth White, the wife of a local landowner, who was described as 'a revered and aged gentlewoman...who had in her house eight sons and eight daughters, who were virgins, and four small grandchildren, in all twenty in number.' With tears in her eyes, Mrs White pleaded with Carbery for protection, reminding him that he was, 'in point of honour...engaged to protect...the chastity of matrons and virgins.' Carbery sneeringly replied that 'it were better her children and family should perish than that the king should want means to perfect his designs.'[20]

Some women were mentally scarred for life by their experiences. Of the two maids who witnessed the massacre at Hopton Castle, one never recovered her reason. On the other side of the country, one noblewoman caught up in the siege of Colchester was so terrified by the constant bombardment that for the rest of her life she was only happy when playing with her dolls. When, during the siege of Raglan Castle, the Countess of Glamorgan witnessed her father-in-law, Lord Worcester, being struck by a spent musket ball, she ran away screaming, an experience she was never likely to forget.[21]

The wars inflicted physical scars too, as both men and women suffered the loss of a limb or an eye or endured other wounds that affected their health. During the siege of Brampton Bryan, Lady Colebourne lost an eye when a bullet sent splinters of stone flying from a wall. For many men coming home from the wars with a missing arm or leg, there was the challenge of finding work to support themselves and their families. For the most seriously injured amongst them, the future was grim indeed.

A system of relief for those who were unable to support themselves had been put in place during the reign of Queen Elizabeth I. The system was administered through the parish and the necessary funds were raised by levying a tax, known as the poor rate, on property owners or comfortably-off tenants in each parish. The impotent poor, who couldn't work at all, were cared for in almshouses, but anyone who was old, lame, blind or otherwise incapacitated were offered relief. This might come in the form of money, clothing or food. Those who were able to undertake work of some kind would be given the materials and tools needed to earn a living. Some maimed soldiers – the term used at the time for injured veterans – and sailors were given permits that allowed them to beg without fear of arrest.

There were obvious drawbacks to the system, which came under strain after the Civil War, with so many maimed soldiers applying for relief. It was clear that something more needed to be done. In 1659, Lord Fairfax presented to Parliament a petition from 2,500 injured soldiers and 4,000 widows, asking for regular payment of pensions. The scheme seems to have been forgotten at the Restoration and it was not until almost two decades had passed that attention was again given to the plight of maimed soldiers.

The provision of pensions became the responsibility of Justices of the Peace, acting through the Quarter and General Sessions. Applicants were to present to the Bench a certificate and a statement or claim, as well as an appearance before the General Sessions to prove that they were not malingerers. If accepted, a man's name would be entered onto a roll. Exceptions were made for those with obvious war-related injuries, as their claim was clearly justified.

The fund for maimed soldiers was administered by an annually appointed treasurer, though sub-committees could be created to deal with matters, if required. All details of pensions granted were kept in an order book, along with information about payments made for road repairs, bridge mending and other expenditures. In 1676, maximum annual payments of £4 were introduced for maimed soldiers.

However, as early as January 1661, the Justices of the Peace in Caernarfonshire instructed those injured soldiers who had fought for the king to appear before a local committee. Amongst those who applied were Hugh Owen of Aberdaron, shot and cut on one shoulder and both arms, and David Owen of Conwy, who had suffered a serious gunshot under one eye, the bullet still lodged under his ear. Harry ap Rees of Llanllechid had lost the use of both hands, whilst eighty-year-old Jane verch Hugh of Caernarfon, whose husband had died serving under Lord Ormond in Ireland, was in great poverty and 'deserveth to be considered'.[22]

The *Brecknockshire Quarter Sessions Order Book 1670–1685* still exists and gives fascinating details of payments made to maimed soldiers in the Brecon area. The list for 1675 mentions thirty-seven names and a total of £78 was paid out. The name of Captain Edward Davies heads the list, with a payment of £10. When this was reduced to the statutory £4 a year later, he was forced to appeal for the previous amount to be restored to him and was successful. If he had raised a company of soldiers during the war, he would have had to bear all the costs of equipping and arming them, which may have ruined his private fortune. The magistrates would have taken this into account when restoring his original pension. Most of the others on the list were probably foot soldiers or mounted troops, such as David Jones of Talgarth, Henry Morris of the Hay, William Evors of Builth and Thomas Herbert of Crickhowell, who were awarded sums of £1 or £2 annually.

In a later list for 1681, the amounts paid out have been considerably reduced. Captain Davies is only receiving £1 per annum, Thomas Herbert is given ten shillings and William Evors of Builth and David Jones of Talgarth are awarded five shillings each.

There is no explanation for the reductions, though the petty constables, who were responsible for collecting the cash from the local parishioners, found to their dismay that not everyone was willing to pay and sometimes had to apply for warrants to distrain the goods of those who refused. Poor relief placed a considerable burden on local communities, many of whom were not wealthy and had limited resources. It was not only maimed soldiers who had to be supported, but widows, orphaned children, the blind, to name but a few.

There were also problems with those who administered the funds. In 1681, the treasurer for that year and his predecessor were asked to account for the money that passed through their hands, as they had neglected to account for the years they had held the post.[23]

Although the Order Books have given no details of where and when these men were injured, it's worth noting that those in receipt of a pension, however small it was, were probably Royalist soldiers. Presumably, there was little provision after the Restoration for men who had fought against the king, and they probably had to depend on the kindness and charity of friends and family.

The people of Wales who lived through the Civil Wars had experienced a series of events that were bewildering, terrifying and, for some, exhilarating. They had seen their nation scoured by the fires of war, stripped of its men to provide armies in which fathers, sons and brothers often fought against one another, spilling their blood on unfamiliar fields for ideals that were far removed from their daily concerns of family and community. The Wales we have today owes a great debt to the struggles of that long-ago generation and to generations since then who have fought for equality, justice and peace.

Bibliography

Archaeologia Cambrensis, 1853.

Ashton, R., *Counter Revolution; The Second Civil War and its Origins* (Yale University Press, 1994).

Barratt, J., *The Great Siege of Chester* (Tempus, 2003).

Barratt, J., *Cavalier Generals; King Charles I and His Commanders in the English Civil War* (Pen and Sword, 2004).

Bennett, M., *Dampnified Villagers, Taxation in Wales during the First Civil War* (Welsh Historical Review, Vol 19, 1, pp.29-43).

Bracher, Emmett, R., *Shropshire in the Civil War* (Shropshire Books, 2000).

Braddick, M., *God's Fury, England's Fire* (Allen Lane, 2008).

British Library Historical Collection *Letters from a subaltern officer of the Earl of Essex's Army written in the summer and autumn of 1642.*

Brown, E., *Learned Friend and Loyal Fellow Prisoner* (The National Library of Wales Journal, Vol XVIII No 4, pp.374-381).

Carlton, C., *Going to the Wars; the Experience of the English Civil Wars 1638–1651* (Routledge, 1992).

Carlyle, T., *Oliver Cromwell's Letters and Speeches,* Vol II (London: Chapman and Hall, 1872).

Chandler, J. (ed.), *Travels through Stuart Britain; The Adventures of John Taylor, the Water Poet* (Sutton Publishing, 1999).

Charles, B.G., *Calendar of the Records of the Borough of Haverfordwest 1539–1660* (University of Wales Press, 1967).

Deanweb; The Forest of Dean Local History; www.deanweb.info/civil war.html.

Dore, R.N. (ed.), *The Letter Books of Sir William Brereton, Vol 1* (Record Society of Lancashire and Cheshire, 1984).

Durant, H., *The Somerset Sequence* (Hughes and Son, 1976).

Emberton, W., *The English Civil War Day by Day* (Alan Sutton Publishing, 1995).

Fletcher, A., *The Outbreak of the English Civil War* (Edward Arnold, 1993 reprint).

Fraser, A., *The Weaker Vessel; Women's Lot in seventeenth-century England* (Weidenfeld and Nicolson, 1984).

Fulton, H. (ed.), *Urban Culture in Medieval Wales* (University of Wales Press, 2012).

Gaunt, P., *A Nation Under Siege* (HMSO, 1991).

Guest, K. & D., *British Battles* (HarperCollins, 1996).

Gwynfor Jones, J., *The Welsh Gentry 1536–1640* (University of Wales Press, 2016).

Gwynfor Jones, J., *Early Modern Wales 1525–1640* (St Martin's Press, 1994).

Gwynne Williams, J., *Sir John Vaughan of Trawscoed 1603–1674* (The National Library of Wales Journal, Vol VIII, No 3 pp.225-241).

Howells, B. (ed.), *Elizabethan Pembrokeshire; the Evidence of George Owen.* (Pembrokeshire Record Society, 1973).

Hunt, T., *The English Civil Wars at First–Hand* (Weidenfeld and Nicolson, 2002).

Hutton, Ronald, *The Royalist War Effort 1642–1646* (Routledge, 2003).

Jenkins, G.H., *The Foundations of Modern Wales 1642–1780* (Oxford University Press, 1993).

John, T., *The Civil War in Pembrokeshire* (Logaston, Press 2008).

Knight, J., *Civil War and Restoration in Monmouthshire* (Logaston Press, 2005).

Leach, A.L., *History of the Civil War 1642–1649 in Pembrokeshire* (London, 1937).

Lewis, J., *Fire and Sword along the Marches* (Jacobus Publications, 1996).

De Lisle, L., *The White King; Charles I, Traitor, Murderer, Martyr* (Chatto and Windus, 2018).

Lawrence, Dr K., The Barthomley Incident (Nantwich Museum, no date).

Lloyd, H.A., *The Gentry of South-West Wales 1540–1640* (University of Wales Press, 1968).

Lynch, J., *For King and Parliament; Bristol and the Civil War* (Sutton Publishing, 1999).

McKenna, J. (ed.), *A Journal of the English Civil War; The Letter Book of Sir William Brereton* (McFarland & Company, Inc, North Carolina and London, 2012).

Matthews, R., *A Storme out of Wales; The Second Civil War in South Wales 1648* (Cambridge Scholars Publishing, 2012).

Morris, R.H., *The Siege of Chester during the Civil War 1643–46* (Journal of the Chester Archaeological Society 25, Vol 25, pp.215-53, https://doi.org/10.5284/1070062).

Parker, K., *Radnorshire; From Civil War to Restoration* (Logaston Press, 2000).

Pembrokeshire County History, Volume III.

Phillips, J.R., *Memoirs of the Civil War in Wales and the Marches 1642–1649* (Volumes 1 and 2 Longmans, Green, 1874; Elibron Classics reprint, 2006).

Porter, S., *Destruction in the English Civil Wars* (Sutton, 1994).

Porter, S., Marsh, S., *The Battle for London* (Amberley, 2010).

Purkiss, D., *The English Civil War; A People's History* (Harper Press, 2006).

Raymond, J. (ed.), *Making the News; An Anthology of the Newsbooks of Revolutionary England 1641–1660* (The Windrush Press, 1993).

Reid, S., *All the King's Armies; A Military History of the English Civil War 1642–1651* (Spellmount, 1998).

Roberts, K., Tinsey, J., *Edgehill 1642* (Osprey Military, 2001).

Roberts, S.K., *How the West was Won; Parliamentary Politics, Religion and the Military in South Wales* (Welsh Historical Review, Vol 21, 4, pp.646-703).

Rees, J.F., *Studies in Welsh History* (University of Wales Press, 1965 2nd Edition).

Royle, T., *Civil War; The Wars of the Three Kingdoms* (Little, Brown, 2004).

Scott, C., Turton, A., von Arni, E., *Edgehill; the battle reinterpreted* (Pen and Sword, 2004).

Stoyle, M., *West Britons; Cornish Identities and the Early Modern British State* (University of Exeter, 2002).

Stoyle, M., *Soldiers and Strangers; An Ethnic History of the English Civil War* (Yale University Press, 2005).

Thomas, W.S.K., *Stuart Wales* (Gomer Press, 1988).

Tucker, N., *Brecknockshire's Maimed Soldiers* (The National Library of Wales Journal, Vol XIV, No 6, pp.397-406).

Tucker, N., *Civil War Aftermath in Caernarfonshire* (The National Library of Wales Journal, Vol XIII, No 3, pp.235-251).

Tucker, N., *Richard Griffiths at the Siege of Chester* (The National Library of Wales Journal, Vol XIII, No 1, pp.57-66).

Tucker, N., *North Wales and Chester in the Civil War* (Landmark, 2003).

Webb, D., *The Battle of St Fagans 1648* (Stuart Press, 1998).

Willliams, G., *Renewal and Reformation Wales 1415–1642* (Oxford University Press, 1993).

Woolrych, A., *Britain in Revolution (*Oxford University Press, 2002).

Worton, J., *The Battle of Montgomery, 1644* (Helion and Company, 2016).

Young, *Edgehill 1642 (*The Roundwood Press, 1995, The Windrush Press reprint, 1995).

Endnotes

Chapter 1: Wales, Land and People

1. Chandler, quoted, 267, 272.
2. Williams, 408.
3. Gwynfor Jones, J., 36.
4. Gaunt, 8.
5. *Ibid.*
6. Howells, 16.
7. Williams, 475.
8. Gwynfor Jones, *Welsh Gentry,* 14.
9. Phillips, I., 31.
10. Fulton, 171–72.
11. Barratt, 14.
12. John, quoted, 20.
13. Lewis, 6.
14. Williams, 432.
15. Knight, 53.
16. Lhuyd, 20.
17. Parker, 16.
18. Gwynfor Jones, *Welsh Gentry,* 8.
19. Williams, 442.
20. De Lisle, 59.
21. Phillips, I., 37.
22. Woolrych, 54.
23. PRO, CSPD, 28 August 1627.
24. PRO, CSPD, 25 September 1627.
25. de Lisle, 59–60.
26. Phillips, I., 43.
27. PRO, CSPD, 23 October 1628.
28. Phillips I, 50.
29. Thomas, 11.

30. Lloyd, 111.
31. Woolrych, 65.
32. *Ibid.,* 66.
33. Phillips, I., 73–4.
34. Lloyd, 122.
35. Gwynfor Jones, *Welsh Gentry,* 200.
36. Lewis, 6.
37. de Lisle, 114.
38. *Ibid.,* 115.
39. Royle, 128.
40. John, 31.
41. Hunt, 62.
42. Braddick, 172.
43. Royle, 154.
44. DOP, 2–10 January 1641(2).
45. Phillips, 8–9.
46. John, quoted, 36.

Chapter 2: 1642

1. Jenkins, G.H., 5.
2. Phillips, Vol 1, 342.
3. Gaunt, 17.
4. Stoyle, 11.
5. Philips II, 4–5.
6. Tucker, 19.
7. AC, 1853.
8. Phillips 1, 139.
9. *Ibid.*, 108.
10. BLHC, 19.
11. Knight, 59.
12. Durant, 61.
13. Phillips 1, 121.
14. *Ibid.*, 124.
15. Knight, 64.
16. Parker, 61–2.
17. Phillips, I., 133.
18. *Ibid.*, 133–4.

19. Royle, 190–1.
20. Phillips II, 128.
21. Royle, 190.
22. Scott, Turton, von Arni, 80.
23. *Ibid.*, 84.
24. Phillips, Vol 2, 36–7.
25. Porter, Marsh, 75.
26. Barratt, 33.
27. *Ibid.*
28. Phillips II, 44–5.
29. *Ibid.*, 42–3.

Chapter 3: 1643

1. Phillips, Vol I, 147.
2. Reid, 32.
3. Stoyle, quoted, 154.
4. Knight, 66.
5. *Ibid.*
6. Phillips I, 149.
7. www.deanweb.info/civilwar.html.
8. Stoyle, 28.
9. Knight, 69.
10. Durant, 66.
11. Lewis, 22.
12. Phillips I, 141.
13. Barratt, 35.
14. Lewis, 20.
15. Barratt, 40.
16. Tucker, 22.
17. *Ibid.*, Lewis, 22.
18. Phillips I, 144.
19. Knight, 72.
20. *Ibid.*, 73.
21. Stoyle, 157.
22. *Ibid.*, 158.
23. John, 50–1.

24. NLW, MSS, 1377b.
25. Tucker, 23–4.
26. *Ibid.*, 24.
27. Phillips I, 162.
28. Tucker, 26.
29. Parker, 67.
30. Lewis, 8.
31. Tucker, 30.
32. Phillips I, 182, Barratt, 47.
33. Phillips II, 93–100.
34. Phillips I, 184.
35. *Ibid.*, II, 108.
36. Barratt, 50–1.
37. Lawrence, 34.
38. Royle, 215.

Chapter 4: 1644

1. Phillips I, 192–3.
2. Lewis, quoted, 10.
3. Phillips II, 128.
4. Barratt, 54–5.
5. *Ibid.*, 56.
6. Phillips II, 134.
7. *Ibid.*, 135.
8. *Ibid.*, I, 218.
9. Parker, 82.
10. John, 11.
11. Phillips II, 120.
12. NLW, Thomason Tracts, E42.
13. NLW, MSS, 1377b.
14. NLW, Thomason Tracts, E42.
15. *Ibid.*
16. *Ibid.*
17. Leach, 76–7.
18. *Ibid.*, 80–1.
19. Stoyle, 59.

20. Stoyle, 60; Gaunt, 44.
21. Stoyle, 60.
22. Parker, 85.
23. Knight, 75–6.
24. Phillips II, 158–160.
25. Phillips II, 175.
26. *Ibid.*, I, 226.
27. Tucker, 37.
28. Phillips I, 239.
29. *Ibid.*, II, 197.
30. Lynch, 109.
31. Worton, 39.
32. *Ibid.*, 87.
33. Phillips II, 209.
34. Worton, 94.
35. Phillips II, 205–6.
36. Worton, 96.
37. *Ibid.*, 98.
38. Hutton, 139.
39. Phillips II, 190.
40. John, 78.
41. PRO, CSPD, I July 1644.
42. PRO, CSPD, 27 July, 1 August 1644.
43. Knight, 76.
44. *Ibid.*, 77.
45. Phillips II, 211.
46. Phillips I, 263.
47. *Ibid.*, I, 271.
48. John, 81.
49. Phillips II, 229.

Chapter 5: 1645

1. Barratt, 69.
2. *Ibid.*, 71.
3. Dore, 74.
4. Lewis, 56.
5. Phillips II, 240.

6. Barratt, 74.
7. Phillips II, 242.
8. Morris, JCAS, 222–3.
9. Barratt, 76.
10. Phillips II, 243–4.
11. *Ibid.*, 245–6.
12. Tucker, 47.
13. *Ibid.*, 50.
14. Dore, 380–1.
15. Barratt, 80.
16. Phillips II, 229.
17. Parker, 96.
18. NLW, Thomason Tracts, E285.
19. Phillips II, 249.
20. Leach, 109.
21. AC, 1988.
22. AC, 1882.
23. PRO, CSPD, 26 May 1645.
24. PRO, CSPD, 30 June 1645.
25. PRO, CSPD, 2 July 1645.
26. PRO, CSPD, 1 August 1645.
27. WHR, Bennet, 36.
28. Phillips II, 139.
29. Knight, 84.
30. Parker, 93–4.
31. Knight, 87.
32. *Ibid.*, 91.
33. Durant, 83.
34. Phillips I, 317–8.
35. Knight, 97.
36. Leach, 113.
37. Phillips II, 274–6.
38. *Ibid.*, 273–4.
39. Phillips I, 340.
40. *Ibid.*, 340–1, Knight, 100.
41. Barratt, 84–5.
42. *Ibid.*, 88.
43. *Ibid.*, 91.
44. Guest, quoted, 163.

45. Lewis, 17–8.
46. Morris, 234.
47. Tucker, 60.
48. Lewis, 18.
49. Barratt, 141.
50. Royle, 371–3.

Chapter 6: 1646

1. Phillips I, 356.
2. Knight, 103–4.
3. *Ibid.*, 103.
4. Phillips II, 298–300.
5. *Ibid.*
6. *Ibid.*
7. John, 97.
8. Phillips II, 305.
9. Knight, 112.
10. Durant, 96.
11. Knight, 112.
12. Durant, 97.
13. *Ibid.*, 98.
14. Phillips I, 374.
15. Durant, 104.
16. Parker, 115.
17. Barratt, 151.
18. *Ibid.*, 154.
19. Phillips I, 352.
20. Barratt, 164; Phillips I, 354.
21. Tucker, 85.
22. *Ibid.*, 88.
23. *Ibid.*, 93.
24. Phillips II, 326.
25. Tucker, 78.
26. Parker, 126.
27. Leach, 191.
28. Charles, 76.

Chapter 7: 1647–49

1. John, 107.
2. De Lisle, 225.
3. Knight, 122; Phillips II, 340.
4. Knight, 123.
5. Tucker, 94.
6. NLW, MSS, 1377 (b).
7. Matthews, 45.
8. PRO, CSPD, 25 January 1648.
9. Phillips II, 345–6.
10. Leach, 146.
11. *Ibid.*, 161.
12. Phillips II, 362.
13. *Ibid.*, 363–4.
14. Webb, 12; Gaunt, 68.
15. Phillips II, 365.
16. *Ibid.*
17. *Ibid.*
18. Webb, 19.
19. Ashton, 347.
20. Matthews, 127.
21. Knight, 125–8.
22. Thomason Tracts, E446 (27).
23. Carlyle II, 10.
24. Phillips II, 396.
25. Tucker, quoted, 104–5.
26. *Ibid.*, 109–112.

Chapter 8: After the War

1. Chandler, 271.
2. Porter, 78.
3. *Ibid.*, 65.
4. Parker, 133–7.
5. Knight, 137.
6. *Ibid.*, 138–9.

7. Durant, 103.
8. Tucker, 123.
9. HC, MSS, 262.
10. John, 154.
11. HC, MSS, 532.
12. PCH III, 210.
13. Knight, 140–1.
14. Tucker, 121.
15. HC, MSS, 265.
16. Scott, Turton, von Arni, 152.
17. Carlton, 214.
18. *Ibid.*, 260.
19. Parker, 105.
20. Laws, 325.
21. Durant, 98.
22. Tucker, 124–5.
23. Tucker, NLWJ, XIV, 397–406.

Index

Fairfax, Sir William, 92, 93-4
Farrar, Captain Robert, 104
Feilding, Basil, Earl of Denbigh,
   57, 84-6, 106
Feilding, Richard, 38
Fellowship, Bristol ship, 54
Fitzgerald, Richard, 188
Five Members, attempted arrest
   of, 23
Fleming, Colonel, 163, 164, 165,
   166, 167, 168, 169
Flint, 1, 61, 136, 140, 150,
   153, 184
Flintshire, 2, 9, 15, 25, 29, 32, 57,
   60, 62, 108, 109, 115, 135
Forster, Captain, 133
Forth, Earl of, 37
Framilode, 46
France, 4, 9, 14, 15, 77, 159, 167

Gallows Point, 183
Gamull, Francis, 68-9
Gardiner, Sir Thomas, 89
Gerard, Colonel Charles, 82,
   84, 96, 97, 101, 102, 103,
   105, 116, 117, 118, 119, 120,
   125, 127
Glamorgan, Countess of, 191
Glamorgan, Vale of, 2
Glamorganshire, 3, 5, 9, 11, 15,
   16, 27, 98, 124, 126, 130,
   132, 143, 155, 160, 165,
   167, 169
Glasbury, 126
Glasgow, 18, 19
Globe, warship, 73, 74, 76
Gloucester, 4, 36, 44, 45, 46, 47,
   52, 53, 64, 82, 98, 99, 101,

132, 133, 164, 165, 172, 173,
   174, 175
Gloucestershire, 44, 82
Golden Grove, 4
Goodrich, 82, 148
Gower, the, 2
Grand Remonstrance, 22
Grandison, Lord, 31
Grigson, Major, 173
Gunter, John of Lamphey, 38
Gunter, James, of Abergavenny, 124
Gwasnewydd, 48
Gwernyfed, 126
Gwynne, Colonel, 79
Gwynne, John, Governor of
   Tenby, 78-9
Gwynn, Sir John, 1
Gwysaney, 112

Halchdyn, 139
Hamilton, Marquis of, 178
Hammond, David, Mayor of
   Tenby, 29
Hammond, Colonel Robert, 159
Hampden, John, 23
Hampshire, 159
Hampton Court Palace, 24, 159
Handbridge, Chester, 61, 112, 184
Hanmer, 57
Harlech, 145, 153, 157, 184
Harley, Lady Brilliana, 71, 101
Harley, Colonel Edward, 101, 102
Harley, Sir Robert, 7
Harry ap Rees, of
   Llanllechid, 192
Hart, Bristol ship, 54
Haselrig, Arthur, 23
Hatton Heath, 136, 138